# HASMONEAN REALITIES BEHIND
# EZRA, NEHEMIAH, AND CHRONICLES

# ANCIENT ISRAEL AND ITS LITERATURE

Thomas C. Römer, General Editor

*Editorial Board:*
Susan Ackerman
Mark G. Brett
Marc Brettler
Tom Dozeman
Cynthia Edenburg
Konrad Schmid

Number 34

# HASMONEAN REALITIES BEHIND EZRA, NEHEMIAH, AND CHRONICLES

Israel Finkelstein

**SBL PRESS**

**Atlanta**

Copyright © 2018 by Israel Finkelstein

All rights reserved. No part of this work may be reproduced or transmitted in any form or by any means, electronic or mechanical, including photocopying and recording, or by means of any information storage or retrieval system, except as may be expressly permitted by the 1976 Copyright Act or in writing from the publisher. Requests for permission should be addressed in writing to the Rights and Permissions Office, SBL Press, 825 Houston Mill Road, Atlanta, GA 30329 USA.

Library of Congress Cataloging-in-Publication Data

Names: Finkelstein, Israel, author.
Title: Hasmonean realities behind Ezra, Nehemiah, and Chronicles : archaeological and historical perspectives / by Israel Finkelstein.
Description: SBL Press, [2018] | Series: Ancient Israel and its literature ; number 34 | Includes bibliographical references and index.
Identifiers: LCCN 2018020288 (print) | LCCN 2018020576 (ebook) | ISBN 9780884143093 (ebk.) | ISBN 9780884143079 (pbk. : alk. paper) | ISBN 9780884143086 (hbk. : alk. paper)
Subjects: LCSH: Jews—History—586 B.C.-70 A.D. | Bible. Chronicles—Criticism, interpretation, etc. | Bible. Ezra—Criticism, interpretation, etc. | Bible. Nehemiah—Criticism, interpretation, etc. | Maccabees.
Classification: LCC DS121.7 (ebook) | LCC DS121.7 .F56 2018 (print) | DDC 222/.095—dc23
LC record available at https://lccn.loc.gov/2018020288

Printed on acid-free paper.

# Contents

List of Figures ..................................................................................... vii
Abbreviations ...................................................................................... ix

Introduction ........................................................................................ 1

1. Jerusalem in the Persian (and Early Hellenistic) Period and
   the Wall of Nehemiah ................................................................... 3

2. Archaeology of the List of Returnees in the Books of Ezra
   and Nehemiah ............................................................................. 29

3. The Territorial Extent and Demography of Yehud/Judea
   in the Persian and Early Hellenistic Periods ............................. 51

4. Nehemiah's Adversaries ............................................................. 71

5. The Historical Reality behind the Genealogical Lists in
   1 Chronicles ................................................................................ 83

6. Rehoboam's Fortified Cities (2 Chr 11:5–12) .......................... 109

7. The Expansion of Judah in 2 Chronicles ................................ 129

Conclusions .................................................................................... 159
Bibliography ................................................................................... 165

Biblical References Index ............................................................. 193
Modern Authors Index .................................................................. 197
Place Names Index ........................................................................ 203
Ancient Figures Index ................................................................... 207

# List of Figures

1.1. The topography of Jerusalem, marking the main sectors of the ancient site, including the hypothesized old mound on the Temple Mount (for the latter, see addendum)

2.1. Sites mentioned in the list of returnees

3.1. Places mentioned in Neh 3 (in bold) versus main area with Persian period Yehud seal impressions (85 percent of the finds in solid line; 90 percent in dotted line)

3.2. Places mentioned in relation to the Hasmonean expansion; sites referred to in 1 Maccabees as locations of the battles of Judas Maccabeus and forts built by Bacchides are in bold. Question mark signals tentative identification.

4.1. Nehemiah's adversaries

5.1. Places mentioned in the Genealogies in 1 Chr 2–9

6.1. Sites mentioned in the list of Rehoboam's fortresses (in bold), with the addition of the sites fortified by Bacchides according to 1 Macc 9 (in italics). Question mark denotes sites whose identification is not secure.

# Abbreviations

| | |
|---|---|
| AASOR | Annual of the American Schools of Oriental Research |
| AB | The Anchor Bible |
| ABD | Freedman, David Noel, ed. *Anchor Bible Dictionary*. 6 vols. New York: Doubleday, 1992. |
| ABS | Archaeology and Biblical Studies |
| AcBib | Academia Biblical |
| AJSL | *American Journal of Semitic Languages and Literatures* |
| A.J. | Josephus, *Antiquitates judaicae* |
| ATD | Das Alte Testament Deutsch |
| BA | *Biblical Archaeologist* |
| BAIAS | *Bulletin of the Anglo-Israeli Archaeoloigcal Society* |
| BARIS | BAR (British Archaeological Reports) International Series |
| BASOR | *Bulletin of the American Schools of Oriental Research* |
| BBB | Bonner biblische Beiträge |
| BEATAJ | Beiträge zur Erforschung des Alten Testaments und des Antiken Judentum |
| Bib | *Biblica* |
| B.J. | Josephus, *Bellum judaicum* |
| BN | Biblische Notizen |
| BWANT | Beiträge zur Wissenschaft vom Alten und Neuen Testament |
| BZAW | Beihefte zur Zeitschrift für die alttestamentliche Wissenschaft |
| ESI | *Excavations and Surveys in Israel* |
| CAH | *Cambridge Ancient History* |
| DCLS | Deuterocanonical and Cognate Literature Studies |
| DJD | Discoveries in the Judaean Desert |
| DMOA | Documenta et Monumenta Orientis Antiqui |
| ErIsr | *Eretz-Israel* |
| HAT | Handbuch zum Alten Testament |

| | |
|---|---|
| *HeBAI* | *Hebrew Bible and Ancient Israel* |
| HNT | Handbuch zum Neuen Testament |
| HSM | Harvard Semitic Monographs |
| HTR | *Harvad Theological Review* |
| IAA Reports | Israel Antiquity Authority Reports |
| IEJ | *Israel Exploration Journal* |
| JAJSup | Journal of Ancient Judaism Supplements |
| JAOS | *Journal of the American Oriental Society* |
| JBL | *Journal of Biblical Literature* |
| JHS | *Journal of Hebrew Scripture* |
| JSJ | *Journal for the Study of Judaism* |
| JJS | *Journal of Jewish Studies* |
| JNES | *Journal of Near Eastern Studies* |
| JNSL | *Journal of Northwest Semitic Languages* |
| JQR | *Jewish Quarterly Review* |
| JSJSup | Supplements to the Journal for the Study of Judaism |
| JSNTSup | Journal for the Study of the New Testament Supplement Series |
| JSOT | *Journal for the Study of the Old Testament* |
| JSOTSup | Journal for the Study of the Old Testament Supplement Series |
| JTS | *Journal of Theological Studies* |
| LHBOTS | Library of Hebrew Bible/Old Testament Studies |
| MSIA | Monograph Series of the Institute of Archaeology Tel Aviv University |
| NEA | *Near Eastern Archaeology* |
| NEAEHL | Ephraim, Stern, ed. *The New Encyclopedia of Archaeological Excavations in the Holy Land*. 4 vols. Jerusalem: Israel Exploration Society & Carta; New York: Simon & Schuster, 1993. |
| NSJ | *New Studies on Jerusalem* |
| OBO | Orbis Biblicus et Orientalis |
| Od. | Homer, *Odyssey* |
| OJA | *Oxford Journal of Archaeology* |
| OtSt | Oudtestamentlische Studiën |
| PEQ | *Palestine Exploration Quarterly* |
| PJ | *Palästinajahrbuch* |
| RB | *Revue biblique* |
| SBLDS | Society of Biblical Literature Dissertation Series |

| | |
|---|---|
| SBLStBL | Society of Biblical Literature Studies in Biblical Literature |
| SJ | Studia Judaica |
| SJLA | Studies in Judaism in Late Antiquity |
| SJOT | *Scandinavian Journal of the Old Testament* |
| SNTSMS | Society for New Testament Studies Monograph Series |
| SSN | Studia Semitica Neerlandica |
| SymS | Symposium Series |
| TA | *Tel Aviv* |
| TMO | Travaux de la Maison de l'Orient |
| TSAJ | Texte und Studien zum antiken Judentum |
| *Transeu* | *Transeuphratène* |
| *UF* | *Ugarit Forschungen* |
| *VT* | *Vetus Testamentum* |
| VTSup | Supplements to Vetus Testamentum |
| WMANT | Wissenschaftliche Monographien zum Alten und Neuen Testament |
| *ZAW* | *Zeitschrift für die Alttestamentliche Wissenschaft* |
| *ZDPV* | *Zeitschrift des Deutschen Palästina-Vereins* |
| *ZPE* | *Zeitschrift für Papyrologie und Epigraphik* |

# Introduction

Over the last decade, I published seven articles concerning texts in the books of Ezra, Nehemiah, and Chronicles. They deal with the construction of Jerusalem's city wall, described in Neh 3; the lists of returnees in Ezra 2:1–67 and Neh 7:6–68; the adversaries of Nehemiah; the genealogies in 1 Chr 2–9; the towns fortified by Rehoboam according to 2 Chr 11:5–12; and the unparallel accounts in 2 Chronicles that relate the expansion of Judah. An additional article gives an overview of the territorial extent of Yehud/Judea in the Persian and Hellenistic periods.

My interest in this material stemmed from a sense of a déjà vu: for many years, I dealt—directly or indirectly—with biblical texts that recount the history of Israel and Judah and noticed circular arguments in research regarding their dating. My way out of this impasse was to deploy archaeology and extrabiblical texts in the study of these materials. The case with Ezra, Nehemiah, and Chronicles is similar: some scholarly discussion is mired in circular arguments and uncritical reliance on what the texts say. In this case, too, the solution is to consult data not directly related to the texts—first and foremost archaeology.

The biblical materials discussed in these articles include geographical information, which may shed light on the historical background behind the texts and the goals of their authors. This historical setting can be reached by deploying archaeology in order to verify the settlement history of the sites mentioned in the texts and by comparing the information given by these verses and chapters to extrabiblical written sources.

The articles reprinted in this book were published over a period of several years (2008–2015), with no preplanned scheme, meaning that one theme led to another. But during the process of writing them, it became clear to me that the articles depict a similar picture regarding the historical background behind them—later than assumed by most scholars. And since the geographical texts discussed in the articles constitute significant parts of the books of Nehemiah and Chronicles, they bear on broader issues than the date of a specific text, including the stratigraphy and chronology of the books involved. This is the reason for my decision to publish the articles as a book: to suggest to the reader their overall significance.[1]

The original articles are reprinted here with no change, except for adaptation to SBL style in both the text and the footnotes. This means that I have not added bibliographical entries that appeared after the given article was published. Yet, at the end of five of the seven chapters, I have included an addendum, with archaeological updates and references to specific articles published on the matter discussed in the given chapter. To make reading easier, I have also added several maps, which were not included in the original publications. Evidently in a collection of articles that deal with the same general theme there are certain repetitions, for instance, in references to the archaeology of Gibeon and Beth-zur and the list of places fortified by Bacchides (1 Macc 9:50–52), or in summaries of issues related to the genealogies and Rehoboam fortified towns in the article on the expansion of Judah in Chronicles. This is unavoidable; eliminating these repetitions would have ruined the structures of the articles.

The original articles included in this book are listed below in the order in which they appear here:

- "Jerusalem in the Persian (and Early Hellenistic) Period and the Wall of Nehemiah." *JSOT* 32 (2008): 501–20.
- "Archaeology of the List of Returnees in the Books of Ezra and Nehemiah." *PEQ* 140 (2008): 7–16.
- "The Territorial Extent and Demography of Yehud/Judea in the Persian and Early Hellenistic Periods." *RB* 117 (2010): 39–54.
- "Nehemiah's Adversaries: A Hasmonaean Reality?" *Transeu* 47 (2015): 47–55.
- "The Historical Reality behind the Genealogical Lists in 1 Chronicles." *JBL* 131 (2012): 65–83.
- "Rehoboam's Fortified Cities (II Chr 11, 5–12): A Hasmonean Reality?" *ZAW* 123 (2011): 92–107.
- "The Expansion of Judah in II Chronicles: Territorial Legitimation for the Hasmoneans?" *ZAW* 127 (2015): 669–95.

---

1. I wish to thank my student Na'ama Walzer and Shimrit Salem for helping me in transforming the original articles to SBL style, to Ido Koch and Assaf Kleiman for preparing the maps (maps 1 and 2–7, respectively), and to Sabine Kleiman for proofreading the book and preparing the index.

# 1
# Jerusalem in the Persian (and Early Hellenistic) Period and the Wall of Nehemiah

Knowledge of the archaeology of Jerusalem in the Persian (and early Hellenistic) period—the size of the settlement and whether it was fortified—is crucial to understanding the history of the province of Yehud, the reality behind the book of Nehemiah, and the process of compilation and redaction of certain biblical texts.[1] It is therefore essential to look at the finds free of preconceptions (which may stem from the account in the book of Nehemiah) and only then attempt to merge archaeology and text.

## 1. The Current View

A considerable number of studies dealing with Jerusalem in the Persian period have been published in recent years.[2] Although the authors were

---

   1. On the latter see, e.g., William M. Schniedewind, "Jerusalem, the Late Judaean Monarchy and the Composition of the Biblical Texts," in *Jerusalem in the Bible and Archaeology: The First Temple Period*, ed. Andrew G. Vaughn and Ann E. Killebrew, SymS 18 (Atlanta: Society of Biblical Literature, 2003), 375–94; Schniedewind, *How the Bible Became a Book: The Textualization of Ancient Israel* (Cambridge: Cambridge University Press, 2004), 165–78; Diana V. Edelman, *The Origins of the 'Second' Temple: Persian Imperial Policy and the Rebuilding of Jerusalem* (London: Equinox, 2005), 80–150.
   2. E.g., Charles E. Carter, *The Emergence of Yehud in the Persian Period: A Social and Demographic Study*, JSOTSup 294 (Sheffield: Sheffield Academic Press, 1999); Hanan Eshel, "Jerusalem under Persian Rule: The City's Layout and the Historical Background" [Hebrew], in *The History of Jerusalem: The Biblical Period*, ed. Shmuel Ahituv and Amihai Mazar (Jerusalem: Yad Ben-Zvi, 2000), 327–44; Ephraim Stern, *The Assyrian, Babylonian, and Persian Periods (732–332 B.C.E.)*, vol. 2 of *Archaeology of the Land of the Bible* (New York: Doubleday, 2001), 434–36; Edelman, *Origins of the 'Second' Temple*; Oded Lipschits, *The Fall and Rise of Jerusalem: Judah under Babylo-*

aware of the results of recent excavations, which have shown that the settlement was limited to the eastern ridge (the "City of David," fig. 1.1), they continued to refer to a meaningful, fortified "city" with a relatively large population.

Carter argued that Jerusalem grew from a built-up area of 30 dunams in the Persian I period to 60 dunams "after the mission of Nehemiah"[3] and estimated the peak population to have been between 1250 and 1500 people.[4] Based on detailed archaeological data from excavations and surveys and using a density coefficient of twenty-five people per one built-up dunam (a number which may be somewhat too high; see below), Carter reached a population estimate of circa 20,000 people for the entire province of Yehud in the Persian period.[5] Carter rightly asked: if Yehud "was this small and this poor, how could the social and religious elite sustain the literary activity attributed to the Persian period?... How could such a small community have built a temple and/or refortified Jerusalem."[6] Based on "historical and sociological parallels"—in fact almost solely on the biblical text—Carter answered in the positive, arguing that the urban elite was large enough for both the production of a large body of texts and for the fortification of Jerusalem.[7]

Eshel reconstructed the history of Jerusalem in the Persian period almost solely according to the biblical texts, arguing that the "Jerusalem of Nehemiah was a small town ... nevertheless it had eight gates ... much

---

*nian Rule* (Winona Lake, IN: Eisenbrauns, 2005); Lipschits, "Achaemenid Imperial Policy, Settlement Processes in Palestine, and the Status of Jerusalem in the Middle of the Fifth Century B.C.E.," in *Judah and the Judeans in the Persian Period*, ed. Oded Lipschits and Manfred Oeming (Winona Lake, IN: Eisenbrauns, 2006), 19–52; David Ussishkin, "The Borders and *De Facto* Size of Jerusalem in the Persian Period," in Lipschits and Oeming, *Judah and the Judeans in the Persian Period*, 147–66.

3. Carter, *Emergence of Yehud*, 200.

4. Carter, *Emergence of Yehud*, 288.

5. Carter, *Emergence of Yehud*, 195–205, compared to circa 30,000 according to Oded Lipschits, "Demographic Changes in Judah between the Seventh and the Fifth Centuries B.C.E.," in *Judah and the Judeans in the New-Babylonian Period*, ed. Oded Lipschits and Joseph Blenkinsopp (Winona Lake, IN: Eisenbrauns, 2003), 364, also using the twenty-five people one per built-up dunam coefficient.

6. Carter, *Emergence of Yehud*, 285; see the same line of thought in Schniedewind, "Jerusalem, the Late Judaean Monarchy"; Schniedewind, *How the Bible Became a Book*, 165–78.

7. Carter, *Emergence of Yehud*, 288.

more than the real need of the town at that time."⁸ Eshel acknowledged that the population of Jerusalem was depleted (in line with Neh 7:4), but in the same breath argued that it was populated by Levites and others, who were brought to Jerusalem by Nehemiah (13:4–14; 11:1). He compared the demographic actions taken by Nehemiah to the *synoikismos* policy of Greek tyrants.⁹ Regarding the rebuilding of the walls, following Neh 3, Eshel envisioned a major operation, which involved many groups of builders.

Stern began the discussion of the archaeology of Jerusalem in the Persian period with a sentence based solely on the biblical text: "Persian period Jerusalem was bounded by walls erected by Nehemiah."¹⁰ At the same time, he acknowledged that "only a few traces have survived of the city wall of Nehemiah along the course described in the Bible."¹¹ Stern referred to a segment of a city wall at the top of the eastern slope of the City of David, which was dated by Kenyon¹² to the Persian period (see below).

Edelman accepted Neh 3 as accurately reflecting "the names of individuals and settlements in Yehud at the time the walls of Jerusalem were constructed during the reign of Artaxerxes I."¹³ Edelman, like Lipschits (below), saw the construction of the walls by Nehemiah as a turning point in the history of Yehud—marking the transfer of the capital from Mizpah to Jerusalem. The walls provided "protection for the civilian population and government officials who would man the fort and carry out the administration of the province."¹⁴ Edelman saw a major construction effort in Jerusalem under Persian auspices in the days of Artaxerxes I—an effort far greater than the reconstruction of the city walls that also included the temple and a fort.¹⁵

---

8. Eshel, "Jerusalem under Persian Rule," 341.
9. Also Joel P. Weinberg, *The Citizen-Temple Community*, JSOTSup 151 (Sheffield: Sheffield Academic Press, 1992), 43; Weinberg, "Jerusalem in the Persian Period" [Hebrew], in Ahituv and Mazar, *History of Jerusalem, The Biblical Period*, 308–9, 313–16.
10. Stern, *Assyrian, Babylonian, and Persian Periods*, 434.
11. Stern, *Assyrian, Babylonian, and Persian Periods*, 435.
12. Kathleen M. Kenyon, *Digging Up Jerusalem* (London: Ernest Benn, 1974), 183–84.
13. Edelman, *Origins of the 'Second' Temple*, 222.
14. Edelman, *Origins of the 'Second' Temple*, 206.
15. Edelman, *Origins of the 'Second' Temple*, 344–48.

Ussishkin declared that "the corpus of archaeological data should be the starting point for the study of Jerusalem.... This source of information should take precedence, wherever possible, over the written sources, which are largely biased, incomplete, and open to different interpretations."[16] Reviewing the archaeological data, he rightly concluded that the description in Neh 3 must relate to the maximal length of the city walls, including the western hill. But then, solely according to the textual evidence in Neh 3, he accepted that the Persian period settlement was indeed fortified: "When Nehemiah restored the city wall destroyed by the Babylonians in 586 B.C.E., it is clear ... that he restored the city wall that encompassed the Southwestern Hill, as suggested by the 'maximalists.'"[17]

Lipschits's reconstruction of the history of Jerusalem in the Persian period revolved around the rebuilding of the city wall by Nehemiah.[18] Though "there are no architectural or other finds that attest to Jerusalem as an urban center during the Persian Period,"[19] "the real change in the history of Jerusalem occurred in the middle of the fifth century B.C.E., when the fortifications of Jerusalem were rebuilt. Along with scanty archaeological evidence, we have a clear description of this event in the Nehemiah narrative...."[20] Lipschits saw the construction of the city wall as the turning point in the history of Jerusalem—when it became the capital of Yehud: "The agreement of the Persians to build fortifications in Jerusalem and to alter the status of the city to the capital of the province was the most dramatic change in the history of the city after the Babylonian destruction in 586."[21] Lipschits described Jerusalem as a "city" of 60 dunams, with a population of circa 1,500 inhabitants.[22]

Obviously, all the scholars who dealt with the nature of Jerusalem in the Persian period based their discussion on the biblical text, mainly on the description of the reconstruction of the city wall in Neh 3.

---

16. Ussishkin, "Borders and *De Facto* Size of Jerusalem," 147–48.
17. Ussishkin, "Borders and *De Facto* Size of Jerusalem," 159; also 160.
18. Lipschits, "Achaemenid Imperial Policy."
19. Lipschits, "Achaemenid Imperial Policy," 31.
20. Lipschits, "Achaemenid Imperial Policy," 34.
21. Lipschits, "Achaemenid Imperial Policy," 40.
22. Lipschits, "Achaemenid Imperial Policy," 32; also Lipschits, "Demographic Changes in Judah," 330–31; Lipschits, "Achaemenid Imperial Policy," 212; see a different number, 3,000 people, in "Achaemenid Imperial Policy," 271.

1. Jerusalem and the Wall of Nehemiah        7

2. The Finds

Intensive archaeological research in Jerusalem in the past forty years has shown that:

1. The southwestern hill (fig. 1.1) was part of the fortified city in the late Iron II and the late Hellenistic periods.[23]
2. The southwestern hill *was not* inhabited in the Persian and early Hellenistic periods. This has been demonstrated by excavations in the Jewish Quarter,[24] the Armenian Garden,[25] the Citadel,[26]

---

23. For the Iron II see Hillel Geva, "The Western Boundary of Jerusalem at the End of the Monarchy," *IEJ* 29 (1979): 84–91; Geva, "Summary and Discussion of Findings from Areas A, W and X-2," in *Jewish Quarter Excavations in the Old City of Jerusalem*, ed. Hillel Geva, vol. 2 (Jerusalem: Israel Exploration Society, 2003), 505–18; Geva, "Western Jerusalem at the End of the First Temple Period in Light of the Excavations in the Jewish Quarter," in Vaughn and Killebrew, *Jerusalem in the Bible and Archaeology*, 183–208; Nahman Avigad, *Discovering Jerusalem* (Nashville: Nelson, 1983), 31–60; Ronny Reich and Eli Shukron, "The Urban Development of Jerusalem in the Late Eight Century B.C.E.," in Vaughn and Killebrew, *Jerusalem in the Bible and Archaeology*, 209–18. For the late Hellenistic period see Hillel Geva, "Excavations in the Citadel of Jerusalem, 1979–1980: Preliminary Report," *IEJ* 33 (1983): 55–71; Geva, "Excavations at the Citadel of Jerusalem, 1976–1980," in *Ancient Jerusalem Revealed*, ed. Hillel Geva (Jerusalem: Israel Exploration Society, 1994), 156–67; Geva, "Summary and Discussion of Findings," 526–34; Magen Broshi and Shimon Gibson, "Excavations along the Western and Southern Walls of the Old City of Jerusalem," in Geva, *Ancient Jerusalem Revealed*, 147–55; Doron Chen, Shlomo Margalit, and Bagil Pixner, "Mount Zion: Discovery of Iron Age Fortifications below the Gate of the Essens," in Geva, *Ancient Jerusalem Revealed*, 76–81; Renee Sivan and Giora Solar, "Excavations in the Jerusalem Citadel, 1980–1988," in Geva, *Ancient Jerusalem Revealed*, 168–76; Gregory J. Wightman, *The Walls of Jerusalem: From the Canaanites to the Mamluks* (Sydney: Meditarch, 1993), 111–57.

24. Avigad, *Discovering Jerusalem*, 61–63; Hillel Geva, "General Introduction to the Excavations in the Jewish Quarter," in *Jewish Quarter Excavations in the Old City of Jerusalem*, ed. Hillel Geva, vol. 1 (Jerusalem: Israel Exploration Society, 2000), 24; Geva, "Summary and Discussion of Findings," 524; Geva, "Western Jerusalem at the End," 208.

25. Shimon Gibson, "The 1961–67 Excavations in the Armenian Garden, Jerusalem," *PEQ* 119 (1987): 81–96; Geva "Summary and Discussion of Findings," 524–25.

26. Ruth Amiran and Avraham Eitan, "Excavations in the Courtyard of the Citadel, Jerusalem, 1968–1969 (Preliminary Report)," *IEJ* 20 (1970): 9–17.

and Mt. Zion.²⁷ Apart from a few possible isolated finds,²⁸ there is no evidence of any activity in any part of the southwestern hill between the early sixth century and the second century BCE. The Persian and early Hellenistic settlement should therefore be sought on the southeastern ridge—the City of David.

In the City of David, too, the evidence is fragmentary. Most finds from the Persian and early Hellenistic periods were retrieved from the central part of the ridge, between Areas G and D of the Shiloh excavations.²⁹ The Persian period is represented by Stratum 9, which fully appears, according to Shiloh³⁰ in Areas D1,³¹ D2, and G,³² and which is partially represented in Area E1. According to De Groot, the most significant finds were retrieved from Area E.³³ But even in these areas the finds were meager and poor; most of them came from fills and quarrying refuse.³⁴ De Groot describes a possible reuse in one late Iron II building in Area E.³⁵ Persian-period sherds and a few seal impressions were found in Reich and Shukron's Areas A and B, located in the Kidron Valley and midslope respectively, circa 200–250 m south of the Gihon Spring; they seem to have originated in the settlement located on the ridge.³⁶

Stratum 8 stands for the early Hellenistic period. It is fully represented only in Area E2, partially represented in Areas E1 and E3, and scarcely

---

27. Magen Broshi, "Excavations on Mount Zion, 1971–1972 (Preliminary Report)," *IEJ* 26 (1976): 82–83.

28. Geva, "Summary and Discussion of Findings," 525.

29. Yigal Shiloh, *Excavations at the City of David*, vol. 1, Qedem 19 (Jerusalem: Institute of Archaeology, 1984), 4.

30. Shiloh, *Excavations at the City of David*, 4, table 2.

31. Donald T. Ariel, Hannah Hirschfeld and Neta Savir, "Area D1: Stratigraphic Report," in *Extramural Areas*, vol. 5 of *Excavations at the City of David*, ed. Donald T. Ariel, Qedem 40 (Jerusalem: Institute of Archaeology, The Hebrew University of Jerusalem, 2000), 59–62.

32. Shiloh, *Excavations at the City of David*, 20.

33. Alon De Groot, "Jerusalem during the Persian Period" [Hebrew], *NSJ* 7 (2001), 77–82.

34. See the difficulty to distinguish the "limestone chops layer" in Ariel, Hirschfeld, and Savir, "Area D1," 59.

35. De Groot, "Jerusalem during the Persian Period."

36. Ronny Reich and Eli Shukron, "The Yehud Seal Impressions from the 1995–2005 City of David Excavations," *TA* 34 (2007): 59–65.

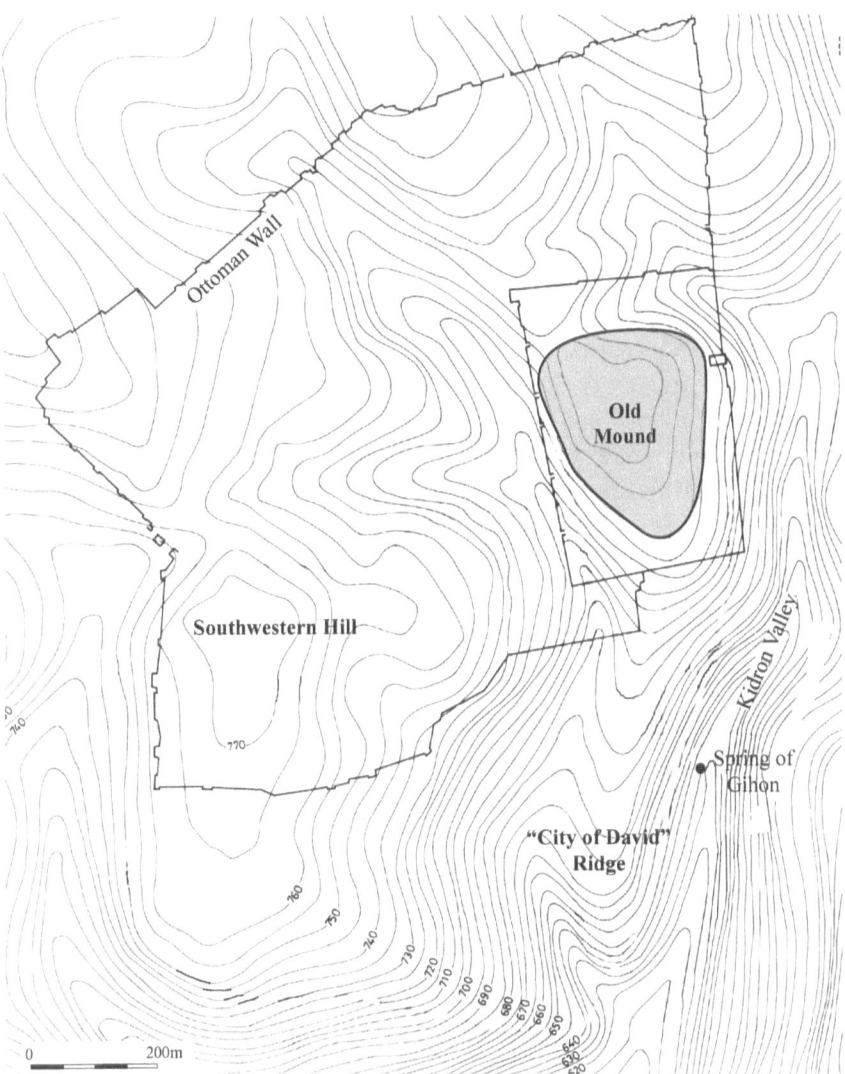

Figure 1.1. The topography of Jerusalem, marking the main sectors of the ancient site, including the hypothesized old mound on the Temple Mount (for the latter, see addendum).

represented in Areas D1 and D2.[37] In this case, too, the finds are meager. They are comprised of three *columbaria*[38] and a structure that yielded the only assemblage of early Hellenistic pottery from Jerusalem.[39]

In the case of the City of David, too, the negative evidence is as important as the positive. No Persian or early Hellenistic finds were found in Area A on the southern tip of the ridge. It is significant to note that in Area A1 early Roman remains were found over Iron II remains.[40] In Kenyon's Site K, located on the southwestern side of the City of David, circa 50 m to the north of the Siloan Pool, Iron II sherds were found on bedrock, superimposed by late Hellenistic finds.[41]

As for the northern part of the ridge, the Persian and early Hellenistic periods were not represented in B. and E. Mazar's excavations to the south of the southern wall of the Temple Mount, which yielded late Hellenistic and mainly early Roman finds superimposed over Iron II buildings.[42] It is also significant that Persian and early Hellenistic finds were not reported from B. Mazar's excavations near the southwestern corner of the Temple Mount.[43] A few finds, but no architectural remains or *in-situ* assemblages of pottery, were retrieved by Crowfoot in the excavation of the "Western

---

37. Shiloh, *Excavations at the City of David*, 4, table 2.

38. Alon De Groot, "Jerusalem in the Early Hellenistic Period" [Hebrew], *NSJ* 10 (2004): 67–70.

39. In Area E1—Shiloh, *Excavations at the City of David*, 15.

40. Alon De Groot, David Cohen, and Arza Caspi, "Area A1," in *Stratigraphic, Environmental, and Other Reports*, vol. 3 of *Excavations at the City of David 1978–1985*, ed. Alan De Groot and Donald T. Ariel, Qedem 33 (Jerusalem: Institute of Archaeology, The Hebrew University of Jerusalem, 1992), 1–29.

41. Kathleen M. Kenyon, "Excavations in Jerusalem, 1965," *PEQ* 98 (1966): 84. Shiloh's Area K, located on the ridge 90 m to the north of Area A, in roughly the same line as Kenyon's Site K, was excavated to bedrock. The earliest remains date to the early Roman period. In this case a large-scale clearing operation, which could have destroyed the earlier remains, seems to have taken place in the Roman period [also Kathleen M. Kenyon, "Excavations in Jerusalem, 1964," *PEQ* 97 (1965), 14; Kenyon, "Excavations in Jerusalem, 1965," 88 for her excavations nearby].

42. Eilat Mazar and Benjamin Mazar, *Excavations in the South of the Temple Mount: The Ophel of Biblical Jerusalem*, Qedem 29 (Jerusalem: Institute of Archaeology, The Hebrew University of Jerusalem, 1989), XV–XVI.

43. Benjamin Mazar, "The Excavations in the Old City of Jerusalem near the Temple Mount—Second Preliminary Report, 1969–1970 Seasons" [Hebrew], *ErIsr* 10 (1971): 1–34.

Gate"[44] and by Macalister and Duncan[45] in the excavation immediately to the west of Shiloh's Area G. The 8–10 m thick dump-debris removed by Reich and Shukron on the eastern slope of the City of David, near the Gihon Spring,[46] yielded ceramic material from the Iron II and "late Second Temple period," but no Persian and early Hellenistic pottery. Reich and Shukron interpret this as evidence that Area G, located upslope from their dig, was uninhabited at that time. Finally, it is noteworthy that sifting of debris from the Temple Mount recovered almost no Persian period finds.[47]

Reich and Shukron[48] also noted that seventy-five of the eighty-five *Yehud* seal impressions from the Shiloh excavations published by Ariel and Shoham[49] originated from Areas B, D, and E. They concluded that the settlement of the Persian and early Hellenistic periods was restricted to the top of the ridge, to the south of Area G.[50]

All this seems to indicate that:

1. In the Persian and early Hellenistic periods activity on the Temple Mount was not strong[51] and in any event did not include intensively inhabited areas;

---

44. John W. Crowfoot and Gerald M. Fitzgerald, *Excavations in the Tyropoeon Valley, Jerusalem 1927*, Palestine Exploration Fund Annual 5 (London: Palestine Exploration Fund, 1929).

45. Robert A. S. Macalister and John G. Duncan, *Excavation on the Hill of Ophel, Jerusalem, 1923–1925*, Palestine Exploration Fund Annual 4 (London: Palestine Exploration Fund, 1926).

46. Ronny Reich and Eli Shukron, "Yehud Seal Impressions"; also Reich and Shukron, "The History of the Gihon Spring in Jerusalem," *Levant* 36 (2004): 211–23.

47. Compared to a significant number of finds from the Iron II and from the Hellenistic–early Roman periods—Gabriel Barkay and Yitzhak Zweig, "The Temple Mount Debris Sifting Project: Preliminary Report" [Hebrew], *NSJ* 11 (2006): 213–37.

48. Reich and Shukron, "Yehud Seal Impressions."

49. Donald T. Ariel and Yair Shoham, "Locally Stamped Handles and Associated Body Fragments of the Persian and Hellenistic Periods," in *Inscriptions*, vol. 6 of *Excavations at the City of David 1978–1985*, ed. Donald T. Ariel, Qedem 41 (Jerusalem: Institute of Archaeology, 2000), 137–71.

50. See a somewhat similar view in Ariel and Shoham, "Locally Stamped Handles," 138.

51. Compare the Iron II finds to the south of the southern wall of the Temple Mount to the negative evidence for the Persian and early Hellenistic periods, see Barkay and Zweig, "Temple Mount Debris Sifting Project."

2. The northern part of the ridge of the City of David was uninhabited;
3. The southern part of the ridge was probably uninhabited as well.

The Persian and early Hellenistic settlement was confined to the central part of the ridge, between Shiloh's Area G (which seems to be located on the margin of the inhabited area) and Shiloh's Areas D and E. The settlement was located on the ridge, with the eastern slope outside the built-up area. Even in this restricted area, a century of excavations, by a number of archaeologists, failed to yield even a single (!) house or proper floor from the Persian period, and only one structure from the early Hellenistic period was found. The idea that the settlement was eradicated because of later activity and erosion[52] must be rejected in the light of the reasonable preservation of the late Hellenistic and Iron II remains.

The maximal size of the Persian and early Hellenistic settlement was therefore circa 240 (N–S) × 120 (E–W) m, that is, circa 20–25 dunams.[53] Calculating the population according to the broadly accepted density coefficient of twenty people per one built-up dunam[54]—a number that may be too high for what seems to have been a sparsely-settled ridge[55]—one reaches an estimated population of four hundred to five hundred people, that is, circa one hundred adult men.[56] This stands in sharp contrast to

---

52. E.g., De Groot, "Jerusalem in the Early Hellenistic Period," 67.

53. Contra to the idea of a 60-dunam settlement (excluding the Temple Mount) in Carter, *Emergence of Yehud*, 200; Lipschits, "Achaemenid Imperial Policy," 32; and a 30-acre settlement (possibly including the Temple Mount), in Nahman Avigad, "Jerusalem: The Second Temple Period," *NEAEHL* 2 (1993): 720.

54. Israel Finkelstein, "A Few Notes on Demographic Data from Recent Generations and Ethno-archaelogy," *PEQ* 122 (1990): 47–52 and bibliography. This coefficient is based on ethnoarchaeological and ethnohistorical data, which stand against Jeffrey R. Zorn, "Estimating the Population Size of Ancient Settlements: Methods, Problems, Solutions, and a Case Study," *BASOR* 295 (1994): 31–48. Zorn reached inflated numbers, which do not fit the demographic data on premodern societies. His error may have stemmed from the assumption that all buildings at Tell Nasbeh were inhabited at the same time; yet, no stratigraphic sequence has been established for the settlement, which was inhabited continuously for centuries, throughout the Iron and Babylonian periods.

55. On this problem, see Finkelstein, "A Few Notes on Demographic Data."

56. Philip J. King and Lawrence E. Stager (*Life in Biblical Israel* [Louisville: Westminster, 2001], 389) are the only scholars to speak about a small settlement with "a few hundred inhabitants"; in the same breath they accepted the description of the construction of the city wall by Nehemiah as historical (see below).

1. Jerusalem and the Wall of Nehemiah    13

previous, even minimal estimates of 1,250, 1,500, or 3,000 inhabitants,[57] estimates which call for a large settlement of 75–150 dunams—more than the entire area of the City of David.[58] These data fit well the situation in the immediate environs of Jerusalem, where the number of spots with archaeological remains dropped from 140 in the Iron II to 14 in the Persian period.[59] They also fit the general demographic depletion in the entire area of the province of Yehud—a maximum of 20,000–30,000 people in the Persian period according to Carter[60] and Lipschits,[61] circa 15,000 according to my own calculations—about a third or a fourth of the population of that area in the late Iron II.[62]

### 3. Nehemiah's Wall

Archaeologists have accepted the description of the reconstruction of the wall in Neh 3 as an historical fact and have been divided only about the course of the fortifications. The minimalists restricted them to the City of David, and the maximalists argued that the description included the southwestern hill.[63] Two finds in the field have been perceived as indications for the course of Nehemiah's city wall: one on the crest above the eastern slope of the City of David and the other on the western side of that ridge.

---

57. Carter, *Emergence of Yehud*, 288; Lipschits, "Achaemenid Imperial Policy," 32; Lipschits, *Fall and Rise of Jerusalem*, 271; "a few thousands" in Avigad, "Jerusalem," 720.

58. Not to mention Weinberg's estimate, based on his interpretation of the biblical text, of 15,000 people in Jerusalem and 150,000 in Yehud in the time of Nehemiah (*Citizen-Temple Community*, 43 and 132 respectively).

59. Amos Kloner, *Archaeological Survey of Israel, Survey of Jerusalem: The Northwestern Sector, Introduction and Indices* (Jerusalem: Israel Antiquities Authority, 2003), 28*; Kloner, "Jerusalem's Environs in the Persian Period," [Hebrew], *NSJ* 7 (2001): 92; for the early Hellenistic period, see Kloner, *Archaeological Survey of Israel*, 30*.

60. Carter, *Emergence of Yehud*, 195–205.

61. Lipschits, "Demographic Changes in Judah," 364.

62. Carter, *Emergence of Yehud*, 247, based on Magen Broshi and Israel Finkelstein, "The Population of Palestine in Iron Age II," *BASOR* 287 (1992): 47–60; Avi Ofer, *The Highlands of Judah during the Biblical Period* [Hebrew] (Phd thesis; Tel Aviv: Tel Aviv University, 1993).

63. See summary in Ussishkin, "Borders and *De Facto* Size of Jerusalem."

Kenyon argued that because of the collapse of the late Iron II city wall and buildings on the eastern slope of the ridge as a result of the Babylonian destruction, the city wall of Nehemiah was built higher up, at the top of the slope.[64] In her Square A XVIII (adjacent to Shiloh's Area G) she identified a short segment in the city wall that had first been uncovered by Macalister and Duncan[65]—a wall that was later unanimously dated to the late Hellenistic period[66]—as the city wall built by Nehemiah. Her dating of this segment of the wall was based on pottery found in a layer dumped against its outer face; this pottery was dated by Kenyon to the fifth–early third centuries BCE.[67] Shiloh, too, argued—without any archaeological evidence—that the city wall was built "on the bedrock at the top of the eastern slope."[68] Stern accepted Kenyon's identification and dating of this segment as Nehemiah's wall.[69] Ussishkin, on the other hand, suggested that Nehemiah reconstructed the Iron II wall, which runs on the lower part of the eastern slope of the City of David.[70]

The only piece of information from the western side of the City of David comes from Crowfoot's 1927 excavations. A massive structure that had been founded on bedrock, under thick layers of later occupations and debris, was identified as a Bronze Age gatehouse that continued to be in use until Roman times.[71] Albright[72] identified Crowfoot's "gatehouse" with the Dung Gate of Neh 3:13, while Alt[73] proposed equating it with the Valley Gate of Nehemiah 3: 13. Alt's proposal has been accepted by most authorities.[74]

---

64. Kenyon, *Digging Up Jerusalem*, 183–84; Kenyon, *Jerusalem: Excavating Three Thousand Years of History* (London: Thames & Hudson, 1967), 111.
65. Macalister and Duncan, *Excavation on the Hill of Ophel*.
66. See literature on the First Wall above.
67. Kenyon, *Digging Up Jerusalem*, 183; the sixth–fifth centuries BCE in caption to pl. 79.
68. Shiloh, *Excavations at the City of David*, 29; also Avigad, "Jerusalem," 720; De Groot, "Jerusalem during the Persian Period," 78.
69. Stern, *Assyrian, Babylonian, and Persian Periods*, 435.
70. Ussishkin, "Borders and *De Facto* Size of Jerusalem," 160.
71. Crowfoot and Fitzgerald, *Excavations in the Tyropoeon Valley*, 12–23.
72. William F. Albright, "Excavations at Jerusalem," *JQR* 21 (1930): 167.
73. Albrecht Alt, "Das Taltor von Jerusalem," *PJ* 24 (1928): 74–98.
74. E.g., Michael Avi Yonah, "The Walls of Nehemiah: A Minimalist View," *IEJ* 4 (1954): 244–45; Yoram Tzafrir, "The Walls of Jerusalem in the Period of Nehemiah"

Yet, both finds—the wall uncovered by Kenyon and the structure unearthed by Crowfoot—cannot be dated to the Persian period.

Kenyon's identification of Nehemiah's wall was based on (yet unpublished) pottery found in a small sounding, in a fill or a dump thrown against the outer face of the wall.[75] As rightly argued by De Groot, such a layer cannot be used for dating a city wall.[76] This material could have been taken from any dump on the slope and put there in order to support the wall.[77] Shiloh reexamined this segment of the city wall and found late Bronze material on the bedrock, close to its inner face; he therefore suggested that this part of the wall may have originated from a pre-Persian period.[78] Excavations immediately to the west of this spot by Macalister and Duncan[79] and E. Mazar[80] did not unearth architectural remains of the Persian and early Hellenistic periods. But they made clear that this segment is part of the late Hellenistic city wall, first uncovered by Macalister and Duncan.[81] Had it not been for Neh 3, I doubt very much whether Kenyon would have dated a short segment in the well-preserved late Hellenistic wall to the Persian period.

Ussishkin has recently dealt in detail with the structure excavated by Crowfoot and identified by him as a gatehouse.[82] Ussishkin has cast doubt on the identification of the structure as a gate, and convincingly argued that it probably dates to the late Hellenistic or early Roman period.[83]

---

[Hebrew], *Cathedra* 4 (1977): 39; Hugh G. M. Williamson, "Nehemiah's Walls Revisited," *PEQ* 116 (1984): 81–88; Eshel, "Jerusalem under Persian Rule," 333.

75. Kenyon, *Digging Up Jerusalem*, pl. 79.

76. De Groot, "Jerusalem during the Persian Period," 78.

77. For the same situation in the Outer Wall of Gezer, see Israel Finkelstein, "Penelope's Shroud Unraveled: Iron II Date of Gezer's Outer Wall Established," *TA* 21 (1994): 278.

78. Jane M. Cahill and David Tarler, "Excavations Directed by Yigal Shiloh at the City of David, 1978–1985," in Geva, *Ancient Jerusalem Revealed*, 41.

79. Macalister and Duncan, *Excavation on the Hill of Ophel*.

80. Eilat Mazar, *The Excavations in the City of David, 2005* [Hebrew] (Jerusalem: Shoham, 2007).

81. Macalister and Duncan, *Excavation on the Hill of Ophel*; see in details Israel Finkelstein, Ze'ev Herzog, Lily Singer-Avitz and David Ussishkin, "Has King David's Palace Been Found in Jerusalem?," *TA* 34 (2007): 142–64.

82. Ussishkin, "Borders and *De Facto* Size of Jerusalem."

83. Ussishkin, "Borders and *De Facto* Size of Jerusalem," 159; see also Kathleen M. Kenyon, "Excavations in Jerusalem, 1963," *PEQ* 96 (1964): 13.

To sum-up this issue, there is no archaeological evidence for the city wall of Nehemiah. The wall in the east dates to the late Hellenistic period and the structure in the west—regardless of its function—also postdates the Persian period. Had it not been for the Neh 3 account, no scholar would have argued for a Persian-period city wall in Jerusalem. Three early city walls are known in the City of David, dating to the Middle Bronze Age, the late Iron II and the late Hellenistic period. All three have been easy to trace and have been found relatively well-preserved. No other city wall has ever been found, and I doubt if this situation will change as a result of future excavations.[84]

One could take a different course and argue, with Ussishkin,[85] that Nehemiah merely rebuilt the ruined late-Iron II wall. Yet, in the many sections of the Iron II wall that have been uncovered—on both the southwestern hill and the southeastern ridge—there is no clue whatsoever for a renovation or reconstruction in the Persian period. In the parts of the late-Iron II city wall uncovered on the southwestern hill, the first changes and additions date to the late Hellenistic period.[86] No such reconstruction has been traced in the long line of the Iron II wall uncovered in several excavations along the eastern slope of the City of David south of the Gihon Spring. Archaeologically, Nehemiah's wall is a *mirage*.

This should come as no surprise, judging from what we do know about the Persian period settlement systems in Yehud in particular and the entire country in general. To differ from the construction of the Iron II and late-Hellenistic fortifications in Jerusalem—which represent a well-organized territorio-political entity with significant wealth and population, evidence for high-level bureaucracy and clear ideology of sovereignty[87]—the small community of several hundred inhabitants of Persian-period Jerusalem

---

84. Theoretically, one could argue that Neh 3 relates to the walls of the temple compound. Yet, the description of a city wall with many gates and towers does not comply with this possibility.

85. Ussishkin, "Borders and *De Facto* Size of Jerusalem."

86. Avigad, *Discovering Jerusalem*, 65–72; Geva, "General Introduction to the Excavations," 24; Geva, "Summary and Discussion of Findings," 529–32.

87. Most scholars date the construction of the Late Hellenistic city wall (Josephus's First Wall) to the time of the Hasmoneans [e.g., Avigad, *Discovering Jerusalem*, 75–83; Hillel Geva, "The 'First Wall' of Jerusalem during the Second Temple Period— An Architectural-Chronological Note" [Hebrew], *ErIsr* 18 (1985): 21–39; Geva, "Summary and Discussion of Findings," 533–34]. Benjamin Mazar and Hanan Eshel ["Who Built the First Wall of Jerusalem?," *IEJ* 48 (1998): 265–68] suggested that the wall was

(that is, not many more than one hundred adult men), with a depleted hinterland and no economic base, could not have possibly engaged in the reconstruction of the circa 3.5-km-long(!) Iron II city wall with many gates.[88] And why should the Persian authorities allow the reconstruction of the old, ruined fortifications and make Jerusalem the only fortified town in the hill country? The explanations of scholars who have dealt with this issue—that this was made possible because of the pressure of the Delian League on the Mediterranean coast, revolt in Egypt, et cetera[89]—seem farfetched, given the location of Jerusalem, distant from Egypt, international roads, coastal ports or other strategic locations.[90] Indeed, Persian-period fortifications are known only along the coastal plain.[91]

4. The Reality behind Nehemiah 3

So what *is* the historical reality behind the description of Nehemiah's rebuilding of the walls of Jerusalem?

Scholars have noted the independent nature of the list in Neh 3 as compared to the rest of the "Nehemiah Memoir,"[92] but are divided on the question of whether Nehemiah used an earlier or a contemporary source that was kept in the temple archives,[93] or whether a later editor

---

built earlier, in the days of Antiochus III. For reasons that are beyond the scope of this article, I would adhere to the former option.

88. Accepting Ussishkin's reconstruction—"Borders and *De Facto* Size of Jerusalem."

89. Summaries in Kenneth G. Hoglund, *Achaemenid Imperial Administration in Syria-Palestine and the Missions of Ezra and Nehemiah*, SBLDS 125 (Atlanta: Scholars Press, 1992), 61–64, 127–28; Edelman, *Origins of the 'Second' Temple*, 334–40; Lipschits, "Achaemenid Imperial Policy," 35–38.

90. Lipschits, "Achaemenid Imperial Policy," 35–38.

91. Stern, *Assyrian, Babylonian, and Persian Periods*, 464–68.

92. Charles C. Torrey, *Ezra Studies* (Chicago: University of Chicago Press, 1910), 225; Frank Michaeli, *Les Livres des Chroniques, d'Esdras et de Néhémie*, Commentaire de l'Ancien Testament 16 (Neuchâtel: Delachaux & Niestlé, 1967), 318–19; Hugh G. M. Williamson, *Ezra, Nehemiah*, WBC 16 (Waco, TX: Word Books, 1985), 200; Joseph Blenkinsopp, *Ezra/Nehemiah: A Commentary* (Philadelphia: Westminster, 1988), 231; Mark A. Throntveit, *Ezra-Nehemiah* (Louisville: John Knox, 1992), 74–75; Lester L. Grabbe, *Ezra-Nehemiah* (London: Routledge, 1998), 157.

93. Michaeli, *Les Livres des Chroniques*, 319; Ulrich Kellermaan, *Nehemia: Quellen Überlieferung und Geschichte*, BZAW 102 (Berlin: Töpelmann, 1967), 14–17;

inserted the text into the book of Nehemiah.[94] Taking into consideration the archaeological evidence presented in this paper, an existing source from the Persian period, which described a genuine construction effort at that time, is not a viable option. We are left, therefore, with the following possibilities:

1. That the description in Neh 3 is utopian; it was based on the geographical reality of the ruined Iron II city wall but does not reflect actual work on the wall. The text may describe a symbolic act rather than an actual work, similar to symbolic acts connected to the founding of Etruscan and Roman cities. And it may correspond to an ascriptive, ideal-type of a city that ought to include a wall (cf. *Od.* 6.6–10).[95]
2. That a Persian-period author used an early source, which described the late eighth century construction or a pre-586 renovation of the Iron II city wall and incorporated it into the Nehemiah text.
3. That the description was inspired by the construction of the late Hellenistic, Hasmonean city wall.

The first possibility is difficult to accept. The detailed description of the construction of the city wall and the prominence of the story of the wall throughout the Nehemiah Memoirs (Neh 1:3; 2:4, 8, 13, 17; 3:33, 38; 4:5, 9; 5:16; 6:1, 6, 15; 7:1; 12:27) renders it highly unlikely. Moreover, the description in Neh 3—which includes reference to many gates, towers, pools and houses—seems to refer to a true reality of a big city; in the light of what has already been said, the late Iron II and Hasmonean periods are the only options.

The second possibility should probably be put aside: (1) There is no evidence—historical or archaeological—of major work on the Iron II city wall in the late seventh or early sixth centuries, and it is doubtful if a source

---

Williamson, *Ezra, Nehemiah*, 201; Throntveit, *Ezra-Nehemiah*, 75; Blenkinsopp, *Ezra/Nehemiah*, 231.

94. E.g., Charles C. Torrey, *The Composition and Historical Value of Ezra-Nehemiah* (Giessen: Ricker, 1896), 37–38; Torrey, *Ezra Studies*, 249, who identified the editor with the Chronist; Sigmund Mowinckel, *Studien zu dem Buche Ezra-Nehemia* (Oslo: Universitetsforlaget, 1964), 109–16, who opted for a postchronist redactor.

95. I am grateful to my colleague and friend Irad Malkin for drawing my attention to these possibilities.

from the late eighth century would have survived until the fifth or fourth centuries without being mentioned in any late-monarchic biblical source. (2) Most names of gates, towers and pools in the list do not correspond to the many such names in late-monarchic biblical texts.[96]

The third option would put Neh 3 with what scholars see as late redactions in Ezra and Nehemiah, which can be dated as late as the Hasmonean period.[97] Böhler explicitly put the rebuilding of Jerusalem story in Nehemiah on Hasmonean background.[98] The usage of words such as the province *Beyond the River* (עבר הנהר, Neh 3:7), *pelekh*, and פחת (Neh 3:11) does not present difficulty for such a late dating, as they appear in late Jewish sources.[99]

Dating the insertion of this text to the Hasmonean period may correspond to the importance given to the figure of Nehemiah in the first two chapters of 2 Maccabees (as the builder of the temple!), which Bergren interpreted as an attempt to bolster the figure of Judas Maccabeus, the hero of 2 Maccabees, by comparing him to Nehemiah—a prominent

---

96. Except for the Tower of Hananel and the Horse Gate, mentioned in Jer 31:38 and 31:40 respectively. The Fish Gate and the Valley Gate appear in 2 Chr (33:14 and 26:9 respectively), but not in late-monarchic texts.

97. Williamson, *Ezra, Nehemiah*, xxxv; Jacob L. Wright, *Rebuilding Identity: The Nehemiah Memoir and Its Earliest Readers*, BZAW 348 (Berlin: de Gruyter, 2004); Wright, "A New Model for the Composition of Ezra-Nehemiah," in *Judah and the Judeans in the Fourth Century B.C.E.*, ed. Oded Lipschits, Gary N. Knoppers, and Rainer Albertz (Winona Lake, IN: Eisenbrauns, 2007), 333–48. According to Neh 3, the population of Jerusalem included 3,044 men, a number which translates to a total of 12,000–15,000 inhabitants (Weinberg, "Jerusalem in the Persian Period," 316). If this number has any credibility, if fits a city of circa 600 dunams—the size of Jerusalem in the late Iron II and the second century BCE.

98. Dieter Böhler, *Die heilige Stadt in Esdras α und Esra-Nehemia: Zwei Konzeptionen der Wiederherstellung Israels*, OBO 158 (Fribourg: Universitätsverlag, 1997), 382–97.

99. For עבר הנהר, see 1 Macc 7:8—Uriel Rappaport, *The First Book of Maccabees: Introduction, Hebrew Translation, and Commentary* [Hebrew] (Jerusalem: Yad Ben-Zvi, 2004), 281. For *pelekh* in the rabbinical literature [without entering the discussion on the meaning of the word—Aaron Demsky, "*Pelekh* in Nehemiah 3," *IEJ* 33 (1983): 242–44; Moshe Weinfeld, "Pelekh in Nehemiah 3," in *Studies in Historical Geography and Biblical Historiography*, ed. Gershon Galil and Moshe Weinfeld, VTSup 81 (Leiden: Brill, 2000), 249–50; Edelman, *Origins of the 'Second' Temple*, 213–14]; see Alexander Kohut, *Aruch Completum* (Vienna: Hebräischer Verlag Menorah, 1926), 346; Demsky, "*Pelekh* in Nehemiah 3," 243. For פחת see Dan 3:27.

figure in the restoration, a builder, a political leader, a zealot for the law, and a paradigm of piety.[100] Nehemiah could have been chosen as such a model for the Hasmoneans because he represented a non-Davidide, non-Zadokite leadership.

Clues that Neh 3 does not reflect Persian-period realities may be found in the archaeology of two of the three well-identified and excavated (rather than surveyed) sites mentioned in the list—Beth-zur and Gibeon.

The archaeology of Beth-zur (Neh 3:16) in the Persian period has been debated. Funk,[101] Paul and Nancy Lapp,[102] and Carter,[103] argued that the site was very sparsely, in fact, insignificantly inhabited in the Persian and early Hellenistic periods. Funk noted that the "interpretation of the Persian-Hellenistic remains at Beth-zur is dependent in large measure on the extant literary references...."[104] Based on a single locus (!), Stern adhered to the notion of a significant activity at the site in the Persian period.[105] Reich argued in the same line according to an architectural analysis.[106] The published material from the excavations[107] includes only a limited number of finds—sherds, vessels and coins—that can safely be dated to the Persian period,[108] while most forms belonging to the Persian-period repertoire are

---

100. Theodore A. Bergren, "Nehemiah in 2 Maccabees 1:10–2:18," *JSJ* 28 (1997): 249–70; also Bergren, "Ezra and Nehemiah Square off in the Apocrypha and Pseudepigrapha," in *Biblical Figures Outside the Bible*, ed. Michael E. Stone and Theodore A. Bergren (Harrisburg: Trinity Press International, 1998), 340–65. It may be noteworthy that Ben Sira (49:13), an early second century author, also emphasizes Nehemiah as a builder.

101. Robert W. Funk, "Beth-Zur," *NEAEHL* 1 (1993): 261.

102. Paul Lapp and Nancy Lapp, "Iron II—Hellenistic Pottery Groups," in *The 1957 Excavation at Beth-Zur*, by Orvid R. Sellers et al., AASOR 38 (Cambridge: American Schools of Oriental Research, 1968), 70; Paul Lapp, "The Excavation of Field II," in Sellers et al., *1957 Excavation at Beth-Zur*, 29.

103. Carter, *Emergence of Yehud*, 157.

104. Robert W. Funk, "The History of Beth-Zur with Reference to Its Defenses," in Sellers et al., *1957 Excavation at Beth-Zur*, 9.

105. Stern, *Assyrian, Babylonian, and Persian Periods*, 437–38; see also Stern, *Material Culture of the Land of the Bible in the Persian Period, 538–332 B.C* (Warminster: Aris & Phillips, 1982), 36.

106. Ronny Reich, "The Beth-Zur Citadel II—A Persian Residency?," *TA* 19 (1992): 113–23.

107. Ovid R. Sellers, *The Citadel of Beth-Zur* (Philadelphia: Westminster, 1933); Sellers et al., *1957 Excavation at Beth-Zur*.

108. Stern, *Assyrian, Babylonian, and Persian Periods*, 437.

missing altogether. Hence, though archaeology may have revealed traces of some Persian-period activity at the site, it is clear that it was an important place only in the late Iron II and the late Hellenistic periods. It should be noted that Beth-zur—supposedly the headquarters of half a district in the province of Yehud—did not yield even a single Yehud seal impression.[109]

Gibeon (Neh 3:7) did not yield unambiguous Persian-period finds either. Without going into the debate over the dating of the Gibeon winery and inscriptions—late monarchic or sixth century[110]—the *mwsh* seal impressions and wedge-shaped and reed impressed sherds found at the site[111] attest to a certain activity in the Babylonian or Babylonian/early Persian period. Yet, typical Persian-period pottery and Yehud seal impressions were not found.[112] Late Hellenistic pottery and coins are attested. According to Pritchard, there is "only scant evidence of occupation from the end of the sixth century until the beginning of the first century B.C.E." at Gibeon.[113] Still, in an attempt to provide evidence for the Gibeon of Neh 3:7 he argued that "scattered and sporadic settlements" did exist there during the Persian and Hellenistic periods.[114] Stern rightly interpreted the Gibeon finds as evidence for only sixth century and possibly early Persian period activity at the site.[115]

---

109. Over 530 have so far been recorded—Oded Lipschits and David Vanderhooft, "Yehud Stamp Impressions: History of Discovery and Newly-Published Impressions," *TA* 34 (2007): 3.

110. See summaries in Stern, *Material Culture of the Land of the Bible*, 32–33; Stern, *Assyrian, Babylonian, and Persian Periods*, 433.

111. James B. Pritchard, *Winery, Defenses and Soundings at Gibeon* (Philadelphia: University Museum, University of Pennsylvania, 1964), figs 32:7, 48:17.

112. For the latter see Lipschits, *Fall and Rise of Jerusalem*, 180.

113. James B. Pritchard, "Gibeon," *NEAEHL* 2 (1993): 513.

114. James B. Pritchard, *Gibeon, Where the Sun Stood Still: The Discovery of the Biblical City* (Princeton: Princeton University Press, 1962), 163.

115. Stern, *Material Culture of the Land of the Bible*, 32–33; Stern, *Assyrian, Babylonian, and Persian Periods*, 433; Lipschits, *Fall and Rise of Jerusalem*, 243–45—sixth century. Three other sites in the list, which are well identified, yielded both Persian and Hellenistic finds: Jericho [Stern, *Material Culture of the Land of the Bible*, 38; Ehud Netzer, *Hasmonean and Herodian Palaces at Jericho I* (Jerusalem: Israel Exploration Society, 2001) respectively], Zanoah [Yehuda Dagan, *The Shephelah during the Period of the Monarchy in Light of Archaeological Excavations and Surveys* [Hebrew] (MA thesis; Tel Aviv: Tel Aviv University, 1992), 92] and Tekoa [Ofer, *Highland of Judah*, appendix IIA: 28]. Keilah poses a problem, as thus far surveys of the site seem to have yielded only Persian period pottery [Moshe Kochavi, "The Land of Judah,"

There are several problems regarding the Hasmonean option for the background of Neh 3. First, the toponyms in the description of the First Wall in Josephus's *B.J.* 5.4.2—especially the "gate of the Essenes" (as well as names of gates mentioned by Josephus elsewhere)—are different from the toponyms in Neh 3. But the change may be assigned to post-Hasmonean, mainly Herodian times. A more severe problem is the prominence of the story on the construction of the city wall throughout the Nehemiah Memoirs. Accepting a Hasmonean reality behind the city-wall account in Nehemiah would therefore call for a drastic new approach to the entire book of Nehemiah.[116]

## 5. Conclusion

The Persian-period finds in Jerusalem and the search for Nehemiah's wall are additional cases in which archaeologists have given up archaeology in favor of an uncritical reading of the biblical text. The dearth of archaeological finds and the lack of extrabiblical texts on Persian period Yehud open the way to circular reasoning in reconstructing the history of this period.

The finds indicate that in the Persian and early Hellenistic periods Jerusalem was a small village that stretched over an area of circa 20 dunams, with a population of a few hundred people, that is, not much more than one hundred adult men. This population—and the depleted population of the Jerusalem countryside in particular and the entire territory of Yehud in general—could not have supported a major reconstruction effort of the ruined Iron II fortifications of the city. In addition, there is no archaeological evidence whatsoever for any reconstruction or renovation of fortifications in the Persian period. Taking these data into consideration, there are three ways to explain Neh 3: (1) that it is a utopian list; (2) that it preserves a memory of an Iron Age construction or renovation of the city wall; (3) that the list is influenced by the construction of the First Wall in the Hasmonean period. All three options pose significant difficulties—the first two more than the third. In any event, the archaeology of Jerusalem in the Persian period—as presented above—must be the starting point for any future discussion.

---

in *Judaea, Samaria and the Golan, Archaeological Survey 1967–1968* [Hebrew], ed. Moshe Kochavi (Jerusalem: Carta, 1972), 49; Dagan, *Shephelah*, 161.

116. On this, see Böhler, *Die heilige Stadt in Esdras*.

On a broader issue, the archaeological evidence from Jerusalem casts severe doubt on the notion that much of the biblical material was composed in the Persian and early Hellenistic periods. But this crucial issue is beyond the scope of this paper and will be discussed elsewhere.

Addendum

Understanding the Negative Evidence

In a rejoinder to the article reprinted above, Lipschits suggested that Jerusalem of the Persian period included the area of the "Ophel"—between the Temple Mount and Shiloh's Area G.[117] Here one faces a methodological problem: What should rule—archaeological facts, even negative evidence (also a fact), or hypotheses?[118] Lipschits writes (my comments in *italics* in brackets): "The importance of the Ophel hill as the main built-up area in the Persian and Early Hellenistic periods was never discussed in the archaeological and historical research. The reason was the scarcity of finds [*in fact, no finds*] in this area, of about 20 dunams.... This is the only flat, easy-to-settle area in the city. Its proximity to the Temple Mount on the one hand and the easy option to fortify it ... [*no fortification has ever been found*] made it the preferred option for settlement in the Persian period. In spite of the scarcity of finds [*in fact, no finds*] in this area ... [it] should be considered part of the settled area of Jerusalem during the Persian and Early Hellenistic periods. The absence of Persian period finds in the Ophel hill ... is an indication of the limitations of archaeological

---

117. Oded Lipschits, "Persian Period Finds from Jerusalem: Facts and Interpretations," *JHS* 9 (2009): art. 20.

118. For two views regarding this issue see: Nadav Na'aman, "Text and Archaeology in a Period of Great Decline: The Contribution of the Amarna Letters to the Debate on the Historicity of Nehemiah's Wall," in *The Historian and the Bible: Essays in Honour of Lester L. Grabbe*, ed. Philip R. Davies and Diana Vikander Edelman (New York: T&T Clark, 2010), 20–30; Na'aman, "Does Archaeology Really Deserve the Status of a 'High Court' in Biblical Historical Research?," in *Between Evidence and Ideology: Essays on the History of Ancient Israel Read at the Joint Meeting of the Society for Old Testament Study and the Oud Testamentisch Werkgezelschap, Lincoln, July 2009*, ed. Bob Becking and Lester L. Grabbe, OtSt 59 (Leiden: Brill, 2010), 165–84; Israel Finkelstein, "Archaeology as High Court in Ancient Israelite History: A Reply to Nadav Na'aman," *JHS* 10 (2010): art. 19.

research."[119] Needless to say, hypotheses rather than facts on the ground dictate Lipschits's interpretation: there are no finds, but since, according to the author's logic, the area must have been settled then a settlement must have existed there.

## The Mound on the Mount

Three years after the publication of the original article, Koch, Lipschits, and I suggested that the mound of Jerusalem should be sought on the Temple Mount rather than on the southeastern (City of David) ridge.[120] This idea calls for several modifications vis à vis the chapter reprinted above:[121]

1. The settlement of the Persian and early Hellenistic periods was located on the ancient mound on the Temple Mount.
2. This settlement provides a solution for the location of Jerusalem mentioned in an Elephantine letter[122] and a venue for compilation of biblical texts in post-586 and pre- circa 130 BCE Jerusalem.
3. Still, activity in the Persian and early Hellenistic periods on the mound on the Temple Mount was weak. This can be deduced from the sparse finds representing these periods retrieved around the Temple Mount. I refer to the eastern slope of the Temple Mount and the "Ophel" excavations south of it, as well as the debris sifted from the area of the al-Aqsa Mosque.[123]
4. The description of the construction/repair of the wall of Jerusalem in the "Nehemiah Memoir," with no reference to specific places, probably relates to the old, Iron Age fortifications on the Temple

---

119. Lipschits, "Persian Period Finds," 19–20.

120. Israel Finkelstein, Ido Koch, and Oded Lipschits, "The Mound on the Mount: A Solution to the 'Problem with Jerusalem'?," *JHS* (2011): art. 12; following Axel E. Knauf, "Jerusalem in the Late Bronze and Early Iron Ages: A Proposal," *TA* 27 (2000): 75–90.

121. It also answers the concerns expressed in Na'aman, "Text and Archaeology in a Period of Great Decline."

122. Bezalel Porten, *The Elephantine Papyri in English: Three Millennia of Cross-Cultural Continuity and Change*, DMOA 22 (Leiden: Brill, 1996), 135–37.

123. Itzhak Dvira (Zweig), Gal Zigdon, and Lara Shilov, "Secondary Refuse Aggregates from the First and Second Temple Periods on the Eastern Slope of the Temple Mount" [Hebrew], *NSJ* 17 (2011): 68; personal communication from Eilat Mazar; Barkay and Zweig, "The Temple Mount Debris Sifting Project," 222, respectively.

Mount, while the detailed description in Neh 3 refers to the Hellenistic fortifications, which encircle the southeastern ridge and the southwestern hill.[124] Hence, to differ from what I write before the conclusions of the reprinted article above, dating the reality behind Neh 3 to the late Hellenistic period does not necessarily call for a revision regarding the Nehemiah Memoir.

5. The Persian and early Hellenistic pottery and seal impressions found on the eastern slope of the City of David ridge should now be understood as representing activity around the spring rather than a settlement; they may also originate from late Hellenistic and early Roman fills.

Archaeology Updates

The "Northern Tower": A Persian Period City Wall?

Eilat Mazar has recently revived Kenyon's dating of the Northern Tower in Area G, above the eastern slope of the City of David ridge, to the Persian period.[125] Mazar bases her dating of the fortification on finds retrieved *under* the tower, which date to the end of the sixth and the first half of the fifth centuries BCE.[126] Needless to say, these layers provide no more than a *terminus post quem* for the construction of the tower—later than the late sixth/early fifth century BCE. The most logical date for the towers and the wall is the late Hellenistic (Hasmonean) period, as suggested by many authorities (above, in the reprinted article).

---

124. According to Lipschits, the verses in Neh 3 that describe the construction of gates are unique in their sentence structure, word-order, and verbs used; they differ from the usual formula deployed to describe the construction of the wall itself. Without the burden of the many gates, the original account (without Neh 3) described the course of the city wall of the small mound of Jerusalem on the Temple Mount [Finkelstein, Koch, and Lipschits, "Mound on the Mount"; for an analysis of the text of Neh 3 see Oded Lipschits, "Nehemiah 3: Sources, Composition and Purpose," in *New Perspectives on Ezra-Nehemiah: History and Historiography, Text, Literature, and Interpretation*, ed. Isaac Kalimi (Winona Lake, IN: Eisenbrauns, 2012), 73–100.

125. Eilat Mazar, *The Summit of the City of David: Excavations 2005-2008* (Jerusalem: Shoham Academic Research and Publication, 2015), 189–202.

126. Yiftah Shalev, "The Early Persian Period Pottery," in Mazar, *Summit of the City of David*, 203–41.

## Publication of Finds from Area E in the City of David

Finds from Shiloh excavations in Area E were published a few years ago. Persian period finds were uncovered in four squares and early Hellenistic remains were unearthed in several spots.[127] These remains do not change the picture presented in my 2008 article reprinted above. The same holds true for Persian period pottery found in several places in the Armenian and Christian quarter of the Old City;[128] most of this material originated from fills.

## Finds in the Givati Parking Lot

Recent excavations in the Givati Parking Lot, located in the northwestern sector of the City of David ridge, shed light on issues discussed in the article reprinted above:[129]

1. Strong late Hellenistic activity in this area of the city supports the notion that the remains excavated by Crowfoot in the "Western Gatehouse," immediately to the south indeed dates to late Hellenistic or early Roman times, as proposed by Ussishkin.
2. If the late Hellenistic fortification uncovered here—the tower and the glacis—indeed belongs to the Akra, the late Hellenistic First Wall, which is later than this fortification, cannot date before the late second century BCE.

---

127. Alon De Groot, "Discussion and Conclusions," in *Area E: Stratigraphy and Architecture Text*, vol. 7A of *Excavations at the City of David 1978–1985 Directed by Yigal Shiloh*, by Alon De Groot and Hannah Bernick-Greenberg, Qedem 53 (Jerusalem: Institute of Archaeology, The Hebrew University of Jerusalem, 2012), 173–79; Sharon Zuckerman, "The Pottery of Stratum 9 (the Persian Period)," in *Area E: The Finds*, vol. 7B of *Excavations at the City of David 1978–1985 Directed by Yigal Shiloh*, by Alon De Groot and Hannah Bernick-Greenberg, Qedem 54 (Jerusalem: Institute of Archaeology, The Hebrew University of Jerusalem, 2012), 31–50; Andrea Berlin, "The Pottery of Strata 8–7 (The Hellenistic Period)," in De Groot and Bernick-Greenberg, *Area E: The Finds*, 5–30.

128. De Groot, "Discussion and Conclusions," 173–74.

129. Doron Ben-Ami and Yana Tchekhanovets, "The Seleucid Fortification System in the Givati Parking Lot, City of David" [Hebrew], *New Studies in the Archaeology of Jerusalem and Its Region* 9 (2015): 313–22.

3. Early Hellenistic remains revealed here may represent the beginning of expansion of Hellenistic Jerusalem from the mound on the Temple Mount to the south and southwest (similar to the early expansion of the city in the late Iron IIA).
4. Persian period pottery (for now with no architectural remains) was found here during excavations in 2018. The exact date and significance of these finds have not been clarified yet (personal information, Yuval Gadot).

2

# Archaeology and the List of Returnees in the Books of Ezra and Nehemiah

### 1. Introduction

In the first chapter I questioned Neh 3's description of the construction of the Jerusalem wall in the light of the archaeology of Jerusalem in the Persian period.[1] The finds indicate that the settlement was small and poor. It covered an area of circa 2–2.5 hectares and was inhabited by four hundred–five hundred people. The archaeology of Jerusalem shows no evidence for construction of a wall in the Persian period or renovation of the ruined Iron II city wall. I concluded with three alternatives for understanding the discrepancy between the biblical text and the archaeological finds: (1) that the description in Neh 3 is utopian; (2) that it preserves a memory of an Iron Age construction or renovation of the city wall; (3) that the description is influenced by the construction of the First Wall in the Hasmonean period. All three options pose significant difficulties, but the third one seems to me the least problematic. In any event, I argued, the archaeology of Jerusalem in the Persian period must be the starting point for any future discussion of this issue. Accordingly, I believe it is now time to deal with the other lists in the books of Ezra and Nehemiah in the light of modern archaeological research—first and foremost with the list of the returnees to Zion (Ezra 2:1–67; Neh 7:6–68).

The list of returnees forms one of the cornerstones for the study of the province of Yehud in the Persian period. Scholars have debated the relationship between the two versions of the list, the historical authenticity of this source, its date, whether it represents one wave of returnees or a

---

1. Israel Finkelstein, "Jerusalem in the Persian (and Early Hellenistic) Period and the Wall of Nehemiah," *JSOT* 32 (2008): 501–20.

summary of several waves, and its value for estimating the population of Yehud.[2] Because of the lack of ancient Near Eastern sources on Yehud, discussion has focused primarily on the biblical texts and has thus, in certain cases, become trapped in circular reasoning. The only source of information that can break this deadlock is archaeology. Yet until now, archaeology has been brought in only in order to reconstruct settlement patterns and establish the population of Yehud.[3] The archaeology of the sites mentioned in the list of returnees has never been dealt with systematically. It is the aim of this article to do so.

Twenty places are mentioned in the list. They are located in the highlands of Benjamin, the vicinity of Jerusalem (to Bethlehem in the south), and the areas of Lod in the west and Jericho in the east (fig. 2.1). The location of three of these places—Netophah, Nebo (Nob), and Senaah—is not sufficiently well established, while the rest are well (or reasonably well) identified and hence their archaeology can be consulted. In each case I intend to review the finds from the late Iron II, Persian, and Hellenistic periods. In the case of thorough excavations, the discussion may go into subphases within these periods; obviously, this cannot be done in the case of survey material. In addition, I will mention safely dated sources from the late Iron II (biblical material) and Hellenistic periods (the books of Maccabees) that refer to these places. I will commence with the excavated sites and continue with the surveyed sites.

## 2. Sites Excavated

### 2.1. Jerusalem

In the late Iron II, Jerusalem extended over both the "City of David" ridge and the southwestern hill, an area of circa 60 hectares.[4]

---

2. For the latest discussions, see Charles E. Carter, *The Emergence of Yehud in the Persian Period: A Social and Demographic Study*, JSOTSup 294 (Sheffield: Sheffield Academic Press, 1999), 77–78; Diana V. Edelman, *The Origins of the 'Second' Temple: Persian Imperial Policy and the Rebuilding of Jerusalem* (London: Equinox, 2005), 175–76; and especially Oded Lipschits, *The Fall and Rise of Jerusalem: Judah under Babylonian rule* (Winona Lake, IN: Eisenbrauns, 2005), 158–68 with extensive bibliography.

3. Carter, *Emergence of Yehud*; Lipschits, *Fall and Rise of Jerusalem*, 258–71.

4. E.g., Hillel Geva, "Summary and Discussion of Findings from Areas A, W and X-2," in *Jewish Quarter Excavations in the Old City of Jerusalem*, ed. Hillel Geva, vol. 2 (Jerusalem: Israel Exploration Society, 2003), 501–52; Ronny Reich and Eli Shukron,

## 2. Archaeology and the List of Returnees

In the Persian period, the settlement was restricted to a sector of the City of David. Most finds were retrieved from the central part of the ridge, between Areas G and D of the Shiloh excavations.[5] The Persian period (Stratum 9) fully appears, according to Shiloh,[6] in Areas D1,[7] D2, and G[8] and is partially represented in Area E1. But even in these areas the finds were meager and poor; most came from fills and quarrying refuse. Persian-period sherds and a few seal impressions were found in Reich and Shukron's Areas A and B, located in the Kidron Valley and mid-slope respectively, circa 200–250 m south of the Gihon Spring; they seem to have originated in the settlement located on the ridge.[9] Reich and Shukron[10] also note that seventy-five of the eighty-five Yehud seal impressions from the Shiloh excavations published by Ariel and Shoham[11] originated from Areas B, D, and E. They conclude that the settlement of the Persian and early Hellenistic periods was restricted to the top of the ridge, to the south of Area G.[12] Different excavation fields in the southern tip of the City of David and in its northern sector yielded negative evidence for the Persian period; in several of these places late-Hellenistic remains were found superimposed over Iron II remains.[13]

---

"The Urban Development of Jerusalem in the Late Eight Century B.C.E.," in *Jerusalem in the Bible and Archaeology: The First Temple Period*, ed. Andrew G. Vaughn and Ann E. Killebrew, SymS 18 (Atlanta: Society of Biblical Literature, 2003), 209–18.

5. Yigal Shiloh, *Excavations at the City of David*, vol. 1, Qedem 19 (Jerusalem: Institute of Archaeology, 1984), 4.

6. Shiloh, *Excavations at the City of David*, table 2.

7. Donald T. Ariel, Hannah Hirschfeld, and Neta Savir, "Area D1: Stratigraphic Report," in *Extramural Areas*, vol. 5 of *Excavations at the City of David*, ed. Donald T. Ariel, Qedem 40 (Jerusalem: Institute of Archaeology, The Hebrew University of Jerusalem, 2000), 59–62.

8. Shiloh, *Excavations at the City of David*, 20.

9. Ronny Reich and Eli Shukron, "The Yehud Stamp Impressions from the 1995–2005 City of David Excavations," *TA* 34 (2007): 59–65.

10. Reich and Shukron, "Yehud Stamp Impressions."

11. Donald T. Ariel, and Yair Shoham, "Locally Stamped Handles and Associated Body Fragments of the Persian and Hellenistic Periods," in *Inscriptions*, vol. 6 of *Excavations at the City of David 1978–1985*, ed. Donald T. Ariel, Qedem 41 (Jerusalem: Institute of Archaeology, 2000), 137–71.

12. See a somewhat similar view in Ariel and Shoham, "Locally Stamped Handles," 138.

13. See in detail Finkelstein, "Jerusalem in the Persian (and Early Hellenistic) Period" (ch. 1 in this volume).

The early Hellenistic settlement (Stratum 8) is restricted to approximately the same area of the City of David. It fully appears only in Area E2, partially represented in Areas E1 and E3, and scarcely represented in Areas D1 and D2.[14] In this case, too, the finds are meager, consisting of three *columbaria*[15] and a structure that yielded the only assemblage of early Hellenistic pottery from Jerusalem.[16]

The maximal size of the Persian and early Hellenistic settlement was therefore circa 240 (N–S) × 120 (E–W) m, that is, circa 2–2.5 hectares.[17]

In the late Hellenistic period, Jerusalem expanded again, to cover the entire area of the previous Iron II city, that is, the City of David and the southwestern hill.[18]

2.2. Gibeon

Gibeon prospered in the late Iron II. It produced wine, was surrounded by strong fortifications, and was equipped with a sophisticated water system.[19] An elaborate late-Iron II cemetery lies to the east of the mound.[20]

Gibeon did not yield unambiguous Persian-period finds. Without going into the debate over the dating of the Gibeon winery and inscriptions—late monarchic or sixth century[21]—the *mwsh* seal impressions and

---

14. Shiloh, *Excavations at the City of David*, 4, table 2.

15. Alon De Groot, "Jerusalem in the Early Hellenistic Period" [Hebrew], *NSJ* 10 (2004): 67–70.

16. In Area E1—Shiloh, *Excavations at the City of David*, 15.

17. Contra to the idea of a 6-hectare settlement (excluding the Temple Mount) in Carter, *Emergence of Yehud*, 200; Oded Lipschits, "Achaemenid Imperial Policy, Settlement Processes in Palestine, and the Status of Jerusalem in the Middle of the Fifth Century B.C.E.," in *Judah and the Judeans in the Persian Period*, ed. Oded Lipschits and Manfred Oeming (Winona Lake, IN: Eisenbrauns, 2006), 32; and a 30-acre settlement (possibly including the Temple Mount) in Nahman Avigad, "Jerusalem: The Second Temple Period," *NEAEHL* 2 (1993): 720.

18. Summaries in Hillel Geva, "Western Jerusalem at the End of the First Temple Period in Light of the Excavations in the Jewish Quarter," in Vaughn and Killebrew *Jerusalem in the Bible and Archaeology*, 183–208; Geva, "Summary and Discussion of Findings," 526–34; Gregory J. Wightman, *The Walls of Jerusalem: From the Canaanites to the Mamluks* (Sydney: Meditarch, 1993), 111–57.

19. James B. Pritchard, *Gibeon, Where the Sun Stood Still, The Discovery of the Biblical City* (Princeton: Princeton University Press, 1962), 53–99.

20. Hanan Eshel, "The Late Iron Age Cemetery of Gibeon," *IEJ* 37 (1987): 1–17.

21. See summaries in Ephraim Stern, *Material Culture of the Land of the Bible in*

## 2. Archaeology and the List of Returnees 33

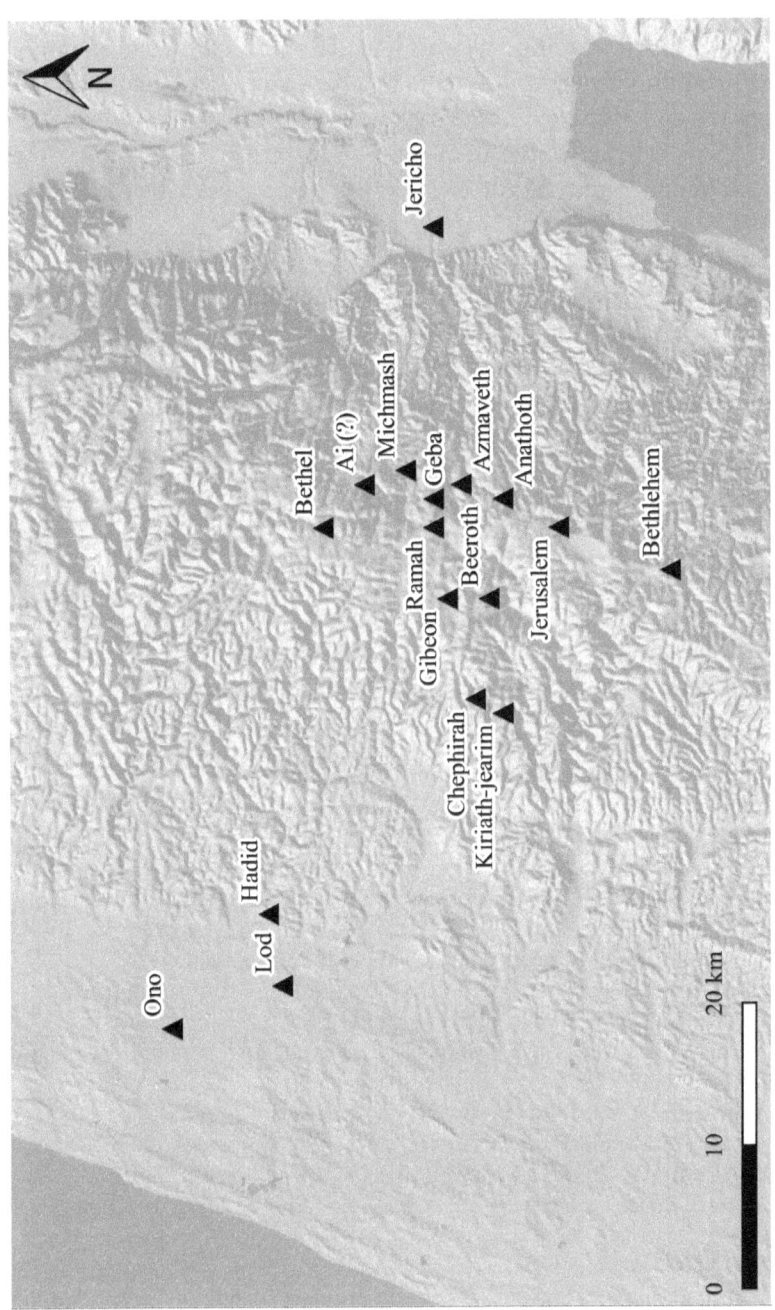

Figure 2.1. Sites mentioned in the list of returnees

wedge-shaped and reed impressed sherds found at the site[22] attest to a certain activity in the Babylonian or Babylonian/early Persian period. Yet, typical Persian-period pottery and Yehud seal impressions were not found.[23] According to Pritchard, there is "only scant evidence of occupation from the end of the sixth century until the beginning of the first century B.C.E." at Gibeon.[24] Still, in an attempt to provide evidence for the Gibeon of Neh 3, 7 and the list of returnees he proposed that "scattered and sporadic settlements" did exist there during the Persian and Hellenistic periods.[25] Stern rightly interpreted the Gibeon finds as evidence for only sixth century and possibly early Persian-period activity.[26]

Late Hellenistic pottery and coins dated to the days of Antiochus III and John Hyrcanus are attested at Gibeon.[27]

Gibeon is mentioned in late monarchic biblical sources—in the list of towns of Benjamin (Josh 18:25), unanimously dated to the late seventh century BCE,[28] and in the book of Jeremiah (28:1; 41:16).

## 2.3. Bethel

Bethel was fully settled in the late Iron II.[29] A wedge-shaped and reed-impressed sherd found at the site[30] and a Babylonian seal bought from the villagers of Beitin[31] seem to indicate that the site continued to be inhabited

---

*the Persian Period, 538–332 B.C* (Warminster: Aris & Phillips, 1982), 32–33; Stern, *The Assyrian, Babylonian, and Persian Periods (732–332 B.C.E.)*, vol. 2 of *Archaeology of the Land of the Bible* (New York: Doubleday, 2001), 433; Oded Lipschits, "The History of the Benjaminite Region under Babylonian Rule" [Hebrew], *Zion* 64 (1999): 287–91.

22. James B. Pritchard, *Winery, Defenses and Soundings at Gibeon* (Philadelphia: University Museum, University of Pennsylvania, 1964), figs. 32, 7, 48, 17.

23. For the latter, see Lipschits, *Fall and Rise of Jerusalem*, 180.

24. James B. Pritchard, "Gibeon," *NEAEHL* 2 (1993): 513.

25. Pritchard, *Gibeon, Where the Sun Stood Still*, 163.

26. Stern, *Material Culture of the Land of the Bible*, 32–33; Stern, *Assyrian, Babylonian, and Persian Periods*, 433; Lipschits, *Fall and Rise of Jerusalem*, 243–45—sixth century.

27. Pritchard, *Gibeon, Where the Sun Stood Still*, 163.

28. Albrecht Alt, "Judas Gaue unter Josia," *PJ* 21 (1925): 100–116; Nadav Na'aman, "Kingdom of Judah under Josiah," *TA* 18 (1991): 3–71, with previous literature.

29. James L. Kelso, *The Excavation of Bethel (1934–1960)*, AASOR 39 (Cambridge: American Schools of Oriental Research, 1968), 36–37.

30. Kelso, *Excavation of Bethel*, pl. 67, 8.

31. Kelso, *Excavation of Bethel*, 37; Stern, *Material Culture of the Land of the Bible*, 31.

in the sixth century BCE (and see below for the reference in Zech 7:2). Kelso[32] suggested that the town was destroyed in the second half of the sixth century.

No unambiguous evidence for a Persian-period occupation was found at Bethel; there were no architectural remains, no pottery, and no seal impressions. Moreover, the foundations of the Hellenistic walls penetrated into the Iron II remains.[33] The excavators speculated that a Persian-period settlement may have been located under the built-up area of the village of Beitin, near the spring, in the southern part of the site,[34] but such a settlement should have left a clear ceramic imprint at the site. The only such clue is a tiny sherd identified by Illiff as part of a fifth century BCE Greek lekythos.[35]

A prosperous Hellenistic settlement was uncovered at Bethel.[36]

Bethel is mentioned in a large number of late-monarchic biblical sources, such as the list of towns of Benjamin (Josh 18:22), which dates to the late seventh century,[37] and the description of the days of Josiah (2 Kgs 23). Papyrus Amherst 63 mentions deportees by the Assyrians, who were probably settled at Bethel.[38] If the mention of Bethel in Zech 7:2 refers to a place[39] and is not part of a name of a person,[40] it testifies to the fact that the site was inhabited in the late sixth century. Bethel is mentioned in the list of forts built by Bacchides (1 Macc 9:50).

---

32. Kelso, *Excavation of Bethel*, 37, 38.
33. Kelso, *Excavation of Bethel*, 36.
34. Kelso, *Excavation of Bethel*, 38.
35. Kelso, *Excavation of Bethel*, 80, pl. 37, 10. I wish to thank Dr. Oren Tal of Tel Aviv University for checking this sherd and confirming its date as suggested decades ago by Illiff.
36. Kelso, *Excavation of Bethel*, 36, 40, 52; Paul W. Lapp, "Bethel Pottery of the Late Hellenistic and Early Roman Periods," in Kelso, *Excavation of Bethel*, 77–80.
37. Alt, "Judas Gaue unter Josia"; Na'aman, "Kingdom of Judah."
38. Richard C. Steiner, "The Aramaic Text in Demotic Script: The Liturgy of a New Year's Festival Imported from Bethel to Syene by Exiles from Rash," *JAOS* 111 (1991): 362–63.
39. E.g., Carol L. Meyers and Eric M. Meyers, *Haggai, Zechariah 1–8*, AB 25B (Garden City: Doubleday, 1987), 382–83.
40. E.g., Peter R. Ackroyd, *Exile and Restoration, A Study of Hebrew Thought of the Sixth Century BC* (London: SCM Press, 1968), 207.

## 2.4. Hadid

Hadid is safely identified in the mound of el-Haditheh northeast of Lod. Salvage excavations at the site indicate that the late Iron Age settlement extended over the main mound and its northwestern slope.[41] The excavation yielded two seventh century BCE Neo-Assyrian cuneiform tablets.[42] The site was occupied in both the Persian and Hellenistic periods.[43]

Hadid is mentioned in connection with the history of the Hasmoneans; it was fortified by Simeon the Hasmonean (1 Macc 12:38; 13:13; Josephus, *A.J.* 13.203, 392).

## 2.5. Jericho

Tell es-Sultan was intensively settled in the seventh century BCE. Yehud seal impressions and attic vessels[44] indicate that the site was inhabited in the Persian period. The late Hellenistic settlement was located at Tulul Abu el-Alayiq to the southwest of Tell es-Sultan.[45]

Jericho is mentioned in the list of towns of Benjamin (Josh 18:21), which dates to the late seventh century BCE.[46] It is referred to in various Hellenistic sources—the Zenon papyri, 1 and 2 Maccabees, Diodorus, and Strabo.[47]

---

41. Etty Brand, *Salvage Excavation on the Margin of Tel Hadid, Preliminary Report* [Hebrew] (Tel Aviv: Tel Aviv Institute of Archaeology, 1998), 27–29.

42. Nadav Na'aman and Ran Zadok, "Assyrian Deportations to the Province of Samaria in the Light of the Two Cuneiform Tablets from Tel Hadid," *TA* 27 (2000): 159–88.

43. Etty Brand, "el-Haditha" [Hebrew], *ESI* 19 (1997): 44*–46*; for the Hellenistic settlement, see also Alla Nagorsky, "Tel Hadid," *ESI* 117 (2005): http://www.hadashot-esi.org.il/report_detail_eng.aspx?id=173&mag_id=110.

44. David Vanderhooft and Oded Lipschits, "A New Typology of the Yehud Stamp Impressions," *TA* 34 (2007): 12–37; Stern, *Material Culture of the Land of the Bible*, 38, respectively.

45. Ehud Netzer, *Hasmonean and Herodian Palaces at Jericho I* (Jerusalem: Israel Exploration Society, 2001).

46. Alt, "Judas Gaue unter Josia"; Na'aman, "Kingdom of Judah."

47. Yoram Tzafrir, Leah Di Segni, and Judith Green, *Tabula Imperii Romani Judaea Palaestina, Maps and Gazetteer* (Jerusalem: Israel Academy of Sciences and Humanities, 1994), 143.

## 2.6. Lod

The mound of Lod has never been properly excavated; in fact, its exact extent under the premodern Arab town is not very clear.[48] Still, enough finds have been unearthed to show that Lod was inhabited from Neolithic to Ottoman times.[49] Excavations at Neve Yarak, a neighborhood of modern Lod situated near the ancient mound, yielded Iron II, Persian, and Hellenistic finds.[50] It is quite clear, then, that the site was inhabited in all three periods discussed in this paper.

Lod is mentioned in 1 Macc 11:34 as one of the three toparchies added to the Hasmonean territory in 145 BCE.

## 3. Sites Surveyed

### 3.1. Bethlehem

The mound occupies the eastern sector of the ridge overbuilt by the town of Bethlehem. It seems to have been fully occupied in the Iron II.[51] A recent survey of parcels of land still available for research to the east of the Church of Nativity revealed Iron II and Byzantine sherds;[52] no other period is mentioned.

The only quantitative survey at the site was conducted by Ofer, who collected twenty-six rims from the late Iron II, two rims from the Persian period, and one or two rims from the Hellenistic period.[53] Beyond indicating periods of occupation, these data are insufficient for reconstructing the size of the site and the intensity of activity in the various periods of habitation.

---

48. See Ram Gophna and Itzhak Beit-Arieh, *Archaeological Survey of Israel: Map of Lod (80)* (Jerusalem: Israel Antiquities Authority, 1997), 88.
49. Gophna and Beit-Arieh, *Archaeological Survey of Israel*.
50. Aryeh Rosenberger and Alon Shavit, "Lod, Newe Yaraq," *ESI* 13 (1993): 54*–56*; Amir Feldstein, "Lod, Neve Yaraq (B)," *ESI* 19 (1997): 50*; Hamoudi Khalaily and Avi Gopher, "Lod," *ESI* 19 (1997): 51*; Yoav Arbel, "Lod," *ESI* 116 (2004): 40*.
51. See list of spots with Iron II finds in Kay Prag, "Bethlehem, A Site Assessment," *PEQ* 132 (2000): 170–71.
52. Prag, "Bethlehem."
53. Avi Ofer, "The Highland of Judah during the Biblical Period" [Hebrew] (PhD thesis; Tel Aviv: Tel Aviv University, 1993), appendix IIA, 13.

Bethlehem is mentioned in the LXX version of the list of towns of Judah (Josh 15:59a), which dates to the late seventh century BCE,[54] and in the book of Jeremiah (41:17).

## 3.2. Anathoth

Early studies did not locate pre-Roman remains at the village of Anata.[55] Hence the location of biblical Anathoth was sought at two sites in the vicinity of the village.

Ras el-Kharubeh was both surveyed and excavated.[56] The modern excavation yielded a small number of sherds (forty altogether) from the late Iron II, sherds from the Persian period (about 25 percent of the material from the dig), and a large number of sherds from the late Hellenistic period. The site was found to be eroded and sparsely inhabited.[57] A survey conducted at the site yielded Iron II and Hellenistic sherds, but no Persian-period finds.[58]

Another site suggested for the location of biblical Anathoth is Khirbet Deir es-Sidd, which was also excavated by Biran.[59] It was strongly inhabited in the late-Iron II, but did not yield Persian-period finds. Only a few Hellenistic-Roman sherds were found. A survey conducted at the site yielded a large number of sherds, 70 percent of which were dated to the Iron II. Persian-period sherds were found in a tomb. Hellenistic sherds were also present.[60]

A thorough, modern survey of the village of Anata has shown that it is built on an ancient site.[61] Hence there is no reason to seek the location of Anathoth elsewhere. The survey yielded 242 sherds, 35 percent of which

---

54. Alt, "Judas Gaue unter Josia"; Na'aman, "Kingdom of Judah."
55. Edward P. Blair, "Soundings at 'Anata (Roman Anathoth)," *BASOR* 62 (1936): 18–21; William F. Albright, "Additional Note," *BASOR* 62 (1936): 25–26.
56. For early research, see Avraham Bergman and William F. Albright, "Soundings at the Supposed Site of Old Testament Anathoth," *BASOR* 62 (1936): 22–25.
57. Avraham Biran, "On the Identification of Anathoth," *ErIsr* 18 (1985): 209–11.
58. Uri Dinur and Nurit Feig, "Eastern Part of the Map of Jerusalem" [Hebrew], in *Archaeological Survey of the Hill Country of Benjamin*, ed. Israel Finkelstein and Yitzhak Magen (Jerusalem: Israel Antiquities Authority, 1993), 358.
59. Biran, "On the Identification of Anathoth," 211–13.
60. Dinur and Feig, "Eastern Part of the Map of Jerusalem," 379.
61. Dinur and Feig, "Eastern Part of the Map of Jerusalem," 359–60.

2. Archaeology and the List of Returnees          39

date to the Iron II and 10 percent to the Hellenistic period. The Persian period is not represented.[62]

The mention of Anathoth in the book of Jeremiah attests to its being settled in late-monarchic times.

3.3. Azmaveth

Azmaveth is securely identified with the village of Hizma northeast of Jerusalem. The site was surveyed twice. Kallai reported sherds from the Roman period and later.[63] A more thorough and modern survey was conducted by Dinur and Feig,[64] who reported sherds from the Iron II, Persian, and Hellenistic periods.[65]

3.4. Kirjath-jearim

Kirjath-jearim is securely identified in the mound of Deir el-'Azar, above the village of Abu-Ghosh. A large collection of pottery from the site, stored by the Antiquities Authority, was studied by the author in 1992. It includes 440 sherds, of which 310 date to the Iron II, 1 to the Persian period, 49 to the Persian or Hellenistic period, 23 to the Hellenistic period, and 11 to the Hellenistic or Roman period. The number of sherds collected at the site is sufficient to state that it was strongly inhabited in the late Iron II, very sparsely inhabited—if at all—in the Persian period, and inhabited in the Hellenistic period.

Kirjath-jearim is mentioned in the lists of towns of Judah and Benjamin (Josh 15:60; 18:14), which date to the late seventh century BCE,[66] and in the book of Jeremiah (26:20).

---

62. As an editor of the volume in which the surveys of Dinur and Feig and Felstein et al. where published, the author went over the pottery of all sites. This includes the sites reported here, Anata, Hizma, Kh. el-Kafira, Kh. el-Burj, er-Ram, Jaba, and Mukhmas.

63. Zacharia Kallai, "The Land of Benjamin and Mt. Ephraim" [Hebrew], in *Judaea, Samaria and the Golan, Archaeological Survey 1967–1968*, ed. Moshe Kochavi (Jerusalem: Carta, 1972), 185.

64. Dinur and Feig, "Eastern Part of the Map of Jerusalem," 372–73.

65. See also Uri Dinur, "Hizma," *ESI* 5 (1986): 53.

66. Alt, "Judas Gaue unter Josia"; Na'aman, "Kingdom of Judah."

## 3.5. Chephirah

Chephirah is securely identified with Kh. el-Kafira northwest of Jerusalem. The site was surveyed twice. Vriezen collected a large number of Iron II sherds and several Persian and Hellenistic sherds.[67] Feldstein et al. surveyed the site thoroughly and collected 243 sherds, of which 81 percent date to the Iron II.[68] A few sherds were tentatively dated to the Persian period and 13 percent were assigned to the Hellenistic and Roman periods. It is clear from these data that the main period of occupation was the Iron II, that activity at the site in the Persian period was weak, and that occupation intensified in the Hellenistic period.

Chephirah is mentioned in the list of towns of Benjamin (Josh 18:26) which dates to the late seventh century BCE.[69]

## 3.6. Beeroth

The location of Beeroth was debated in the early years of research[70] but was later safely fixed at the site of Khirbet el-Burj on the outskirts of the modern Jerusalem neighborhood of Ramot.[71] The site was surveyed and partially excavated in a salvage operation.

Kallai was the first to conduct a modern survey at the site.[72] He reported Iron II pottery and a single wedge-shaped and reed-impressed sherd that should probably be dated to the sixth century BCE. Feldstein et al.[73] conducted a more modern and thorough survey at the site and collected 212 sherds, of which 74 percent date to the Iron II, a few to the Persian period, 9 percent to the Persian or Hellenistic period, and 8 percent to the Hellenistic period.

---

67. Karel J. H Vriezen, "Hirbet Kefire—Eine Oberflächenuntersuchung," *ZDPV* 91 (1975): figs. 4, 23–25, and 5 respectively.

68. Amir Feldstein et al., "Southern Part of the Maps of Ramallah and el-Bireh and Northern Part of the Map of 'Ein Kerem'" [Hebrew], in Finkelstein and Magen, *Archaeological Survey of the Hill Country of Benjamin*, 209–11.

69. Alt, "Judas Gaue unter Josia"; Na'aman, "Kingdom of Judah."

70. Summary in Shemuel Yeivin, "The Benjaminite Settlement in the Western Part of their Territory," *IEJ* (1971): 141–42.

71. Yeivin, "Benjaminite Settlement," 141–42.

72. Kallai, "Land of Benjamin," 186–87.

73. Feldstein et al., "Southern Part of the Maps of Ramallah," 231–33.

A salvage excavation was conducted at the site in 1992.[74] Most of the finds belonged to medieval times, but evidence was revealed for a settlement that was occupied from the Iron Age through the Hellenistic period.

It is clear from this data that the settlement was at its peak in the Iron II, that activity in the Persian period was weak, and that a certain recovery occurred in the Hellenistic period.

Beeroth is mentioned in the list of towns of Benjamin (Josh 18:25), which dates to the late seventh century BCE.[75] It is possibly mentioned in 1 Macc 9:4 as Βερεα.[76]

## 3.7. Ramah

Ramah is unanimously identified with the village of er-Ram north of Jerusalem. Only one modern survey was conducted at the site—by Feldstein et al.[77] They collected a large number of 359 sherds, of which 20 percent date to the Iron II, 2 percent to the Persian period, and 13 percent to the Hellenistic period. This means that the site was strongly inhabited in the Iron II, that it declined in the Persian period, and that it recovered in the Hellenistic period.

Ramah appears in the list of towns of Benjamin (Josh 18:25), which dates to the late seventh century BCE,[78] and in the book of Jeremiah (31:15; 40:1).

## 3.8. Geba

Geba is securely identified with the village of Jaba northeast of Jerusalem. The site was surveyed twice. Kallai reported sherds from the Iron II and the Persian period.[79] Feldstein et al. conducted a more thorough survey at the site and collected 284 sherds, of which 23 percent date to the Iron

---

74. Alexander Onn and Yehuda Rapuano, "Jerusalem, Khirbet el-Burj," *ESI* 14 (1994): 88–90.
75. Alt, "Judas Gaue unter Josia"; Na'aman, "Kingdom of Judah."
76. Josephus, *A.J.* 12.422 writes Βηρζεθ, but see discussion in Uriel Rappaport, *The First Book of Maccabees: Introduction, Hebrew Translation, and Commentary* [Hebrew] (Jerusalem: Yad Ben-Zvi, 2004), 233.
77. Feldstein et al., "Southern Part of the Maps of Ramallah," 168–69.
78. Alt, "Judas Gaue unter Josia"; Na'aman, "Kingdom of Judah."
79. Kallai, "Land of Benjamin," 183.

II and 22 percent to the Hellenistic period.[80] It seems, therefore, that the site was strongly inhabited in both the Iron II and the Hellenistic period. It was probably deserted (or very sparsely inhabited) in the Persian period.

Geba appears in the list of towns of Benjamin (Josh 18:24), which dates to the late seventh century BCE.[81]

## 3.9. Michmash

Michmash is securely identified with the village of Mukhmas to the northeast of Jerusalem. The ancient site—Khirbet el-Hara el-Fauqa—is located on the northern edge of the village. The site was thoroughly surveyed by Feldstein et al., who collected 643 sherds (!), of which 14 percent date to the Iron II, 10 percent to the Persian period, and 19 percent to the Hellenistic period.[82] This means that the site was strongly inhabited in all three periods discussed here.

Michmash served for a while as the seat of Jonathan the Hasmonean (1 Macc 9:73; Josephus, *A.J.* 13.34).

## 3.10. Ai

Ai of the list of returnees is a riddle. The site of et-Tell was not inhabited after the Iron I. Assuming that there is a connection between the Ai of the book of Joshua (as a name originally derived from an etiological story) and the Ai of the list, the only sites which may provide an archaeological reality behind this place-name are the village of Deir Dibwan, or better (from the preservation of the name point of view) Khirbet el-Haiyan, located on the southern outskirts of Deir Dibwan.

Deir Dibwan is a large village that has never been properly surveyed. Feldstein et al. managed to collect twenty sherds there, among them a single sherd from the Iron II and all the others from the Roman period and later.[83] This is insufficient to reach conclusions regarding the settlement history of the site.

---

80. Feldstein et al., "Southern Part of the Maps of Ramallah," 177–79.
81. Alt, "Judas Gaue unter Josia"; Na'aman, "Kingdom of Judah."
82. Feldstein et al., "Southern Part of the Maps of Ramallah," 185–86.
83. Feldstein et al., "Southern Part of the Maps of Ramallah," 183–84.

Khirbet el-Haiyan was both excavated and surveyed. Excavation at the site revealed evidence for occupation starting in the Roman period.[84] Kallai's survey revealed sherds from the Roman period and later.[85] Feldstein et al. collected 112 sherds at the site, of which 32 percent were dated to the Hellenistic or Roman period.[86]

These data are not sufficient for this discussion. It seems logical to suggest that Ai of the list of returnees should be sought at Deir Dibwan.

3.11. Ono

Gophna, Taxel, and Feldstein have recently shown that Ono cannot be identified with Kafr Ana, a site that was not occupied from the Chalcolithic to the Byzantine period.[87] Instead, they suggested identifying Ono at the site of Kafr Juna, located 1 km to the northeast of Kafr Ana. Surveys conducted there yielded a large number of Iron II, Persian, and Hellenistic sherds.[88]

4. Discussion

Table 1 summarizes the finds at the sites mentioned in the list of returnees.

Table 1. Summary of the archaeology of the sites mentioned in the list of returnees, including intensity of occupation (V = evidence for activity, but data not sufficient to specify intensity of activity)

|  | Iron II | Persian | Hellenistic |
| --- | --- | --- | --- |
| Jerusalem | Strong | Weak | Strong |
| Bethlehem | V | Weak | Weak |
| Gibeon | Strong | — (except for sixth century)? | Weak |

---

84. Joseph A. Callaway and Murray B. Nicol, "A Sounding at Khirbet Hayian," *BASOR* 183 (1966): 19.

85. Kallai, "Land of Benjamin," 178–79.

86. Feldstein et al., "Southern Part of the Maps of Ramallah," 183.

87. Ram Gophna, Itamar Taxel, and Amir Feldstein, "A New Identification of Ancient Ono," *BAIAS* 23 (2005): 167–76.

88. Gophna, Taxel, and Feldstein, "New Identification of Ancient Ono," 167–76.

|  | Iron II | Persian | Hellenistic |
|---|---|---|---|
| Anathoth | Strong | — | Medium |
| Azmaveth | V | V | V |
| Kirjath-jearim | Strong | Weak | Medium |
| Chephirah | Strong | Weak | Weak |
| Beeroth | Strong | Weak | Medium |
| Ramah | Strong | Weak | Medium |
| Geba | Strong | —? | Strong |
| Michmash | Strong | Medium | Strong |
| Bethel | Strong | — (except for sixth century)? | Strong |
| Ai (if Kh. Haiyan) | — | — | V? |
| (if Deir Dibwan) | V |  |  |
| Lod | V | V | V |
| Hadid | V | V | V |
| Ono | Strong | Strong | Strong |
| Jericho | V | V | V |

Three-to-five places mentioned in the list (including places which were thoroughly excavated) were not inhabited in the Persian period, and at other sites activity was meager. Places which do not appear in the list are also worth mentioning. The best marker for importance of sites in the Persian period is the number of Yehud seal impression found in the course of their excavations.[89] The sites with the largest number of such seal impres-

---

89. I refer to types 1–15 in Vanderhooft and Lipschits, "New Typology of the Yehud Stamp Impressions."

## 2. Archaeology and the List of Returnees

sions are Ramat Rahel, Jerusalem, Mizpah, Nebi Samuel, and En Gedi. Mizpah, En Gedi, and Beth-haccherem[90] do not appear in the list, and the list does not include any name which can fit the location of Nebi Samuel. In other words, four of the five sites with the largest number of Yehud seal impressions are absent from the list—another indication that the list does not fit the reality of the Persian period. Finally, it is evident that the number of returnees which appear in the list[91]—if taken as reflecting a real demographic reality—does not fit the depleted population of Yehud in the Persian period.[92]

All this is sufficient to argue that the list of returnees cannot be seen as an authentic record of the places where returnees settled in the Persian period. The archaeology of the list contradicts the ideas of both those who accept the list as genuinely representing the early settlement, immediately after the return,[93] or in the days of Nehemiah,[94] and those who see it as summarizing several waves of returnees up to the days of Nehemiah.[95] Based on a demographic estimation for Persian-period Yehud, Lipschits[96] rejected the notions of large scale deportations at the end of the Iron II and significant waves of returnees thereafter and suggested that the list is a literary compilation that could have been based on several censuses that were undertaken during the Persian period.[97] The results of this investigation make this suggestion too untenable.

There are several ways to decipher the reality behind the list of returnees. According to the first, it reflects a late Iron II situation, possibly focused on a vague memory of the main areas from which people were deported, or the main areas to which they returned. Another pos-

---

90. Most probably Ramat Rahel—Yohanan Aharoni, *The Land of the Bible: A Historical Geography* (Philadelphia: Westminster Press, 1979), 418.

91. See discussion in Lipschits, *Fall and Rise of Jerusalem*, 161–62.

92. For the latter, see, e.g., Carter, *Emergence of Yehud*, 195–205; Lipschits, *Fall and Rise of Jerusalem*, 270.

93. E.g., Kurt Galling, "The 'Gola-List' according to Ezra 2 // Nehemiah 7," *JBL* 70 (1951): 149–58; Jacob M. Myers, *Ezra Nehemiah*, AB 14 (Garden City: Doubleday, 1965), 14–17.

94. Joseph Blenkinsopp, *Ezra/Nehemiah: A Commentary* (Philadelphia: Westminster, 1988), 83.

95. Summary in Lipschits, *Fall and Rise of Jerusalem*, 159–60, n. 91.

96. Lipschits, *Fall and Rise of Jerusalem*, 160–61.

97. For other scholars who proposed a similar solution, see references in Lipschits, *Fall and Rise of Jerusalem*, 160, n. 92.

sibility is that the list has no historical value at all, and simply mentions important settlements of the late Iron II, in areas that were included in the province of Yehud. A third explanation could be that the list was compiled in the late Hellenistic (Hasmonean) period and reflects the settlement reality of that time, against the background of a vague memory of the territory of the province of Yehud with the addition of the area of Lod (below). The latter possibility would also fit the demographic reality hidden behind the list.[98]

Finally, it is noteworthy that seven of the places in the list appear in the books of Maccabees, including important places in the history of the Hasmoneans such as Beeroth, Michmash, and Hadid. The appearance in the list of Lod, Hadid, and Ono is also significant. According to the distribution of the Persian-period Yehud seal impressions,[99] this area was not part of the province of Yehud. The Samaria district of Lod was added to the Hasmonean territory in 145 BCE (1 Macc 11:34)—another clue that the list may depict a second century BCE reality.

## 5. Summary

The archaeology of the places mentioned in the list of returnees seems to show that it does not represent Persian-period realities. Important Persian-period places not mentioned in the list support this notion. The archaeology of the list leaves two main options for understanding the reality behind it. According to the first, the list portrays late Iron II places. According to the second, it was compiled in the late Hellenistic (Hasmonean) period and represents the reality of the time. The latter solution, also proposed as a possibility for the understanding of Neh 3,[100] raises significant difficulties, as it has far-reaching implications regarding the date of the final redaction of the books of Ezra and Nehemiah. Yet, without extrabiblical sources to support a Persian-period date for the list of returnees, the archaeological evidence cannot be ignored.

---

98. From the text point of view, see Jacob L. Wright, "A New Model for the Composition of Ezra-Nehemiah," in *Judah and the Judeans in the Fourth Century B.C.E.*, ed. Oded Lipschits, Gary N. Knoppers, and Rainer Albertz (Winona Lake, IN: Eisenbrauns, 2007), 347. Wright argues that the list "appears to respond to apocalyptic notions that most likely do not predate the Hellenistic period."

99. Vanderhooft and Lipschits, "New Typology of the Yehud Stamp Impressions."

100. Finkelstein, "Jerusalem in the Persian Period" (ch. 1 in this volume).

## Addendum

Archaeology of Jerusalem

A few years after the publication of the original article, Koch, Lipschits, and I raised the possibility that the ancient mound of Jerusalem was located on the Temple Mount (rather than the "City of David" ridge).[101] In this case too there is enough information to indicate that activity in the Persian and early Hellenistic period was weak; see more in the addendum to chapter 1.

Bethel

A year after the publication of the original article on the list of returnees, Singer-Avitz, and I published a detailed reevaluation of the archaeology of Bethel, which was based on a thorough examination of the pottery from the dig stored in the Pittsburgh Theological Seminary and the The W. F. Albright Institute of Archaeological Research in Jerusalem.[102] We reaffirmed the observation (based on the published material) regarding an occupational gap (or very weak activity) at the site in the Babylonian, Persian, and early Hellenistic periods. Na'aman and Lipschits criticized our findings,[103] arguing that:

1. The site was only partially excavated.

---

101. Israel Finkelstein, Ido Koch, and Oded Lipschits, "The Mound on the Mount: A Solution to the 'Problem with Jerusalem'?," *JHS* 11 (2011): art. 12.

102. Israel Finkelstein and Lily Singer-Avitz, "Reevaluating Bethel," *ZDPV* 125 (2009): 33–48.

103. Nadav Na'aman, "Does Archaeology Really Deserve the Status of a 'High Court' in Biblical Historical Research?," in *Between Evidence and Ideology: Essays on the History of Ancient Israel Read at the Joint Meeting of the Society for Old Testament Study and the Oud Testamentisch Werkgezelschap, Lincoln, July 2009*, ed. Bob Becking and Lester L. Grabbe, OtSt 59 (Leiden: Brill), 180–82; Na'aman, "The Jacob Story and the Formation of Biblical Israel," *TA* 41 (2014): 101; Oded Lipschits, "Bethel Revisited," in *Rethinking Israel: Studies in the History and Archaeology of Ancient Israel in Honor of Israel Finkelstein*, ed. Oded Lipschits, Yuval Gadot, and Matthew J. Adams (Winona Lake, IN: Eisenbrauns, 2017), 233–46. For my initial answer to Na'aman, see Israel Finkelstein, "Archaeology as High Court in Ancient Israelite History: A Reply to Nadav Na'aman," *JHS* 10 (2010): art. 19.

2. In certain periods, Bethel functioned as a temple-only place, and the temple may have been located in unexcavated sectors of the site.
3. Based on Gen 12:8, 13:3, Lipschits suggested that the temple was located east of Bethel; he raised the possibility of identifying its site on a hill about one kilometer away from the mound of Bethel.
4. Lipschits raised the possibility that "periods with a low number of imported, 'nice,' and indicative material (such as the Babylonian, Persian and Early Hellenistic periods, for example) were thrown away …" (sic).[104]
5. Bethel must have been settled at these periods because of the dating of composition of biblical texts to this time slot.

These arguments should all be dismissed:

1. The area that was available for the excavation of Bethel was a significant one. In 1927, Albright estimated it to cover 1.5 hectares,[105] which makes up about half the area of the mound. This sector was explored in several relatively large fields plus a few additional soundings. In some of the excavated areas the dig reached bedrock. This means that Bethel had been excavated more thoroughly than many other sites in the southern Levant and that the finds—including stray sherds—should represent the settlement history of the site.
2. Even if this had been the case, four centuries of activity in a temple should have left some remains—stray sherds here and there.
3. The Genesis verses cannot decide the location of the temple. The authors may have wanted to distance Abraham from the abominable temple of Bethel; the idea could have been to associate Abraham with the important site of Bethel, but locate his altar away from the sinful temple of Jeroboam. In any event, for now, the hill to the east of Bethel, which has recently been excavated,[106] shows no sign of cult activity, and no finds from the Babylonian, Persian, and early Hellenistic periods.

---

104. Lipschits, "Bethel Revisited," 240.
105. Kelso, *Excavation of Bethel*, 2.
106. Aharon Tavger, "E.P. 914 East of Beitin and the Location of the Ancient Cult Site of Bethel" [Hebrew], *In the Highland's Depth* 5 (2015): 49–69.

4. This argument is difficult to understand: why should the excavators decide to throw away the simple (not "nice") sherds from one period and keep similar sherds from another?
  5. A classic circular argument.

Other Sites Mentioned in the List of Returnees

The first season of excavations at the site of Kiriath-jearim (2017) confirmed the description of the finds from the survey reported above: Strong occupation in the Iron IIB–C, weak activity in the Persian and Early Hellenistic periods and significant activity in the late Hellenistic period.[107]

Albright Revividus?

Zevit contested my treatment of the archaeology of sites mentioned in the list of returnees and defended the dating of the list to the Persian period.[108] The debate translates into two contrasting attitudes to the reconstruction of the history of ancient Israel. Zevit—in the footsteps of the Albright School—repeats the biblical testimony in modern (lesser) language; adapts archaeology when it is useful and rejects it when it stands in his way; and fights off any attempt to challenge the historicity of the text. I tend to give archaeology a central, independent role and treat the text as a stratified literary work whose layers are embedded with the ideological goals of their authors and the realities of their time.[109]

Zevit's article demonstrates lack of knowledge—and understanding—of archaeological method and techniques:

  1. Zevit argues against the reliability of archaeological surveys: "Surveys are simply surveys. The accidental origin of what surveyors pick up somewhat randomly cannot be used to determine the actual nature of a site...."[110] It is true that a survey of a given site

---

107. Israel Finkelstein et al., "Excavations at Kiriath-jearim Near Jerusalem, 2017: Preliminary Report," *Semitica* 60 (2018): 31–83.

108. Ziony Zevit, "Is There an Archaeological Case for Phantom Settlements in the Persian Period?," *PEQ* 141 (2009): 124–37.

109. See in detail, Israel Finkelstein, "Persian Period Jerusalem and Yehud: A Rejoinder," *JHS* 9 (2009): art. 24.

110. Zevit, "Is There an Archaeological Case," 131.

may miss periods of occupation later revealed in excavations, but: (a) this is certainly not true in the case of sites which produce hundreds of sherds (see above for Anata, Deir el-ʿAzar, Khirbet el-Kafira, er-Ram, Jaba, and Mukhmas; (b) the case described in this chapter involves a large number of sites and hence the chances of a systematic error in the field—skipping the same periods time and again—are slim. The fact that several of the sites in the list of returnees were thoroughly excavated (rather than surveyed) strengthens my case.

2. "Theoretically an historical presence [in the Persian period—I.F.] could be invisible to archaeology."[111] This is a surprising statement, as walls, floors, sherds, stone vessels, metal implements and other finds do not evaporate. Even faint human activity leaves traces, which can be detected in excavations. Surveys, too, if properly executed, provide a good picture of the settlement history of a site. This is especially true in the highlands, where settlements are usually located on a ridge or a hill and thus sherds are eroded to the slopes, where they can easily be collected in large numbers.

3. What Zevit says about the "two partially overlapping Persian periods" (the historical and the archaeological[112])—is trivial. Similar phenomena were studied long ago regarding other transition periods, for example, from the Roman to Byzantine and from the Byzantine to early Islamic periods. What Zevit states about the transition of pottery traditions between the late Iron II and the sixth century BCE[113] is known to every first-year archaeology student and is taken into consideration in serious studies of the period. In any event, the fifth to fourth centuries BCE pottery repertoire is well-known and easy to identify.[114]

---

111. Zevit, "Is There an Archaeological Case," 125.
112. Zevit, "Is There an Archaeological Case," 132.
113. Zevit, "Is There an Archaeological Case," 125.
114. For instance, Stern, *Material Culture of the Land of the Bible*.

# 3
# The Territorial Extent and Demography of Yehud/Judea in the Persian and Early Hellenistic Periods

The territorial extent of Persian-period Yehud and Hellenistic Judea and estimates of their population are major issues in current research,[1] with far-reaching implications for dating the composition of several biblical works.[2] Recent research on the Yehud seal impressions[3] and my own work on geographical lists in the books of Ezra and Nehemiah[4] raise new questions and call for a fresh treatment of both issues.

## 1. Yehud in the Persian Period

While the borders of the province of Yehud have seemingly been reconstructed according to two pieces of information—the geographical lists in the books of Ezra and Nehemiah, first and foremost among them the list

---

1. For instance, Charles E. Carter, *The Emergence of Yehud in the Persian Period: A Social and Demographic Study*, JSOTSup 294 (Sheffield: Sheffield Academic Press, 1999); Oded Lipschits, *The Fall and Rise of Jerusalem: Judah under Babylonian Rule* (Winona Lake, IN: Eisenbrauns, 2005).

2. For example, William Schniedewind, "Jerusalem, the Late Judaean Monarchy and the Composition of the Biblical Texts," in *Jerusalem in Bible and Archaeology: The First Temple Period*, ed. Andrew G. Vaughn and Ann E. Killebrew, SymS 18 (Atlanta: Society of Biblical Literature, 2003): 375–94; Schniedewind, *How the Bible Became a Book: The Textualization of Ancient Israel* (Cambridge: Cambridge University Press, 2004), 165–90.

3. David Vanderhooft and Oded Lipschits, "A New Typology of the Yehud Stamp Impressions," *TA* 34 (2007): 12–37.

4. Israel Finkelstein, "Jerusalem in the Persian (and Early Hellenistic) Period and the Wall of Nehemiah," *JSOT* 32 (2008): 501–20; Finkelstein, "Archaeology and the List of Returnees in the Books of Ezra and Nehemiah," *PEQ* 140 (2008): 1–10 (chs. 1, 2 in this book).

of the builders of Jerusalem's city wall in Nehemiah, and the distribution of the Persian-period Yehud seal impressions[5]—in reality the main consideration has always been the biblical text. The distribution of the Yehud seal impressions covers only part of the area described in Neh 3, but this has not been thoroughly considered, mainly because scholars have not questioned the Persian-period date of the geographical material in Nehemiah.

Most geographical lists in Ezra and Nehemiah are fragmentary and do not cover the entire supposed area of Yehud. Nehemiah 3 gives a more comprehensive picture, mentioning the division of the territory ruled from Jerusalem into several districts (*pelekh*) and half districts (half *pelekh*). Five places are listed as headquarters in this administrative system (fig. 3.1): Jerusalem, Beth-haccherem, Mizpah, Beth-zur, and Keilah. Several scholars have suggested adding districts in the east (Jericho) and northwest (Gezer).[6] I agree with Liphschits that the province described in the list was divided into five units—those specifically referred to in the text.[7] Accordingly, this province extended from Beth-zur in the south to the area of Mizpah in the north (including the areas around these two sites), and from the Judean desert in the east to Keilah in the west. The latter is the only extension into the Shephelah.

Even so, the list in Neh 3 can hardly serve as the basis for reconstructing the borders of Yehud in the *Persian period*.

(1) Elsewhere I argued that the description of the building of the city wall in Neh 3 does not fit what we know about the archaeology of Jerusalem in the Persian period.[8] While Neh 3 refers to the big city, probably including the southwestern hill (60 hectares, with walls running a length of 3.5 km[9]), that was fortified by a major wall with many towers and gates,

---

5. Types 1–12 in Vanderhooft and Lipschits, "New Typology of the Yehud Stamp Impressions"; for summary of the different opinions, see Carter, *Emergence of Yehud*, 75–90; Lipschits, *Fall and Rise of Jerusalem*, 154–84.

6. See summaries of the different opinions in Ephraim Stern, *Material Culture of the Land of the Bible in the Persian Period, 538–332 B.C.* (Warminster: Aris & Phillips, 1982), 247–49; Carter, *Emergence of Yehud*, 79–80; Lipschits, *Fall and Rise of Jerusalem*, 168–74.

7. Lipschits, *Fall and Rise of Jerusalem*, 168–74.

8. For the original paper, Finkelstein, "Jerusalem in the Persian (and Early Hellenistic) Period" (ch. 1 in this book).

9. David Ussishkin, "The Borders and *De Facto* Size of Jerusalem in the Persian Period," in *Judah and the Judeans in the Persian Period*, ed. Oded Lipschits and Manfred Oeming (Winona Lake, IN: Eisenbrauns, 2006), 147–66.

## 3. Territorial Extent and Demography of Yehud/Judea 53

Persian-period Jerusalem was an *unfortified* village that extended over a very limited area of 2–2.5 hectares—in the central part of the City of David ridge. It seems that the description in Neh 3—which does not belong to the Nehemiah Memoir[10] and was probably inserted into the text of Nehemiah[11]—if not utopian, may represent the reality of the construction of the First Wall by the Hasmoneans in the second century BCE.[12]

(2) The archaeology of Beth-zur, mentioned as the headquarters of half a district (Neh 3:16), poses another problem. Funk, Paul and Nancy Lapp, and Carter argued that the site was very sparsely, in fact, insignificantly inhabited in the Persian and early Hellenistic periods.[13] Funk noted that the "interpretation of the Persian-Hellenistic remains at Beth-zur is dependent in large measure on the extant literary references,"[14] meaning that it was written according to one's understanding of the text rather than the archaeological data. Based on a single locus (!), Stern adhered to the notion of significant activity at the site in the Persian period.[15] Reich argued in the same vein according to an architectural analysis.[16] The published material

---

10. For example, Charles C. Torrey, *Ezra Studies* (Chicago: University of Chicago Press, 1910), 225; Hugh G. M. Williamson, *Ezra, Nehemiah*, WBC 16 (Waco, TX: Word Books, 1985), 200; Joseph Blenkinsopp, *Ezra/Nehemiah: A Commentary* (Philadelphia: Westminster, 1988), 231.

11. For instance, Charles C. Torrey, *The Composition and Historical Value of Ezra-Nehemiah* (Giessen: Ricker, 1896), 37–38; Torrey, *Ezra Studies*, 249; Sigmund Mowinckel, *Studien zu dem Buche Ezra-Nehemia* (Oslo: Universitetsforlaget, 1964), 109–16.

12. Finkelstein, "Jerusalem in the Persian (and Early Hellenistic) Period." Dieter Böhler, *Die heilige Stadt in Esdras a und Esra-Nehemia: Zwei Konzeptionen der Wiederherstellung Israels*, OBO 158 (Fribourg: Universitätsverlag, 1997), 382–97 explicitly put the rebuilding of Jerusalem story in Nehemiah on Hasmonean background.

13. Robert W. Funk, "Beth-Zur," *NEAEHL* 1 (1993): 261; Paul Lapp and Nancy Lapp, "Iron II—Hellenistic Pottery Groups," in *The 1957 Excavation at Beth-Zur*, Orvid R. Sellers et al., AASOR 38 (Cambridge: American Schools of Oriental Research, 1968), 70; Paul Lapp, "The Excavation of Field II," in Sellers et al., *1957 Excavation at Beth-Zur*, 29; Carter, *Emergence of Yehud*, 157.

14. Robert W. Funk, "The History of Beth-Zur with Reference to Its Defenses," in Sellers et al., *1957 Excavation at Beth-Zur*, 9.

15. Ephraim Stern, *The Assyrian, Babylonian, and Persian Periods (732–332 B.C.E.)*, vol. 2 of *Archaeology of the Land of the Bible* (New York: Doubleday, 2001), 437–38; see also Stern, *Material Culture of the Land of the Bible*, 36.

16. Ronny Reich, "The Beth-Zur Citadel II—A Persian Residency?," *TA* 19 (1992): 113–23.

from the excavations[17] includes only a limited number of finds—sherds, vessels and coins—that can safely be dated to the Persian period,[18] while most forms typical of the Persian-period repertoire are missing altogether. Hence, though archaeology may have revealed traces of some Persian-period activity at the site, it is clear that it was an important place only in the late Iron II and more so in the late Hellenistic period.

(3) Gibeon, which is also mentioned in this chapter (Neh 3:7), did not yield unambiguous Persian-period finds either. Without delving into the debate over the dating of the Gibeon winery and inscriptions—late monarchic or sixth century[19]—the *mwsh* seal impressions and wedge-shaped and reed-impressed sherds found at the site attest to a certain activity in the Babylonian or Babylonian/early Persian period.[20] Yet, typical Persian-period pottery and Yehud seal impressions were not found.[21] Late Hellenistic pottery and coins are attested. According to Pritchard, there is "only scant evidence of occupation from the end of the sixth century until the beginning of the first century B.C.E." at Gibeon.[22] Still, in an attempt to provide evidence for the Gibeon of Neh 3:7 he argued that "scattered and sporadic settlements" did exist there during the Persian and Hellenistic periods.[23] Stern rightly interpreted the Gibeon finds as evidence for only sixth century and possibly early Persian-period activity at the site.[24]

(4) Last but not least, the distribution of the Persian-period Yehud seal impressions[25] does not fit the territory described in Neh 3 (fig. 3.1).[26] In

---

17. Ovid R. Sellers, *The Citadel of Beth-Zur* (Philadelphia: Westminster, 1933); Ovid R. Sellers et al., *1957 Excavation at Beth-Zur*.

18. Stern, *Assyrian, Babylonian, and Persian Periods*, 437.

19. Summaries in Stern, *Material Culture of the Land of the Bible*, 32–33; Stern, *Assyrian, Babylonian, and Persian Periods*, 433; Lipschits, "The History of the Benjaminite Region under Babylonian Rule" [Hebrew], *Zion* 64 (1999): 287–91.

20. James B. Pritchard, *Winery, Defenses and Soundings at Gibeon* (Philadelphia: University Museum, University of Pennsylvania, 1964), figs. 32:7, 48:17.

21. For the latter, see Lipschits, *Fall and Rise of Jerusalem*, 180.

22. James B. Pritchard, "Gibeon," *NEAEHL* 2 (1993): 513.

23. James B. Pritchard, *Gibeon, Where the Sun Stood Still: The Discovery of the Biblical City* (Princeton: Princeton University Press, 1962), 163.

24. Stern, *Material Culture of the Land of the Bible*, 32–33; Stern, *Assyrian, Babylonian, and Persian Periods*, 433; Lipschits, *Fall and Rise of Jerusalem*, 243–45—sixth century.

25. Groups 1–12 in Vanderhooft and Lipschits, "New Typology of the Yehud Stamp Impressions."

26. Throughout this article, when describing the distribution of the different

the highlands, these seal impressions are concentrated in Jerusalem and its surroundings, including Ramat Rahel, with only a few (six items) found in the highlands to the north of Jerusalem. No seal impression of this type was found south of Ramat Rahel. In the east, seal impressions of these types were found at Jericho and En-Gedi (six items)—a reasonable reason for the inclusion of this area within the borders of Yehud. In the west they were found at Gezer and Tel Harasim in the western Shephelah (four items altogether)—places clearly outside the borders of Yehud until the expansion of the Hasmonean state in the days of Jonathan and Simeon (below); none was found in the many sites of the upper Shephelah.

Considering the problem of dating the reality behind Neh 3, and with no extrabiblical textual data for the Persian period, one can (should?) try to reconstruct the borders of Yehud *only* according to the distribution of the seal impressions and the fragmentary textual data from the third and second centuries BCE (below).[27] Accordingly, Yehud seems to have included mainly the area of Jerusalem, between Ramat Rahel and the City of David. It could have extended a bit further to the south, but Beth-zur seems to have been outside of the province.[28] In the north, the dearth of seal impressions from the area of Mizpah and Nebi Samuel (six items, which make 5.5 percent of the total of this type, compared to thirty-two items, which make 11 percent of the later Types 13–14 in the work of Vanderhooft and Lipschits[29]) raises the question whether this area was included in Yehud. The list of returnees, which mentions places in this area, should probably be dated to the Hellenistic period.[30] In the east, there was a possible extension to Jericho and En-Gedi. As for the west, in the

---

types of the Yehud seal impressions, I refer to the main concentrations. A single seal impression means nothing, as demonstrated by the impressions found in Babylon and Kadesh-barnea; for the latter, see Vanderhooft and Lipschits, "New Typology of the Yehud Stamp Impressions," 21 and 27 respectively.

27. The genealogies of Judah and Benjamin in 1 Chronicles cannot help reconstructing the "territoriality" (replacing "territory"—a post-modern fad) of Yehud (John W. Wright, "Remapping Yehud: The Borders of Yehud and the Genealogies of Chronicles," in Lipschits and Oeming, *Judah and the Judeans in the Persian Period*, 67–89), because they seem to represent post-Persian-period realities (see ch. 5 in this book).

28. Contra Carter, *Emergence of Yehud*, 98–99.

29. Vanderhooft and Lipschits, "New Typology of the Yehud Stamp Impressions."

30. For the original article, Finkelstein, "Archaeology and the List of Returnees" (ch. 2 in this book).

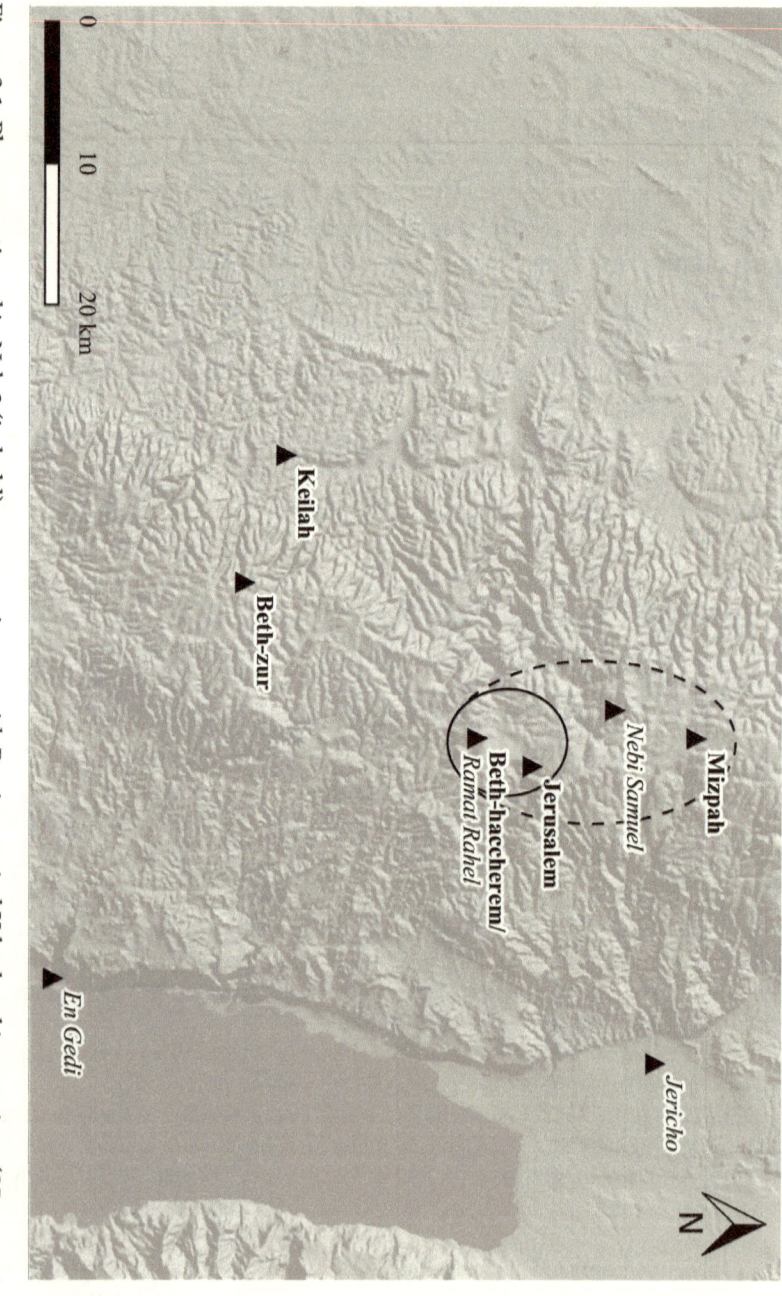

Figure 3.1. Places mentioned in Neh 3 (in bold) versus main area with Persian-period Yehud seal impressions (85 percent of the finds in solid line; 90 percent in dotted line)

## 3. Territorial Extent and Demography of Yehud/Judea 57

time of the Zenon Papyri of the mid-third century BCE, Mareshah and Adoraim belonged to Idumea. The area of Lod and Gezer (which were Israelite rather than Judahite towns in the Iron II), and Ekron in the western Shephelah were annexed to Judea only in the days of Jonathan and Simeon, in the 140s BCE. I therefore tend to agree with Carter that Persian-period Yehud did not extend to the Shephelah.[31]

Yehud was "ruled" from a small temple village in Jerusalem, which had a limited population of a few hundred people.[32] Still, its status as the capital of the province is clear from its mention in the Bagohi papyrus from Elephantine and seemingly also from the high level of silver in the Yehud coins, which seems to be related to their role in the temple economy.[33]

Based on interpretation of the literary sources, the population of Persian-period Yehud had been estimated to have numbered up to 150,000 souls.[34] More reasonable, archaeologically-based studies have estimated the population of the province to have been between 20,000 and 30,000 people.[35] Yet, the latter numbers, too, seem to be somewhat inflated.

(1) The density coefficient of 250 inhabitants per one built-up hectare used by Carter and Lipschits is too high for the sparsely settled highlands villages of the Persian period. A coefficient of 200 inhabitants per one built-up hectare seems to be the maximal possible figure.[36]

---

31. Carter, *Emergence of Yehud*, 91–98.
32. Finkelstein, "Jerusalem in the Persian (and Early Hellenistic) Period" (ch. 1 in this book).
33. Yigal Ronen, "Some Observations on the Coinage of Yehud," *Israel Numismatic Journal* 15 (2003–2006): 29–30; Oren Tal, "Coin Denominations and Weight Standards in Fourth Century B.C.E. Palestine," *Israel Numismatic Research* 2 (2007): 17–28.
34. Joel Weinberg, *The Citizen-Temple Community*, JSOTSup 151 (Sheffield: Sheffield Academic Press, 1992), 132.
35. Carter, *Emergence of Yehud*, 195–205; Oded Lipschits, "Demographic Changes in Judah between the Seventh and the Fifth Centuries B.C.E.," in *Judah and the Judeans in the New-Babylonian Period*, ed. Oded Lipschits and Joseph Blenkinsopp (Winona Lake, IN: Eisenbrauns, 2003), 364 respectively.
36. Israel Finkelstein, "Ethno-historical Background: Land Use and Demography in Recent Generations," in *Highlands of Many Cultures: The Southern Samaria Survey*, ed. Israel Finkelstein, Zvi Lederman, and Shlomo Bunimovitz, MSIA 14 (Tel Aviv: Tel Aviv University Institute of Archaeology, 1997), 121–24.

(2) The population of Jerusalem was less than half of the 1250–1500 advocated by Carter and 1,500 or even 3,000 estimated by Lipschits.[37] It numbered no more than a few hundred people.[38]

(3) Carter and Lipschits included in their calculations areas north of Mizpah and south of Beth-zur, and Lipschits added parts of the Shephelah.

I have now checked this issue afresh. My estimate is based on the archaeological data assembled by Lipschits,[39] yet limiting it to the area described above: from south of Ramat Rahel to Mizpah and from the Dead Sea to the border between the highlands and the Shephelah. I divided the sites according to categories (table 3.1):[40]

Small sites: 0.1–0.3 hectare, with an average of 0.2 hectare
Medium sites: 0.4–1 hectare, with an average of 0.7 hectare
Large sites: 1.1–3 hectares, with an average of 2 hectares

Table 3.1. Number of sites and total built-up area in Persian-period Yehud

|  | Small Sites | Medium Sites | Large Sites |
| --- | --- | --- | --- |
| North of Jerusalem | 25 | 10 | 4 |
| Area of Jerusalem | 17 | 9 | 2 |
| South of Jerusalem | 30 | 13 | 5 |
| Jordan Valley | 2 | — | 1 |
| Total | 74 | 32 | 12 |
| Total built-up area in hectares | 14.8 | 22.4 | 24 |

The results in table 3.1 add to a total built-up area of circa 61 hectares. Deploying a density coefficient of 200 inhabitants per built-up hectare, the

---

37. Carter, *Emergence of Yehud*, 288; Oded Lipschits, "Achaemenid Imperial Policy, Settlement Processes in Palestine, and the Status of Jerusalem in the Middle of the Fifth Century B.C.E.," in Lipschits and Oeming, *Judah and the Judeans in the Persian Period*, 32. For the higher number, see Lipschits, *Fall and Rise of Jerusalem*, 271.

38. Finkelstein, "Jerusalem in the Persian (and Early Hellenistic) Period" (ch.1 in this book).

39. Oded Lipschits, *The 'Yehud' Province under Babylonian Rule (586–539 B.C.E.): Historic Reality and Historiographic Conceptions* [Hebrew] (PhD thesis; Tel Aviv: Tel Aviv University, 1997), 226–318.

40. For an explanation of this method, see Israel Finkelstein, "Methods of the Field Survey and Data Recording," in Finkelstein, Lederman, and Bunimovitz, *Highlands of Many Cultures*, 20–22.

estimate for the entire province of Yehud in the Persian period, including Jerusalem, would be circa 12,000 people (about half of the numbers proposed by Carter and Lipschits)[41]—comparable to the estimate of the population of Jerusalem alone in the late Iron II and the late Hellenistic period. This comes to about 10 percent of the population of the entire kingdom of Judah (including the densely populated Shephelah) in the late eighth century BCE and circa 15 percent of the population of the highlands parts of late eighth-century Judah.[42]

These demographic estimates—for both Judah in general (above) and Jerusalem (for the latter)[43]—have far-reaching implications on the historical research of the sixth to fourth centuries BCE. They work against scholars who tend to belittle the scope of the catastrophe which befell Judah in 586 BCE,[44] and at the same time contradict the notion of massive waves of returnees to Yehud;[45] they seem to lessen the importance of the local population of Yehud (relative to the deportees in Babylonia) in the production of exilic and postexilic biblical texts and in shaping the nature of early postexilic Judaism;[46] and they challenge the notion[47] that much of the historical material in the Bible was written in Persian-period Yehud.[48]

---

41. Carter, *Emergence of Yehud*, 195–205; Lipschits, "Demographic Changes in Judah," 364.

42. Magen Broshi and Israel Finkelstein, "The Population of Palestine in Iron Age II," *BASOR* 287 (1992): 47–60.

43. Finkelstein, "Jerusalem in the Persian (and Early Hellenistic) Period" (ch. 1 in this book).

44. For instance, Hans M. Barstad, *The Myth of the Empty Land: A Study in the History and Archaeology of Judah during the "Exilic" Period* (Oslo: Scandinavian University Press, 1996); Barstad, "After the 'Myth of the Empty Land': Major Challenges in the Study of Neo-Babylonian Judah," in Lipschits and Blenkinsopp, *Judah and the Judeans in the Neo-Babylonian Period*, 3–20; Thomas C. Römer, *The So-Called Deuteronomistic History* (London: T&T Clark, 2005), 110; for different views on this theme, see Lester L. Grabbe, ed., *Leading Captivity Captive: "The Exile" as History and Ideology*, JSOTSup 278 (Sheffield: Sheffield Academic Press, 1998); for overviews, see Rainer Albertz, *Israel in Exile: The History and Literature of the Sixth Century B.C.E.*, SBLStBL 3 (Atlanta: Society of Biblical Literature, 2003); Lipschits, *Fall and Rise of Jerusalem*.

45. See also Lipschits, "Demographic Changes in Judah," 365.

46. Contra, e.g., Römer, *So-Called Deuteronomistic History*.

47. E.g., Philip Davies, *In Search of Ancient Israel* (Sheffield: JSOT Press, 1992).

48. See also Schniedewind, *How the Bible Became a Book*; Schniedewind, "Jerusalem, the Late Judaean Monarchy."

## 2. The Early Hellenistic Period (Until the 160s BCE)

Direct textual information for the Ptolemaic period is meager: the Zenon Papyri reveal that Mareshah in the Shephelah and Adoraim southwest of Hebron belonged to Idumea.

Turning to archaeology, the main concentrations of the Yehud seal impressions of Types 13–15, which seem to belong to the late-fourth and third centuries BCE,[49] are found in Jerusalem and Ramat Rahel, Jericho and En-Gedi, Mizpah and Nebi Samuel. Their distribution north of Jerusalem is especially noteworthy; in this area Impressions 13–14 grow from circa 5.5 percent of the total in the early group (Types 1–12, of the Persian period), to 11 percent in the period under discussion. This may indicate an expansion of the province, or at least of the Jewish population, to the north, to include the highlands around Mizpah.[50]

The borders of Judea in the first half of the second century BCE can be drawn according to several sources: the location of the battles between Judas Maccabeus and the Seleucids, the location of the fortresses built by Bacchides after the death of Judas, and other clues in 1 Maccabees (for the distribution of the *yrslm* and later types of Yehud seal impressions see below).

The importance of the area to the north and northwest of Jerusalem as commanding the main approach to the city, and possibly as the frontier of expansion of Judea, is indicated by the fact that five of the eight battles of Judas Maccabeus took place here, three of them (Beth-horon, Adasa and Kafar Salama) along the Beth-horon–Gibeon road (fig. 3.2). It is reasonable to assume that Judas Maccabeus encountered the Seleucid forces on the borders of Judea or close to them. The two battles in the south—at Beth-zur and Beth-zacharia (slightly to the north of Beth-zur) should probably indicate the southern boundary of the province. First Maccabees seems to point out that Beth-zur switched hands more than once during the wars,[51] which means that it was located on the southern borders of Judea.

---

49. Vanderhooft and Lipschits, "New Typology of the Yehud Stamp Impressions."

50. For the theory that this happened following the Samaritan revolt against Alexander the Great, see Menahem Stern, *The Documents on the History of the Hasmonaean Revolt* [Hebrew] (Tel Aviv: Hakibbutz Hameuchad, 1965), 110; Aryeh Kasher, "Some Suggestions and Comments Concerning Alexander Macedon's Campaign in Palestine" [Hebrew], *Beit Miqra* 20 (1975): 187–208. Against this idea, see, e.g., Albrecht Alt, "Zur Geschichte der Grenze zwischen Judäa und Samaria," *PJ* (1935): 94–97.

51. Beth-zur had been fortified by Judas Maccabeus (1 Macc 4:61), held by Lysias

### 3. Territorial Extent and Demography of Yehud/Judea

Locating the places fortified by Bacchides "in Judea" (1 Macc 9:50–52) is essential for drawing its borders of the province in the 160s BCE. The sites mentioned in the list are: Jericho, Emmaus, Beth-horon, Bethel, Thamnatha, Pharathon, Tephon, Beth-zur, Gazara, and the Akra in Jerusalem (fig. 3.2). The location of most of these sites is self-evident. The difficult places to identify are Thamnatha, Pharathon, and Tephon.

Thamnatha and Pharathon were identified by Abel as two different locations:[52] Thamnatha = biblical Timnath-heres (Kh. Tibne in southwestern Samaria)[53] and Pharathon = biblical Pirathon (= the village of Far'ata west of Shechem).[54] This proposal is difficult to accept as it locates both places outside of Judea.[55] I therefore agree with Avi-Yonah and Roll, who identify Thamnatha with another Timna—probably Kh. Tibna southwest of Jerusalem, on a ridge sloping down into the Elah Valley.[56] The problem with this identification is that an initial survey of the site revealed late Iron II (but not Hellenistic?) sherds.[57]

---

(1 Macc 6:7), fortified by Bacchides (1 Macc 9:52) besieged by Simeon (1 Macc 11:65) and fortified by him (1 Macc 14:33).

52. Félix-Marie Abel, *Les livres des Maccabées* (Paris: Librairie Lecoffre, 1949), 172.

53. Also Zecharia Kallai, *The Northern Boundaries of Judah* [Hebrew] (Jerusalem: Magnes, 1960), 96; Israel Shatzman, *The Armies of the Hasmonaeans and Herod from Hellenistic to Roman Frameworks* (Tübingen: Mohr, 1991), 42.

54. Also, Axel E. Knauf, "Pireathon–Ferata," *BN* 51 (1990): 19–24.

55. Michael Avi-Yonah, *The Holy Land from the Persian to the Arab Conquests (536 B.C. to A.D. 640) A Historical Geography* (Grand Rapids: Baker, 1977), 53. For the same reason—keeping the sites "in Judea"—I would argue against Israel Roll, "Bacchides' Fortifications and the Arteries of Traffic to Jerusalem in the Hellenistic Period" [Hebrew], *ErIsr* 25 (1996): 509–14 and accept the identification of Gazara with Gezer. I find it difficult to agree to the idea that the term *in Judea* is anachronistic—Félix-Marie Abel, "Topographie des campagnes machabéennes," *RB* 34 (1925): 202–8; Jonathan A. Goldstein, *1 Maccabees: A New Translation with Introduction and Commentary* (Garden City: Doubleday, 1976), 386.

56. Roll, "Fortifications and the Arteries."

57. Amihai Mazar, "The Excavations of Khirbet Abu et-Twein and the System of Iron Age Fortresses in Judah" [Hebrew], *ErIsr* 15 (1981): 246. Gershon Galil, "Pirathon, Parathon and Timnatha," *ZDPV* 109 (1993): 49–53 suggested locating Thamnatha in Kh. et-Tawil. But if one does not look for the preservation of the name any Hellenistic site is possible.

Safrai and Na'aman located Pharathon in the village of Farkha near Nahal Shiloh[58] and Galil identified it with Kh. el-Fire west of Hebron.[59] These sites are all outside the boundaries of Judea. Avi-Yonah sought Pharathon in Wadi Fara northeast of Jerusalem,[60] but there is no actual site that can be proposed for this identification. Therefore, the location of Pharathon remains a riddle.

Tephon was identified with Tappuah south of Shechem,[61] the southern Tappuah west of Hebron,[62] Beit Nattif,[63] Tekoa,[64] and Kh. Bad-Faluh north of Tekoa.[65] The first identification should be dismissed, as it puts the fortress far from Judea. Of the Judean places the two latter seem preferable.

Plotting these places (at least those securely identified) on a map one gets a system that surrounds the core area of Judea: Jericho, Bethel and Beth-horon in the north, Gezer and Emmaus in the northwest, Timna near the Elah Valley in the west, and Beth-zur and Tephon/Tekoa in the south.

The book of Maccabees also tells us that in the west, Adullam was probably in the territory of Judea (2 Macc 12:38), while Gezer belonged to Ashdod until it was conquered by Simeon. Ekron and the area of Lod were annexed to Judea only in the time of Jonathan (below).

According to these sources Judea stretches from the area of Beth-zur, or just north of it, to Mizpah and from the Judean desert to the eastern Shephelah. This means that relative to Yehud of the Persian period, Judea of the early Hellenistic period expanded in two directions: in the west to the upper Shephelah and in the north to the area of Mizpah. The population also grew significantly.

In order to estimate the population of Judea at that time, I compared the situation in the Persian period to that in the Hellenistic period in two

---

58. Zeev Safrai, *Borders and Government in the Land of Israel in the Period of the Mishna and the Talmud* [Hebrew] (Tel Aviv: Hakibbutz Hameuchad: 1980), 61–62; Nadav Na'aman, "Pirathon and Ophrah," *BN* 50 (1989): 11–16.

59. Galil, "Pirathon, Parathon and Timnatha."

60. Avi-Yonah, *Holy Land*, 53–54.

61. Abel, *Les livres des Maccabées*, 173.

62. Avraham Kahana, *Hasfarim Hahitzoniim II* [Hebrew] (Tel Aviv: Massada, 1960), 142, n. 50.

63. Christa Möller and Gotz Schmitt, *Siedlungen Palästinas nach Flavius Josephus* (Wiesbaden: Reichert, 1976), 36–37; Galil, "Pirathon, Parathon and Timnatha."

64. Avi Yonah, *Holy Land*, 54—the name appears as such in one of the manuscripts of Josephus.

65. Roll, "Fortifications and the Arteries," 513.

areas, for which the data are comprehensive and comparable—the highlands to the north and south of Jerusalem.[66] I also included the built-up area of Jerusalem. I used the same method of estimating the size of the sites according to categories (see above) and added a category for very large sites (over 3 built-up hectares)—five altogether. The results are summarized in table 3.2:

Table 3.2. Number of sites and total built-up area in the highlands in the Persian and Hellenistic periods

|  | Persian | Hellenistic |
| --- | --- | --- |
| North of Jerusalem Sites | 39 | 106 |
| Built-up area (hectares) | 20 | 110 |
| South of Jerusalem Sites | 48 | 96 |
| Built-up area (hectares) | 25 | 62 |
| Jerusalem Built-up area (hectares) | 2.5 | 60 |
| TOTAL Sites | 88 | 203 |
| Built-up area (hectares) | 47.5 | 232 |

Extrapolating these figures for the entire area (of Yehud), against the 61 built-up hectares in the Persian period, one gets 298 built-up hectares in the Hellenistic period. To this, one should add the Upper Shephelah (not included in the estimate for the Persian period). Dagan reported 254 sites and a total built-up area of 285 hectares for the entire Shephelah in the Hellenistic period.[67] Calculating about a quarter of the latter number—circa 70 hectares—for the eastern strip of the Shephelah seems reasonable,

---

66. According to Israel Finkelstein and Yitzhak Magen, eds. *Archaeological Survey of the Hill Country of Benjamin*, (Jerusalem: Israel Antiquities Authority, 1993); Avi Ofer, *The Highland of Judah during the Biblical Period* [Hebrew] (PhD thesis; Tel Aviv: Tel Aviv University 1993) respectively.

67. Yehuda Dagan, "Results of the Survey: Settlement Patterns in the Lachish

as sites in the more hilly part of this region are somewhat smaller than those located in the more fertile lower Shephelah. This brings us to circa 370 hectares for entire area of Judea.

Yet, in the surveys the "Hellenistic period" also covers the late Hellenistic phase (the late second and first half of the first centuries BCE). In order to reach a reasonable number for the 160s BCE, I took the mean of the growth from the Persian to the late Hellenistic period in the more limited area of Yehud/Judea—180 hectares—and added 30 hectares for the Shephelah. This makes 210 hectares, which translate into a population estimate of circa 42,000 people—about 10 percent (!) of the number proposed by Avi-Yonah and Bar-Kochva.[68]

Using a 10–15 percent figure for the force that could have been drafted for military service from the entire population in classical times,[69] one reaches circa 5,000 men. To this number one should add Jews from outside Judea who may have joined the forces of Judas Maccabeus, for example, from the three toparchies to its north—possibly circa 1,500 men.[70] All in all these numbers show that Judas Maccabeus could have recruited, for short periods of time, a maximum of circa 6,000–7,000 men to his army. Needless to say, an error of 10 percent or even 20 percent will not change these numbers significantly.

---

Region," in *The Renewed Archaeological Excavations at Lachish (1973–1994)*, by David Ussishkin, vol. 5, MSIA 22 (Tel Aviv: Institute of Archaeology, 2004), 2685.

68. Michael Avi-Yonah, "The Hasmonean Revolt and Judah Maccabee's War against the Syrians," in *The Hellenistic Age*, vol. 6 of *The World History of the Jewish People*, ed. Abraham Schalit (New Brunswick: Rutgers University, 1972), 163; Bezalel Bar-Kochva, *Judas Maccabeus: The Jewish Struggle against the Seleucids* (Cambridge: Cambridge University, 1989), 57. More recently Horsley estimated the population of Judea in the early Hasmonean period at 100–200,000 people: Richard A. Horsley, "The Expansion of Hasmonean Rule in Idumea and Galilee: Toward a Historical Sociology," in *Second Temple Studies III: Studies in Politics, Class and Material Culture*, ed. Philip R. Davies and John M. Halligan, JSOTSup 340 (Sheffield: Sheffield Academic Press, 2002), 134.

69. Bar-Kochva, *Judas Maccabeus*, 56.

70. My estimate for the population of the highlands areas of the three toparchies (according to my own survey—Finkelstein, Lederman, and Bunimovitz, *Highlands of Many Cultures*, is circa 15,000. To that one needs to add the population of the toparchy of Lod in the plain—probably a few thousand. An estimate of 10–15 percent of this number makes circa 3,000, but, of course, not all the population in these toparchies was Jewish. I would therefore estimate no more than half of this figure.

### 3. Territorial Extent and Demography of Yehud/Judea

This estimate fits most of the numbers given for the Jewish force in 1 and 2 Maccabees.[71] There were 6,000 men at the beginning of the war (2 Macc 8:1); a maximum of 10,000 in the battle of Beth-zur (1 Macc 4:29); and 3,000 in the battles of Emmaus (1 Macc 4:6), Adasa (1 Macc 7:40), and Elasa; in the latter a smaller number of 800 took part in the actual fighting (1 Macc 9:5-6). At the same time, the figures derived from archaeology challenge numbers given by historians of the period. Based on the mention of 11,000 men in the Jewish expeditions to the Gilead and Galilee (1 Macc 5:20), and assuming that Judas Maccabeus left a similar number of men to defend Judea, Avi-Yonah estimated the overall Jewish force to number 22,000 men.[72] Bar-Kochva and Shatzman accepted this figure.[73]

### 3. The Early Phases of Hasmonean Expansion

In the 140s, the Hasmonean state started expending to the north and west. The three toparchies to the north of Judea—Lod, Ephraim (Apheraema), and Ramathaim (1 Macc 11:34)—and the area of Ekron (1 Macc 10:89) were handed over to Judea in the days of Jonathan,[74] who, in addition, seems to have annexed the Jewish Peraea in Transjordan (fig. 3.2).[75] Gezer and Joppa were then taken by Simeon (1 Macc 13:43, 48; 14:5).[76] The conquest of Joppa was probably the most important at this stage, as it gave Judea an outlet to the sea. Judea now stretched from Beth-zur in the south to Nahal Shiloh in the north; and from the Judean Desert and the Peraea in the east to beyond Ekron and Gezer in the west and to Joppa in the northwest.

The population of the traditional territory of Judea, including the three toparchies, can be estimated at almost 60,000 (see above). To that

---

71. See summary table in Shatzman, *Armies of the Hasmonaeans*, 25–26, disregarding the possibility that the authors played down the Hasmonean force and the Bible-related nature of some of the numbers in 1 and 2 Maccabees (Bar-Kochva, *Judas Maccabeus*, 47; Israel Shatzman, "The Hasmonean Army" [Hebrew], in *The Hasmonean Period*, ed. David Amit and Hanan Eshel (Jerusalem: Yad Ben-Zvi, 1996), 33.

72. Avi-Yonah, "Hasmonean Revolt," 167.

73. Bar-Kochva, *Judas Maccabeus*, 50; Shatzman, *Armies of the Hasmonaeans*, 27.

74. For example, Avi-Yonah, *Holy Land*, 47, 55–57; Joshua J. Schwartz, *Lod (Lydda), Israel from Its Origins through the Byzantine Period, 5600 B.C.E.–640 C.E.*, BARIS 571 (Oxford: B.A.R, 1991), 50–51.

75. Avi-Yonah, *Holy Land*, 57.

76. Avi-Yonah, *Holy Land*, 58–59.

one should add the western Shephelah (210 built-up hectares in the Hellenistic period according to Dagan,[77] about half of this figure—circa 100 hectares—for the mid-second century BCE), the area of Joppa and the Peraea, which may bring the total number of people in Judea in the days of Simeon to over 100,000. It is clear, therefore, that in a short period of time in the 140s Judea expanded dramatically both in territory and in population. The population ruled from Jerusalem was similar now to that of the kingdom of Judah in the seventh century BCE. This figure (and the outlet to the sea) demonstrates the economic and military opportunities that opened to the Hasmoneans in the second half of the second century BCE, opportunities which were exploited to continue the territorial expansion of the Hasmonean state.

It is difficult to establish whether the later types of Yehud seal impressions[78] belong to this phase in the history of Judea (140s) or to the end of the earlier phase—the beginning of the second century, until the 160s BCE. The following arguments should be taken into consideration.

(1) There is no question that the Paleo-Hebrew Yehud seal impressions and the *yrslm* seal impressions date to the second century BCE, first and foremost because of their distribution in the southwestern hill of Jerusalem, which was not inhabited between the early sixth and second centuries BCE.[79] But their relatively modest number there, compared to their number in the City of David,[80] seems to indicate that they went out of use in the early days of the southwestern quarter; otherwise their number there would be expected to be much higher.

---

77. Dagan, "Results of the Survey," 2685.

78. Types 16 and 17 in Vanderhooft and Lipschits, "New Typology of the Yehud Stamp Impressions".

79. Ronny Reich, "Local Seal Impressions of the Hellenistic Period," in *Jewish Quarter Excavations in the Old City of Jerusalem*, ed. Hillel Geva (Jerusalem: Israel Exploration Society, 2003), 2:256–62.

80. Twenty-seven in the southwestern hill, compared to fifty-nine in the City of David for Types 16 and 17—Vanderhooft and Lipschits, "New Typology of the Yehud Stamp Impressions"; ten to twenty-two respectively for the *yrslm* seal impressions—Reich, "Local Seal Impressions of the Hellenistic Period," and Donald T. Ariel, and Yair Shoham, "Locally Stamped Handles and Associated Body Fragments of the Persian and Hellenistic Periods," in *Inscriptions*, vol. 6 of *Excavations at the City of David 1978-1985*, ed. Donald T. Ariel, Qedem 41 (Jerusalem: Institute of Archaeology, The Hebrew University of Jerusalem, 2000), 137–71 respectively.

## 3. Territorial Extent and Demography of Yehud/Judea

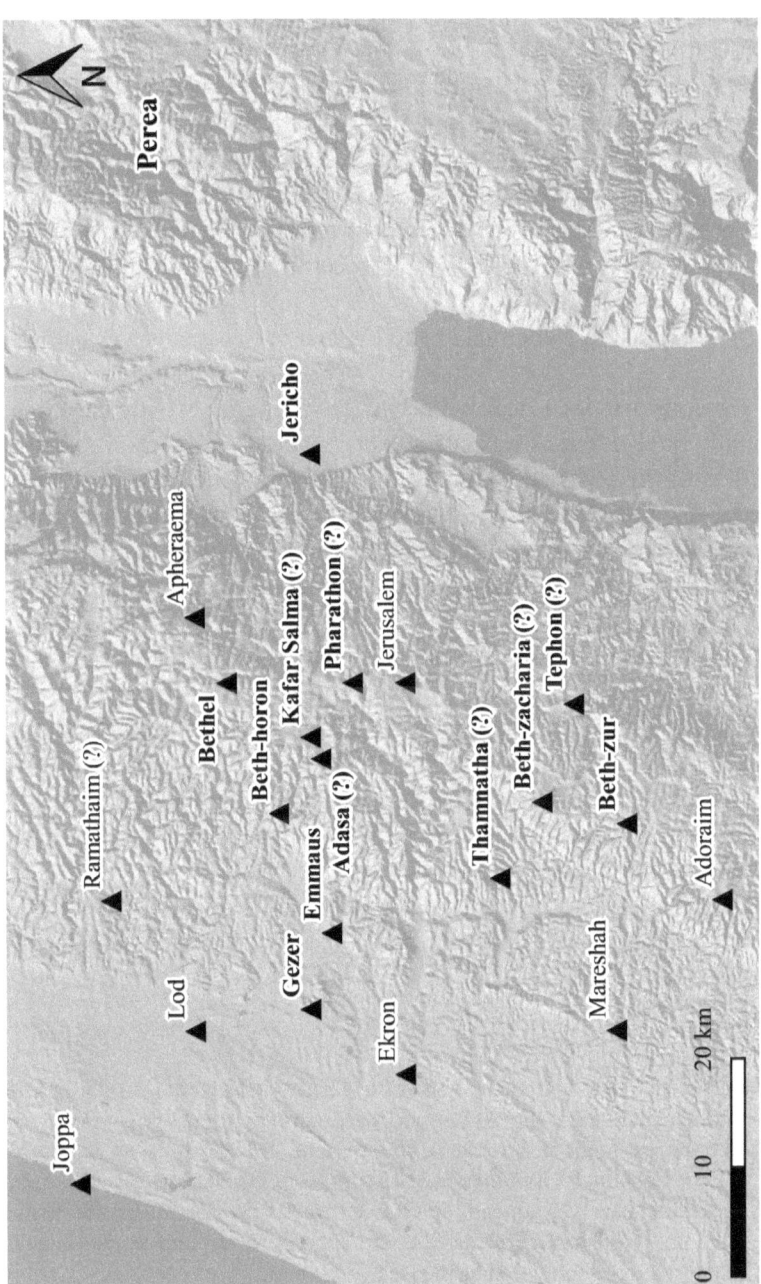

Figure 3.2. Places mentioned in relation to the Hasmonean expansion; sites referred to in 1 Maccabees as locations of the battles of Judas Maccabeus and forts built by Bacchides are in bold. Question mark signals tentative identification.

(2) No seal impression of these types was found at Bethel in the north and Beth-zur in the south. The same holds true for Lod and the entire area of the three toparchies and for Joppa. Only one *yrslm* seal impression is known from the Shephelah (found at Azekah).

It seems, then, that Types 16 and 17 and the *yrslm* seal impressions date to the first half of the second century BCE, before the great expansion of Judea. Their relatively strong appearance at Gezer (five Yehud and two *yrslm* impressions), which was annexed to Judea in the days of Simeon, may be explained as evidence for its strong commercial links to Judea.

## 4. Back to Nehemiah 3 and the List of Returnees

In two previous articles I dealt with two geographical lists in the Bible, traditionally interpreted as reflecting Persian-period realities—the list of the builders of the Jerusalem city wall in Neh 3 and the list of returnees in Ezra 2:1–67 and Neh 7:6–68. Based on the archaeological finds from Jerusalem and from well-identified sites which appear in the list of returnees, I raised the possibility that both reflect Hellenistic, more specifically Hasmonean, realities.[81]

The list of returnees includes places in the highlands to the north of Jerusalem, as far north as Bethel, plus the Lod, Hadid, and Ono niche in the northwest (fig. 2.1). The appearance of the latter sites is another reason, apart from archaeology, to date the list to the Hasmonean period. If this is the case, the list should be dated to the period immediately after the annexation of the three toparchies to Judea in 145 BCE.[82]

Nehemiah 3 is a more complicated case. It mentions the districts of Jerusalem and Beth-haccherem (most probably Ramat Rahel[83]), Mizpah in the north, Beth-zur in the south, and Keilah in the upper Shephelah in the southwest (fig. 3.1). If it indeed reflects realities of the Hellenis-

---

81. Finkelstein, "Jerusalem in the Persian (and Early Hellenistic) Period"; Finkelstein, "Archaeology and the List of Returnees" (chs. 1 and 2 in this book).

82. From the text point of view, see Jacob L. Wright, "A New Model for the Composition of Ezra-Nehemiah," in *Judah and the Judeans in the Fourth Century B.C.E.*, ed. Oded Lipschits, Gary N. Knoppers, and Rainer Albertz (Winona Lake, IN: Eisenbrauns, 2007), 347. Wright argues that the list "appears to respond to apocalyptic notions that most likely do not predate the Hellenistic period."

83. Yohanan Aharoni, *The Land of the Bible: A Historical Geography* (Philadelphia: Westminster, 1979), 418.

tic period, it may be meaningful that the list does not mention a district in the Gezer/Lod area, which implies that it predates the annexation of these cities to Judea in the 140s BCE. The fact that the list does not mention a district of Jericho may correspond to the distribution of the Yehud seal impressions: Jericho and En-Gedi produced a significant number of impression of the Persian period (altogether six impressions of Types 2, 4, 6, and 10 in the work of Vanderhooft and Lipschits) and of Types 13–15, which probably date to the early Hellenistic period (twenty-three items altogether).[84] Yet, the two sites did not yield even a single Paleo-Hebrew seal impression of the second century—Types 16–17 of the Yehud impressions and *yrslm* seal impressions.[85]

## 5. Conclusion

The geographical material in the book of Nehemiah traditionally used to delineate the borders of Yehud seems to date to the Hellenistic period. With no textual evidence, the boundaries of Yehud can be reconstructed only according to the distribution of the Yehud seal impressions. It seems that Yehud stretched around Jerusalem and Ramat Rahel, with a possible extension slightly further north and to Jericho and En-Gedi in the east. It did not include territory in the Shephelah. The population of Yehud can be estimated at circa 12,000 people—even smaller than the limited numbers which have recently been proposed.

Judea of the early Hellenistic period, including the early days of the Hasmoneans, was still limited in territory, though somewhat larger than Persian-period Yehud. It extended from Beth-zur in the south to the area of Mizpah in the north and probably included some territory in the upper, eastern Shephelah. Its population grew dramatically—it is estimated to have numbered circa 40,000 people. This estimate validates the figures given to the forces of Judas Maccabeus in 1 Maccabees, but is significantly smaller than past estimates for both the population of Judea and the overall force of the Hasmoneans in the 160s BCE.

All this changed in the 140s BCE, with the sudden expansion of Judea to the north, east, west, and northwest. Its population almost doubled in a

---

84. Vanderhooft and Lipschits, "New Typology of the Yehud Stamp Impressions."
85. A certain problem is the mention of Beth-zur in the list. Beth-zur did not produce any Yehud seal impressions. In order to date the background of Neh 3 just before the expansion of Judea in the 140s, one needs to argue that this is a coincidence.

few years, reached a number close to that of Judah in the seventh century BCE, and gave it the strength needed for further conquests and economic growth in late-Hasmonean days.

## Addendum

The only major bibliographic addition since the original article was published (2010) is Oded Lipschits and David S. Vanderhooft, *The Yehud Stamp Impressions: A Corpus of Inscribed Impressions from the Persian and Hellenistic Periods in Judah* (Winona Lake, IN: Eisenbrauns, 2011). The book does not change the summary presented in Vanderhooft and Lipschits, "A New Typology of the Yehud Stamp Impressions," which is cited above. For Jerusalem in the Persian period and Neh 3, and the list of returnees, see the relevant chapters.

For the location of Pharathon, discussed above, see Israel Finkelstein, "Major Saviors, Minor Judges: The Historical Background of the Northern Accounts in the Book of Judges," *JSOT* 41 (2017): 440–41.

# 4
# Nehemiah's Adversaries

## 1. Introduction

In chapters 1 and 2, I proposed to identify the geographical, archaeological, and historical realities behind the list of builders of the wall in Neh 3:1–32 and the list of returnees in Neh 7:6–68 (and Ezra 2:1–67) in Hasmonean times.[1] Placing the Neh 3 list in the Hellenistic period should not affect the dating of the Nehemiah Memoir—the backbone of the book.[2] Construction of the wall is a major theme in the Nehemiah Memoir.[3] The reality behind it may be sought in work conducted on the original mound of Jerusalem, which was located on the Temple Mount; apart from activity near the Gihon Spring, which left several pockets of pottery and a scattering of seal impressions in fills,[4] this was the main settlement in the Persian and early Hellenistic periods in Jerusalem.[5] Nehemiah 3:1–32, on

---

1. Chapters 1 and 2 were originally published as Israel Finkelstein, "Jerusalem in the Persian (and Early Hellenistic) Period and the Wall of Nehemiah," *JSOT* 32 (2008): 501–20; and Finkelstein, "Archaeology of the List of Returnees in Ezra and Nehemiah," *PEQ* 140 (2008): 7–15.
2. For its scope, see, e.g., Joseph Blenkinsopp, *Judaism: The First Phase; The Place of Ezra and Nehemiah in the Origins of Judaism* (Grand Rapids: Eerdmans, 2009), 86–108; Reinhard G. Kratz, *The Composition of the Narrative Books of the Old Testament* (London: T&T Clark, 2005), 51.
3. For instance, Hugh G. M. Williamson, *Ezra, Nehemiah* (Waco, TX: Word Books, 1985), xxvii.
4. Finkelstein, "Jerusalem in the Persian (and Early Hellenistic) Period."
5. Israel Finkelstein, Ido Koch, and Oded Lipschits, "The Mound on the Mount: A Possible Solution to the 'Problem with Jerusalem,'" *JHS* 11 (2011), art. 12. The limited number of Persian-period sherds found in the Temple Mount debris (Gabriel Barkay and Itzhak Zweig, "The Temple Mount Debris Sifting Project: Preliminary Report" [Hebrew], *NSJ* 11 [2006]: 222), the eastern slope of the Temple Mount (Itzhak Dvira,

the other hand, is an addition to the Nehemiah Memoir[6] and the reality behind it is the construction of the First Wall of Jerusalem, which encircles the big city of the Second century BCE—including the "City of David" ridge and the Western Hill.[7]

Another prominent theme in the book of Nehemiah, which is tightly related to the subject of the city wall, is the mention of enemies who opposed Nehemiah's building efforts.[8] The story of the enemies, too, appears both as an abstract theme (Neh 4:5, 9; 6:16) and as specific, named adversaries—Sanballat the Horonite, Tobiah the Ammonite, Geshem the Arab (Neh 2:10, 19; 3:33–36; 4:1–3; 6:1–14, 17–19), and the Ashdodites

---

Gal Zigdon and Lara Shilov, "Secondary Refuse Aggregates from the First and Second Temple Periods on the Eastern Slope of the Temple Mount," *NSJ* 17 [2011]: 68) and the "Ophel" excavations south of the Temple Mount (personal communication from Eilat Mazar) seems to indicate that even this relatively restricted settlement was small and under-populated.

6. E.g., Charles C. Torrey, *The Composition and Historical Value of Ezra-Nehemiah* (Giessen: Ricker, 1896), 37–38; Sigmund Mowinckel, *Studien zu dem Buche Ezra-Nehemia* (Oslo: Universitetsforlaget, 1964), 109–16; Jacob L. Wright, "A New Model for the Composition of Ezra-Nehemiah," in *Judah and the Judeans in the Fourth Century B.C.E.*, ed. Oded Lipschits, Gary N. Knoppers, and Rainer Albertz (Winona Lake, IN: Eisenbrauns, 2007), 337; on the independent nature of this source, see, e.g., Williamson, *Ezra, Nehemiah*, 200; Joseph Blenkinsopp, *Ezra/Nehemiah: A Commentary* (Philadelphia: Westminster, 1988), 231; Mark A. Throntveit, *Ezra-Nehemiah* (Louisville: John Knox, 1992), 74–75; Lester L. Grabbe, *Ezra-Nehemiah* (London: Routledge, 1998), 157; Jacob L. Wright, *Rebuilding Identity: The Nehemiah Memoir and Its Earliest Readers*, BZAW 348 (Berlin: de Gruyter, 2004), 118–20; Oded Lipschits, "Nehemiah 3: Sources, Composition and Purpose," in *New Perspectives on Ezra–Nehemiah: History and Historiography, Text, Literature, and Interpretation*, ed. Isaac Kalimi (Winona Lake, IN: Eisenbrauns, 2012), 97–98; for scholars supporting a Persian-period date of the list, see bibliography in Lipschits, "Nehemiah 3," 76–78.

7. For a detailed discussion of Neh 3, with thorough bibliography, see Lipschits, "Nehemiah 3" (he dates the list to the Persian period).

8. Blenkinsopp, *Ezra/Nehemiah*, 225; Blenkinsopp, *Judaism: The First Phase*, 97; on the adversaries, see recently Diana Edelman, "Seeing Double: Tobiah the Ammonite as an Encrypted Character," *RB* 113 (2006): 570–84; Sebastian Grätz, "The Adversaries in Ezra/Nehemiah—Fictitious or Real?," in *Between Cooperation and Hostility: Multiple Identities in Ancient Judaism and the Interaction with Foreign Powers*, ed. Rainer Albertz and Jakob Wöhrle, JAJSup 11 (Göttingen: Vandenhoeck & Ruprecht, 2013), 73–87 and bibliography; for my preliminary notes on this subject, see Israel Finkelstein, "Persian Period Jerusalem and Yehud: A Rejoinder," *JHS* 9 (2009): art. 24.

(Neh 4:1).⁹ It is noteworthy that references to the named adversaries circumscribe the inserted list of the builders of the city wall (Neh 2:19; 3:33–35 [see also 4:1–3]). The question is whether the references to the specific, named adversaries belong to the original Nehemiah Memoir.

The names of the three individuals appear in extrabiblical texts of the Persian and Hellenistic periods. Most scholars identified the named adversaries with Persian-period personage,[10] mainly the Sanballat mentioned in the Elephantine papyri as the governor of Samaria in the end-days of the fifth century BCE and Gashmu king of Qedar, who appears in an Aramaic inscription on a silver vessel ostensibly found at Tell el-Maskhuta in the Delta.[11] Others proposed that the author of the Nehemiah texts took them as symbols of their homelands.[12]

## 2. The Adversaries

Let me start with brief summaries of the appearance of these names in texts which date to (or refer to) the Persian and Hellenistic periods, with reference to information that can help place them in historical context.

### 2.1. Sanballat the Horonite

Individuals named Sanballat appear in the Elephantine papyri as the governor of Samaria in 408 BCE, twice in the Wadi ed-Daliyeh papyri (fourth century BCE) as the father of two governors of Samaria,[13] and in Josephus, *A.J.* 11.302 as a governor of Samaria, ostensibly in the days of Darius III. The Elephantine and Wadi ed-Daliyeh references support the notion that "the Horonite" refers to Beth-horon northwest of Jerusalem,

---

9. For possible layers within this theme, see Wright, *Rebuilding Identity*, 116–17; Kratz, *Composition of the Narrative Books*, 66.

10. E.g., David J. Clines, *Ezra, Nehemiah, Esther* (Grand Rapids: Eerdmans, 1984), 144–45; Williamson, *Ezra, Nehemiah*, 182–84; Blenkinsopp, *Ezra/Nehemiah*, 205, 225.

11. Isaac Rabinowitz, "Aramaic Inscriptions of the Fifth Century B.C.E. from a North-Arab Shrine in Egypt," *JNES* 15 (1956): 1–9; William J. Dumbrell, "The Tell El-Maskhuta Bowls and the 'Kingdom' of Qedar in the Persian Period," *BASOR* 203 (1971): 33–44.

12. Edelman, "Seeing Double," referring to Tobiah of the third century BCE; Grätz, "Adversaries in Ezra/Nehemiah."

13. E.g., Frank M. Cross, "The Discovery of the Samaria Papyri," *BA* 26 (1963): 110–21.

rather than Horonaim in Moab[14] or places farther away in the region.[15] Scholars assume that the Sanballat of Nehemiah was the first in a line of governors of Samaria.[16] The mention of a Sanballat as related to the high priest Eliashib in Neh 13:28 (whether linked to the story in Josephus, *A.J.* 11.7.2 or not) should be noted, as this verse is certainly not part of the Nehemiah Memoir.[17]

2.2. Tobiah the Ammonite

The adjective "Ammonite" is explained by scholars as referring either to the origin of this person, or to his post as a high official in Ammon. Individuals named Tobiah are mentioned in the Bible in connection to "earlier" events in the history of Yehud.[18] Nehemiah 13:7 associates a Tobiah with the high priest Eliashib.[19] A Tobiah is mentioned in the Zenon papyri of the mid-third century BCE as a prominent figure in Ammonitis. The history of the Tobiad family in the late third and early second centuries BCE is told in detail by Josephus (*A.J.* 12.160–236; see references also in 2 Macc 3:11; 1 Macc 5:13). This aristocratic Jewish family from Ammonitis

---

14. Ulrich Kellermann, *Nehemia: Quellen, Überlieferung und Geschichte*, BZAW 102 (Berlin: Topelmann, 1967).

15. Siegfried Mittman, "Tobia, Sanballat und die persische Provinz Juda," *JNSL* 26.2 (2000): 1–49; Oded Tammuz, "Will the Real Sanballat Please Stand Up?," in *Samaritans: Past and Present, Current*, ed. Menahem Mor and Friedrich V. Reiterer, SJ 53 (Berlin: de Gruyter, 2010), 51–58.

16. Frank M. Cross, "Aspects of Samaritan and Jewish History in Late Persian and Hellenistic Times," *HTR* 59 (1966): 201–11; for a different view, see Jan Dušek, "Archaeology and Texts in the Persian Period: Focus on Sanballat," in *Congress Volume Helsinki 2010*, ed. Martti Nissinen (Leiden: Brill, 2012), 117–32.

17. On Sanballat, see, e.g., Cross, "Aspects of Samaritan and Jewish History"; Kellermann, *Nehemia*, 166–67; Hugh G. M. Williamson, "The Historical Value of Josephus' Jewish Antiquities XI," *JTS* 28 (1977): 49–66; Williamson, *Ezra, Nehemiah*, 182–83; Lester L. Grabbe, "Josephus and the Reconstruction of the Judean Restoration," *JBL* 106 (1987): 231–46; Blenkinsopp, *Ezra/Nehemiah*, 216–17; Tammuz, "Will the Real Sanballat Please Stand Up?"

18. Summary in Tamara C. Eskenazi, "Tobiah," *ABD* 6:584; Benjamin Mazar, "The Tobiads," *IEJ* 7 (1957): 137–45; see also Edelman, "Seeing Double."

19. Two Lachish ostraca of circa 600 BCE mention a Tobiyahu as a high official in the administration of Judah ("servant of the king"), possibly belonging to the royal family (Shmuel Ahituv, *Echoes from the Past* [Jerusalem: Carta, 2008], 63, 79 [Ostraca 3 and 5]).

was related to the high priest in Jerusalem and took part in the struggles that led to the Maccabean revolt. They are described as proponents of Hellenistic culture and hence adversaries of the Maccabees.[20]

## 2.3. Geshem the Arab

This is a common name known from Nabataean, Safaitic, Thamudic, and Lihianite inscriptions. Though there must have been a Qedarite king named Geshem sometime in the Persian period,[21] a Lihyanite king with the same name ruled circa 200 BCE;[22] a Lihyanite inscription from el-Ula refers to "Jasm son of Sahr and 'Abd, governor of Dedan."[23]

In an attempt to identify the stage-setting behind the list of named adversaries, attention should be given to the geographical aspect: the location of the adversaries and the threat that they could have posed to Jerusalem, or the menace that the construction of the wall could have caused them. In other words, one must seek the time that best fits a confrontation or tension with Samaria, Ammon, Arabs in the south, and Ashdod. Obviously, the adversaries symbolically represent the areas surrounding Yehud/Judea on all sides (fig. 4.1);[24] still, the idea cannot be detached from

---

20. See, e.g., Mazar, "Tobiads"; Jonathan A. Goldstein, "The Tales of the Tobiads," in *Christianity, Judaism and Other Greco-Roman Cults: Studies for Morton Smith at 60*, ed. Jacob Neusner, SJLA 12 (Leiden: Brill, 1975), 85–123; on Tobiah in the list of adversaries, see also, e.g., Kellermann, *Nehemia*, 167–70; Williamson, *Ezra, Nehemiah*, 183–84; Blenkinsopp, *Ezra/Nehemiah*, 217–19. For a different view, see Dov Gera, *Judaea and Mediterranean Politics 219 to 161 B.C.E.*, Brill's Series in Jewish Studies 8 (Leiden: Brill, 1998), 36–58, who argues that the tale of Josephus cannot be read as an accurate historical account; rather, it is "a piece of propaganda written by a Jew of Ptolemaic Egypt," which was based on the tale of the biblical Joseph.

21. As attested in the Tell el-Maskhuta silver bowl inscription; Rabinowitz, "Aramaic Inscriptions of the Fifth Century B.C.E."; Dumbrell, "Tell el-Maskhuta Bowls."

22. Saba Farès-Drappeau, *Dédan et Liḥyān: Histoire des Arabes aux confins des pouvoirs perse et hellénistique (IVe–IIe s. avant l'ère chrétienne)*, TMO 42 (Lyon: Maison de l'Orient, 2005), 122–23.

23. Israel Ephal, *The Ancient Arabs: Nomads on the Borders of the Fertile Crescent Ninth–Fifth Centuries B.C.* (Jerusalem: Magnes, 1982), 212; Axel E. Knauf, *Ismael: Untersuchungen zur Geschichte Palastinas und nordarabiens im 1. Jahrtausend v. Chr.* (Wiesbaden: Harrassowitz Verlage, 1989), 105; on Geshem as one of the adversaries of Nehemiah, see also, e.g., Kellermann, *Nehemia*, 170–73; Williamson, *Ezra, Nehemiah*, 192; Blenkinsopp, *Ezra/Nehemiah*, 225.

24. Blenkinsopp, *Ezra/Nehemiah*, 225–26.

historical reality. In order to deal with this issue, one should first reconstruct the boundaries of Persian-period Yehud and Hellenistic Judea and estimate their population. I have dealt with this issue in detail elsewhere,[25] so a summary of my main finds will suffice.

### 3. Boundaries of Yehud/Judea

Scholars reconstructed the boundaries of Persian-period Yehud based on the geographical information in the description of the construction of the wall (the location of the district and subdistrict capitals), places mentioned in the list of returnees, and the distribution of the Yehud seal impressions.[26] But if these texts were inserted into the Nehemiah Memoir (in a later period?), using them puts one at risk of circular argumentation. Therefore the only reliable information comes from the distribution of the Persian-period Yehud seal impressions (Types 1–12 in Vanderhooft and Lipschits[27]) and from textual information relating to the early Hellenistic period. Accordingly, the province of Yehud seems to have covered mainly the area of Jerusalem and Ramat Rahel, with possible extension to Jericho and En-Gedi in the east, close to Beth-zur in the south and the area of Mizpha in the north.[28] Its population can be estimated at not much more than 10,000 souls.[29] This small territory, with depleted population, could not have posed a threat to its neighbors, certainly not to the Ashdodites

---

25. Israel Finkelstein, "The Territorial Extent and Demography of Yehud/Judea in the Persian and Early Hellenistic Periods," *RB* 117 (2010): 39–54 (ch. 3 in this book).

26. E.g., Ephraim Stern, *Material Culture of the Land of the Bible in the Persian Period, 538–332 B.C.* (Warminster: Aris & Phillips, 1982), 245–49; Charles E. Carter, *The Emergence of Yehud in the Persian Period: A Social and Demographic Study*, JSOTSup 294 (Sheffield Academic Press, 1999), 75–90; Oded Lipschits, *The Fall and Rise of Jerusalem: Judah under Babylonian Rule* (Winona Lake, IN: Eisenbrauns, 2005), 154–84.

27. For this and other references to this work below, see also the more detailed treatment in David S. Vanderhooft and Oded Lipschits, "A New Typology of the Yehud Stamp Impressions," *TA* 34 (2007): 12–37.

28. One can rightly argue that the seal impressions are related to the administration of the province and are therefore found mainly in/around its hub; still, there is no better way to deal with the borders of Yehud.

29. About half of the numbers presented by Carter, *Emergence of Yehud*, 195–205; Oded Lipschits, "Demographic Changes in Judah between the Seventh and the Fifth Centuries B.C.E.," in *Judah and the Judeans in the New-Babylonian Period*, ed. Oded Lipschits and Joseph Blenkinsopp (Winona Lake, IN: Eisenbrauns, 2003), 364.

in the west and the Arabs in the south; and not to the much more densely populated Samaria.[30]

Information about the situation in the Ptolemaic period (third century BCE) is minimal. The Zenon Papyri reveal that Mareshah in the Shephelah and Adoraim southwest of Hebron belonged to Idumea. The main concentration of the Yehud seal impressions of Types 13–15, which seem to belong to the late fourth and third centuries BCE,[31] is in Jerusalem and Ramat Rahel, Jericho and En-Gedi, Mizpah, and Nebi Samuel. The borders of third century BCE Judea were therefore similar or close to those of Persian-period Yehud.

From the textual perspective, the borders of Judea in the first half of the second century BCE can be plotted according to the location of the spots where the Maccabees confronted their invading enemies and the places fortified by Bacchides.[32] Accordingly, Judea stretches from the area of Beth-zur or close to it in the south to Mizpah in the north and from the Judean desert in the east to the eastern Shephelah in the west. In other words, the main change from the previous period is the possible expansion to the higher Shepehlah. The population seems to have grown to circa 40,000 people.[33]

Archaeologically, the Paleo-Hebrew Yehud seal impressions[34] and the *yrslm* seal impressions clearly date to the second century BCE. But when do they belong within this century? Their relatively modest number in the Western hill of Jerusalem (the Jewish and Armenian Quarters of the

---

30. Adam Zertal, "The Pahwah of Samaria (Northern Israel) during the Persian Period: Types of Settlement, Economy, History and New Discoveries," *Transeu* 2 (1989): 9–30.

31. Vanderhooft and Lipschits, "New Typology of the Yehud Stamp Impressions."

32. Finkelstein, "Territorial Extent and Demography of Yehud," with map; for the location of the Bacchides' fortifications, see 1 Macc 9:50–52 and discussion in Israel Roll, "Bacchides' Fortifications and the Arteries of Traffic to Jerusalem in the Hellenistic Period" [Hebrew], *ErIsr* 25 (1996): 509–14, with references to previous works.

33. About 10 percent of the number proposed by Michael Avi-Yonah, "The Hasmonean Revolt and Judah Maccabee's War against the Syrians," in *The Hellenistic Age*, vol. 6 of *The World History of the Jewish People*, ed. Abraham Schalit (New Brunswick: Rutgers University, 1972), 163; and Bezalel Bar-Kochva, *Judas Maccabeus: The Jewish Struggle against the Seleucids* (Cambridge: Cambridge University, 1989), 57.

34. Types 16–17 in Vanderhooft and Lipschits, "New Typology of the Yehud Stamp Impressions."

Old City) relative to their distribution on the ridge of the City of David[35] seems to indicate that they went out of use in the early days of the western quarter. Also, no seal impression of these types was found at Bethel in the north and Beth-zur in the south. The same holds true for Lod and the entire area of the three toparchies, which were handed over to Jonathan (below), as well as for Joppa. It seems, then, that Types 16–17 and the *yrslm* seal impressions date to the first half of the second century BCE, before the great expansion of Hasmonean Judea. All this indicates that the territory of early second century BCE Judea was not too different from that of Yehud/Judea of the Persian and Ptolemaic periods.

The big change commenced in the 140s, when the Hasmonean state started expanding in all directions. The three toparchies in the north—Lod, Ephraim (Apheraema), and Ramathaim (1 Macc 11:34)—and the area of Ekron (1 Macc 10:89) were handed over to Judea in the days of Jonathan,[36] who, in addition, seems to have annexed the Jewish Peraea in Transjordan,[37] which bordered on Ammonitis. Gezer and Joppa were then taken by Simeon (1 Macc 13:43, 48; 14:5).[38] The population of Judea at that time can be estimated at circa 100,000. It is clear, therefore, that in a short period of time in the 140s Judea expanded dramatically both in territory and in population.

The next step in the expansion of Judea came in the days of John Hyrcanus (134–104 BCE), with the conquest of Madaba in Transjordan, the takeover and destruction of Shechem and the Samaritan temple on Mount Gerizim, and the conquest of Idumea, which included Adoraim (and the Hebron and south Hebron hills) and Mareshah. The later days of John

---

35. Vanderhooft and Lipschits, "New Typology of the Yehud Stamp Impressions"; Ronny Reich, "Local Seal Impressions of the Hellenistic Period," in *Jewish Quarter Excavations in the Old City of Jerusalem*, ed. Hillel Geva (Jerusalem: Israel Exploration Society, 2003), 2:256–62; Donald T. Ariel and Yair Shoham, "Locally Stamped Handles and Associated Body Fragments of the Persian and Hellenistic Periods," in *Inscriptions*, vol. 6 of *Excavations at the City of David 1978–1985*, ed. Donald T. Ariel, Qedem 41 (Jerusalem: Institute of Archaeology, The Hebrew University of Jerusalem, 2000), 137–71.

36. E.g., Michael Avi-Yonah, *The Holy Land from the Persian to the Arab Conquests (536 B.C. to A.D. 640): A Historical Geography* (Grand Rapids: Baker, 1977), 47, 55–57; Seth Schwartz, "Israel and the Nations Roundabout: I Maccabees and the Hasmonean Expansion," *JJS* 42 (1991): 16–38.

37. Avi-Yonah, *Holy Land*, 57.

38. Avi-Yonah, *Holy Land*, 58–59.

Hyrcanus saw the conquest of Samaria, with a possible extension into the Jezreel Valley.[39]

## 4. Enemies Roundabout

Back to the adversaries of Nehemiah, in view of the territorial history of Yehud/Judea, the most logical reality for tension with the four neighbors—Samaria, Ammon east of the Peraea, the Arabs, and Ashdod—is in the days of Jonathan and Simeon, or better, in the early days of John Hyrcanus after the expansion to Idumea and before the conquest of Samaria. Only then were the Judeans concerned with their neighbors on all sides; in fact, this was the time of conflict on all fronts.

Indeed, the description of enemies on all four sides in Nehemiah[40] corresponds well to 1 Maccabees, which was probably composed in the days of John Hyrcanus toward the end of the second century.[41] The book repeatedly refers to the enemies roundabout Judea (1 Macc 1:11), in Samaria (3:10); in Idumea (4:29, 61; 5:3 [also mentioning sons of Esau]; 6:31; 13:20) and the Negev (5:65); in Ammon (5:6, 9 [Gilead but close to Ammon], 13); and in the land of Philistia (3:24, 41; 4:22; 5:66–68), with special emphasis on the role of Ashdod in the conflicts with the Maccabees (5:68; 10:78–84; 11:4; 14:34; 16:10 [also 4:15]). The "enemies roundabout" in 1 Maccabees may be partially conceptual, influenced by biblical references,[42] but the conflicts were real. Incidentally, 2 Maccabees, which was composed about half a century earlier,[43] does not refer to conflicts with the neighbors of Judea—for style and goal, or for real historical reasons.

---

39. On the territorial expansion in the days of John Hyrcanus, see, e.g., Joseph Klausner, "John Hyrcanus I," in Schalit, *Hellenistic Age*, 211–21; Uriel Rappaport, "The Hasmonean State (160–37 B.C.E.)" [Hebrew], in *The History of Eretz Israel: The Hellenistic Period and the Hasmonean State (332–37 B.C.E.)*, ed. Menahem Stern (Jerusalem: Yad Ben-Zvi, 1981), 3:193–273; Tessa Rajak, "The Jews under Hasmonean Rule," *CAH* 9 (1994): 287–96.

40. Blenkinsopp, *Ezra/Nehemiah*, 225–26.

41. Uriel Rappaport, *The First Book of Maccabees: Introduction, Hebrew Translation, and Commentary* [Hebrew] (Jerusalem: Yad Ben-Zvi, 2004), 60–61, with references to earlier literature. The mention of the Plain of Ono as the place where Sanballat and Geshem plan to hurt Nehemiah (Neh 6:2) also seems to fit Hasmonean realities (e.g., 1 Macc 12:38, 13:13).

42. Schwartz, "Israel and the Nations Roundabout," and bibliography.

43. Daniel Schwartz, *The Second Book of Maccabees: Introduction, Hebrew*

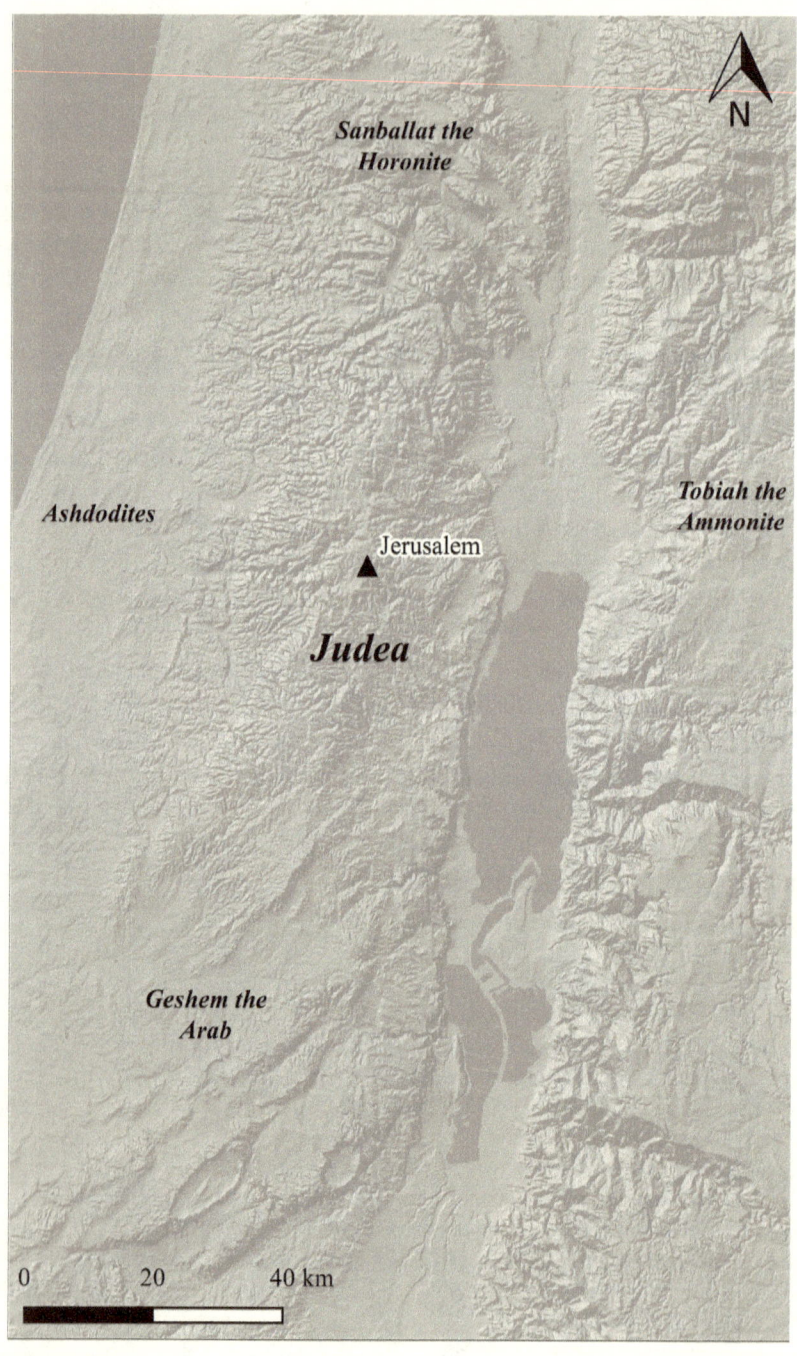

Figure 4.1. Nehemiah's adversaries

## 4. Nehemiah's Adversaries

Needless to say, my proposal does not reflect on the date of the Nehemiah Memoir. The original compilation—the core text of the book—deals with the shameful situation in Jerusalem, the need to fortify it and a certain construction effort carried out there, without details of gates and towers. Similarly, the Nehemiah Memoir (6:16) mentions unnamed opponents from the "nations roundabout." The references to specific, named enemies surrounding Judea was inserted later,[44] in Hasmonean times, together with the detailed description of the construction of a long wall, with its references to specific gates and towers.

This is not to say that the three named adversaries—Sanballat, Tobiah, and Geshem—should be identified with personalities of the mid- to late second century BCE. The author who inserted their names took them each as a symbol of their homelands:[45] Sanballat—possibly the fourth century BCE figure still remembered, or a line of important individuals carrying this name in pre-Hasmonean days—stands for Samaria in the north; the Tobiads—the supporters of Hellenistic culture and adversaries of the Hasmoneans—symbolize Ammon in the east;[46] Geshem—a common name among the Arabs—denotes the population of the desert beyond Idumea in the south; and the Ashdodites stand for the population in the coastal plain, bordering on Hasmonean Gezer and Ekron.

Dating the insertion of the references to the named adversaries (as well as the detailed description of the city wall in Neh 3) to the Hellenistic period should come as no surprise. Scholars noted that the latest redactions and additions in Nehemiah may date as late as the Hasmonean period.[47]

---

*Translation, and Commentary* [Hebrew] (Jerusalem: Yad Ben-Zvi, 2004), 16–19, and bibliography.

44. For the insertion of the theme of the enemies, see Wright, *Rebuilding Identity*, 118, 340—not the latest layer according to him.

45. Also Grätz, "Adversaries in Ezra/Nehemiah," 82, 85.

46. According to Edelman, "Seeing Double," the references to Tobiah meant to criticize Tobiah of the Zenon papyri.

47. Williamson, *Ezra, Nehemiah*, xxxv; Wright, "New Model for the Composition of Ezra-Nehemiah," 334, 347; David M. Car, *The Formation of the Hebrew Bible: A New Reconstruction* (Oxford: Oxford University, 2011), 169; Böhler explicitly put the rebuilding of Jerusalem story in Nehemiah on a Hasmonean background: Dieter Böhler, *Die heilige Stadt in Esdras α und Esra-Nehemia: Zwei Konzeptionen der Wiederherstellung Israels*, OBO 158 (Fribourg: Universitätsverlag, 1997), 382–97.

## 5. Summary

I would suggest, then, that the theme of (unnamed) enemies does appear in the Nehemiah Memoir, which may date to the Persian period. Yet, the specific references to the three named adversaries and the Ashdodites are—together with the detailed description of the construction of the Jerusalem wall—secondary insertions from the Hellenistic period, aimed at representing the real rivals of Judea at a time when the Hasmoneans were expanding in all directions and thus clashing with their neighbors.

# 5
# The Historical Reality behind the Genealogical Lists in 1 Chronicles

The genealogical lists of "the sons of Israel" in 1 Chr 2-9 have been the focus of intensive research from the beginning of modern biblical scholarship.[1] Among other topics, research has centered on the origin of the lists, their purpose, their relationship to other parts of the books of Chronicles and their date. Most scholars agree that the genealogical lists form an independent block, a kind of introduction to history; opinions differ, however, on whether the lists belong to the work of the Chronicler[2] or if they were added after the main substance of the book had already been written.[3] Regarding absolute chronology, scholars have tended to date the lists according to their views on the date of the compilation of the books of Chronicles, with most opting for the fourth century BCE and

---

1. For recent decades, see, e.g., Marshall D. Johnson, *The Purpose of the Biblical Genealogies*, SNTSMS 8 (Cambridge: Cambridge University Press, 1969); Manfred Oeming, *Das wahre Israel: Die "genealogische Vorhalle" 1 Chronik 1-9*, BWANT 128 (Stuttgart: Kohlhammer, 1990); Gary N. Knoppers, *I Chronicles 1-9: A New Translation with Introduction and Commentary*, AB 12 (New York: Doubleday, 2004); James T. Sparks, *The Chronicler's Genealogies: Towards an Understanding of 1 Chronicles 1-9*, AcBib 28 (Atlanta: Society of Biblical Literature, 2008).

2. Johnson, *Purpose of the Biblical Genealogies*, 47-55; Hugh G. M. Williamson, *1 and 2 Chronicles* (Grand Rapids: Eerdmans, 1982), 39; Oeming, *Das wahre Israel*; Sara Japhet, *I and II Chronicles: A Commentary* (London: SCM Press, 1993), 8-9; Steven J. Schweitzer, *Reading Utopia in Chronicles*, LHBOTS 442 (New York: T&T Clark, 2007), 36-40; Sparks, *Chronicler's Genealogies*.

3. For instance, Adam C. Welch, *The Work of the Chronicler: Its Purpose and Date* (London: Milford, 1939), 81-96; Martin Noth, *The Chronicler's History*, JSOTSup 50 (Sheffield: Sheffield Academic Press, 1987), 36-42; Wilhelm Rudolph, *Chronikbücher*, HAT 1 (Tübingen: Mohr, 1955), viii; Frank M. Cross, "A Reconstruction of the Judean Restoration," *JBL* 94 (1975): 4-18.

then looking for a Persian-period Yehud reality behind them[4]—a characteristic circular argument.

Archaeology, which may provide the material reality behind a given text and thus help to date it, has not as yet been consulted. Archaeology is especially strong when many identifiable toponyms (that is, sites) are given. In this article I wish to look at the archaeology and the geographical dispersal of the sites mentioned in the lists and thus shed light on their date.

## 1. The Archaeology of the Places Mentioned in the Lists

Most of the places mentioned in the lists are securely identified (fig. 5.1), which opens the way to check their archaeological record. There is reasonable information on most of these sites from either excavations or surveys. I have collected the information regarding the late Iron II, Persian, and Hellenistic periods—the range of time which can be considered for dating the lists (see below). In many cases survey sites do not allow to reach minute observations within a given period. This is especially true in attempting to distinguish in surveyed sites (as opposed to excavated ones) between Iron IIB and Iron IIC finds (eighth and seventh centuries BCE respectively) and between early and late Hellenistic period finds. In the case of the latter period, it is reasonable to assume that sites which had not been inhabited in the Persian period continued to be deserted in the early Hellenistic period and were resettled only in the second century BCE. This is the case in almost every excavated site in the highlands—Bethel,[5] the northwestern hill in Jerusalem,[6] Gibeon,[7] Moza,[8] and Beth-zur.[9] Tables 5.1-2 summarize the available information.

---

4. E.g., Williamson, *1 and 2 Chronicles*, 39; Yigal Levin, "Who Was the Chronicler's Audience? A Hint from His Genealogies," *JBL* 122 (2003): 229-45; Knoppers, *I Chronicles 1-9*, 253; John W. Wright, "Remapping Yehud: The Borders of Yehud and the Genealogies of Chronicles," in *Judah and the Judeans in the Persian Period*, ed. Oded Lipschits and Manfred Oeming (Winona Lake, IN: Eisenbrauns, 2006), 67-89; Sparks, *Chronicler's Genealogies*, 366.

5. Israel Finkelstein and Lily Singer-Avitz, "Reevaluating Bethel," *ZDPV* 125 (2009): 33-48.

6. E.g., Nahman Avigad, *Discovering Jerusalem* (Nashville: Nelson, 1983), 61-63; Hillel Geva, "Summary and Discussion of Findings from Areas A, W and X-2," in *Jewish Quarter Excavations in the Old City of Jerusalem II* (Jerusalem: Israel Exploration Society, 2003): 524-25.

## 5. Genealogical Lists in 1 Chronicles

Table 5.1. The Archaeology of the Places Mentioned
in the Genealogical Lists in 1 Chronicles 2–9[10]

| Tribe | Place | Bib Ref. | Identification and References to Periods of Activity | | Iron II | Persian Period | Hellenistic Period |
|---|---|---|---|---|---|---|---|
| Judah | Tekoa | 2:24 4:5 | Khirbet et-Tuqu‘[11] | A) B) | V V | V V | — V |
| | Ziph | 2:42 4:16 | Tell Zif[12] | | V | V | V strong |
| | Mareshah | 2:42 4:21 | Tell Sandahannah[13] | | V | V weak | V strong |
| | Hebron | 2:42 | Tell el-Rumeideh[14] | | V | — | V |

7. James B. Pritchard, "Gibeon," *NEAEHL* 2 (1993): 513; Israel Finkelstein, "Jerusalem in the Persian (and Early Hellenistic) Period and the Wall of Nehemiah," *JSOT* 32 (2008): 501–20 (ch. 1 in this book).

8. Zvi Greenhut and Alon de Groot, *Salvage Excavations at Tel Moza: The Bronze and Iron Age Settlements and Later Occupations*, IAA Reports 39 (Jerusalem: Israel Antiquities Authority, 2009).

9. Robert W. Funk, "Beth-zur," *NEAEHL* 1 (1993): 261; Paul Lapp and Nancy Lapp, "Iron II—Hellenistic Pottery Groups," in *The 1957 Excavation at Beth-Zur*, Ovid R. Sellers et al., *AASOR* 38 (Cambridge: American Schools of Oriental Research, 1968), 70; and, in the same volume, Paul W. Lapp, "The Excavation of Field II," in Sellers et al., *1957 Excavation at Beth-Zur*, 29.

10. The table includes only identifiable sites (whose archaeological record can be investigated). The towns of Simeon and Manasseh, taken from the books of Joshua and Judges (below) are excluded from the table. The list of Levites cities (1 Chr 6) is also excluded, as it was probably taken from Josh 21 (regardless of the date of the latter). Note that for column 4, Identification and References to Periods of Activity, when there is more than one survey with different results, the different works are marked in both the table and the references in the footnotes in capital letters (A, B, C).

11. (A) Moshe Kochavi, "The Land of Judah" [Hebrew], in *Judaea Samaria and the Golan: Archaeological Survey 1967–1968* (Jerusalem: Carta, 1972), 47; (B) Avi Ofer, *The Highland of Judah during the Biblical Period* [Hebrew] (PhD thesis; Tel Aviv: Tel Aviv University, 1993), IIA:28.

12. Kochavi, "Land of Judah," 68; Ofer, *Highland of Judah*, IIA:44.

13. Amos Kloner, *Maresha Excavations Final Report I: Subterranean Complexes 21, 44, 70*, IAA Reports 17 (Jerusalem: Israel Antiquities Authority, 2003), 9–30.

14. Ofer, *Highland of Judah*, IIA:30; Avi Ofer, "Hebron," *NEAEHL* 2 (1993): 609;

| Tribe | Place | Bib Ref. | Identification and References to Periods of Activity | | Iron II | Persian Period | Hellenistic Period |
|---|---|---|---|---|---|---|---|
| Judah (cont.) | Tappuah | 2:43 | Tafuh[15] | | V strong | V | V |
| | Maon | 2:45 | Khirbet Ma'in[16] | A) B) | V V strong | — V | V V |
| | Beth-zur | 2:45 | Khirbet et-Tubeiqeh[17] | | V | V weak | V strong |
| | Kiriath-jearim | 2:53 | Deir el-'Azar[18] | | V strong | V weak | V |
| | Zorah | 2:53 | Sar'ah[19] | A) B) C) | V V V | — V — | — — V |
| | Eshtaol | 2:53 | Ishwa'[20] | A) B) | V V | V — | — — |
| | Bethlehem | 2:54 | Beit Lahm[21] | | V strong | V | V |
| | Etam | 4:3 | Khirbet el-Khawkh[22] | | V | V | V |

Emanuel Eisenberg and Alla Nagorski, "Tel Hevron (er-Rumeidi)," *Hadashot Arkheologiyot*/*ESI* 114 (2002): 113; there is no information for the situation under the modern city.

15. Kochavi, "Land of Judah," 59–60; Ofer, *Highland of Judah*, IIA:30.
16. (A) Kochavi, "Land of Judah," 77–78; (B) Ofer, *Highland of Judah*, IIA:43.
17. Finkelstein, "Jerusalem in the Persian Period."
18. Israel Finkelstein, "Archaeology of the List of Returnees in Ezra and Nehmiah," *PEQ* 140 (2008): 5 (ch. 2 in this book).
19.(A) Yehuda Dagan, *The Shephelah during the Period of the Monarchy in Light of Archaeological Excavations and Survey* [Hebrew] (MA thesis; Tel Aviv: Tel Aviv University, 1992): 78; (B) Gunnar Lehmann, Michael H. Niemann, and Wolfgang Zwickel, "Zora und Eschtaol," *UF* 28 (1996): 362–73; (C) personal communication from Rami Raveh, Shlomo Bunimovitz, and Zvi Lederman (I am grateful to them for sharing this information with me).
20. (A) Dagan, *Shephelah*, 77; (B) Lehmann, Niemann, and Zwickel, "Zora und Eschtaol," 353–55.
21. Ofer, *Highland of Judah*, IIA:13.
22. Kochavi, "Land of Judah," 42; Ofer, *Highland of Judah*, IIA:13.

## 5. Genealogical Lists in 1 Chronicles

| Tribe | Place | Bib Ref. | Identification and References to Periods of Activity | Iron II | Persian Period | Hellenistic Period |
|---|---|---|---|---|---|---|
| Judah (cont.) | Gedor | 4:4 4:18 | Khirbet Judur[23] | V strong | V | V |
| | Ophrah | 4:14 | Khirbet et-Tayyibe[24] | V | V | V |
| | Eshtemoa | 4:17 4:19 | es-Samuʿ[25] A) B) | V strong — | — — | — V |
| | Soco | 4:18 | Khirbet Shuweike[26] | V strong | V weak | V strong |
| | Zanoah | 4:18 | Khirbet Zanuʿ[27] | V | V strong | V |
| | Keilah | 4:19 | Khirbet Qila[28] | V | V | V |
| Benjamin | Anathoth | 7:8 | ʿAnata[29] | V strong | — | V |
| | Alemeth | 7:8 8:36 9:42 | Khirbet ʿAlmit[30] | V | V | V |

---

23. Kochavi, "Land of Judah," 46–47; Ofer, *Highland of Judah*, IIA:15.
24. Kochavi, "Land of Judah," 57; Ofer, *Highland of Judah*, IIA:29.
25.(A) Ofer, *Highland of Judah*, IIA:19; only one side of the site was surveyed; (B) John L. Peterson, *A Topographical Surface Survey of the Levitical 'Cities' of Joshua 21 and 1 Chronicles 6: Studies on the Levites in Israelite Life and Religion* (PhD thesis; Chicago: Institute of Advanced Theological Studies; Evanston: Western Theological Seminary, 1977), 507 (one plot was surveyed).
26. Kochavi, "Land of Judah," 77; Ofer, *Highland of Judah*, IIA:33 (but the author of the genealogies could have referred here to Soco of the Shephelah).
27. Dagan, *Shephelah*, 92.
28. Kochavi, "Land of Judah," 48–49; Dagan, *Shephelah*, 161. Hellenistic pottery from this site is kept in the storehouses of the Israel Antiquities Authority and the Archaeological Staff Officer for Judea and Samaria. I am grateful to Yehuda Dagan and Yoav Tzionit for locating this pottery and showing it to me. (Note that this material was not available to me when I wrote my article on Jerusalem in the Persian and early Hellenistic period—Finkelstein, "Jerusalem in the Persian Period.")
29. Uri Dinur and Nurit Feig, "Eastern Part of the Map of Jerusalem" [Hebrew], in *Archaeological Survey of the Hill Country of Benjamin*, ed. Israel Finkelstein and Yitzhak Magen (Jerusalem: Israel Antiquities Authority, 1993), 359–60.
30. Dinur and Feig, "Eastern Part of the Map of Jerusalem," 380–81.

| Tribe | Place | Bib Ref. | Identification and References to Periods of Activity | Iron II | Persian Period | Hellenistic Period |
|---|---|---|---|---|---|---|
| Benjamin (cont.) | Geba | 8:6 | Jaba'[31] | V strong | —? | V strong |
| | Manahath | 8:6 2:54 | el-Malhah[32] | V | no data | no data |
| | Ono | 8:12 | Kafr Juna[33] | V | V | V |
| | Lod | 8:12 | el-Ludd[34] | V | V | V |
| | Aijalon | 8:13 | Yalu[35] A) B) | V V strong | V — | V — |
| | Gibeon | 8:29 9:35 | el-Jib[36] | V | — | V |
| | Azmaveth | 8:36 9:42 | Hizma[37] | V | V | V |
| | Moza | 2:46 8:36 9:42 | Qalunyah[38] | V | — | V |

---

31. Amir Feldstein et al., "Southern Part of the Maps of Ramallah and el-Bireh and Northern Part of the Map of 'Ein Kerem," in Finkelstein and Magen, *Archaeological Survey of the Hill Country of Benjamin*, 177–79; Persian-period pottery reported only in Zecharia Kallai, "The Land of Benjamin and Mt. Ephraim" [Hebrew], in *Judaea Samaria and the Golan: Archaeological Survey 1967–1968*, ed. Mosheh Kochavi (Jerusalem: Carta, 1972), 183.

32. *Hadashot Arkheologiot* 10 (1964): 12.

33. Ram Gophna, Itamar Taxel, and Amir Feldstein, "A New Identification of Ancient Ono," *BAIAS* 23 (2005): 167–76.

34. Finkelstein, "Archaeology and the List of Returnees."

35. (A) Ram Gophna and Yosef Porat, "The Land of Ephraim and Manasseh" [Hebrew], in Kochavi, *Judaea Samaria and the Golan*, 236; (B) Alon Shavit, *The Ayalon Valley and Its Vicinity during the Bronze and Iron Ages* [Hebrew] (MA thesis, Tel Aviv: Tel Aviv University, 1992), 100–101.

36. Finkelstein, "Jerusalem in the Persian (and Early Hellenistic) Period," 513.

37. Finkelstein, "Archaeology and the List of Returnees," 5.

38. Greenhut and de Groot, *Salvage Excavations at Tel Moza*.

## 5. Genealogical Lists in 1 Chronicles

| Tribe | Place | Bib Ref. | Identification and References to Periods of Activity | Iron II | Persian Period | Hellenistic Period |
|---|---|---|---|---|---|---|
| Ephraim | Upper Beth-horon | 7:24 | Beir ʿUr el-Fauqa[39] | V strong | V weak | V |
| | Lower Beth-horon | 7:24 | Beir ʿUr et-Tahta[40] | V strong | V weak | V strong |
| | Bethel | 7:28 | Beitin[41] | V | —? | V strong |
| | Naaran | 7:28 | Ein Duk? | no data | no data | no data |
| | Gezer | 7:28 | Tel Gezer[42] | V | V weak | V |
| | Shechem | 7:28 | Tell Balata[43] | V | V weak | V strong |
| | Ayyah | 7:28 | Khirbet Haiyan?[44] | — | — | V? |
| Asher | Birzaith | 7:31 | Khirbet Bir Zeit[45] | V strong | — | V |
| Reuben | Aroer | 5:8 | ʿAraʿir[46] | V | — | V |
| | Nebo | 5:8 | Khirbet el-Mukhayyat[47] | V | — | V |
| | Baal-meon | 5:8 | Khirbet Main | no data | no data | no data |

---

39. Israel Finkelstein, Zvi Lederman, and Shlomo Bunimovitz, *Highlands of Many Cultures: The Southern Samaria Survey*, MISA 14 (Tel Aviv: Tel Aviv University Institute of Archaeology, 1997), 303–5.
40. Finkelstein, Lederman, Bunimovitz, *Highlands of Many Cultures*, 161–64.
41. Finkelstein and Singer-Avitz, "Reevaluating Bethel"; there was weak occupation in the late Iron II.
42. William G. Dever, "Gezer," *NEAEHL* 2 (1993): 506.
43. Edward F. Campbell, "Shechem, Tell Balatah," *NEAEHL* 4 (1993): 1352–54.
44. Finkelstein, "Archaeology and the List of Returnees," 7.
45. Finkelstein, Lederman, and Bunimovitz, *Highlands of Many Cultures*, 417; Kallai, "Land of Benjamin," 173–74; Khaled Nashef, "Khirbet Birzeit 1996, 1998–1999: Preliminary Report," *Journal of Palestinian Archaeology* 1 (2000): 25–27.
46. Emilio Olavarri, "Aroer (in Moab)," *NEAEHL* 1 (1993): 92–93.
47. Sylvester J. Saller and Bellarmino Bagatti, *The Town of Nebo (Khirbet el-Mekhayyat), with a Brief Survey of Other Ancient Christian Monuments in Transjordan*, Publications of the Studium Bibilicum Franciscanum 7 (Jerusalem: Franciscan Press, 1949).

Table 5.2. Sites Mentioned in the Genealogical Lists in 1 Chronicles 2–9: Summary of Activity in the Late Iron II, Persian, and Hellenistic Periods

|  | Strong | Weak | Strength of activity not decided | No evidence for activity |
|---|---|---|---|---|
| Iron II | 13 | 1 | 21 | 1 |
| Persian | 1 | 8 | 16 | 11 |
| Hellenistic | 8 | 0 | 27 | 1 |

If one sees the genealogical lists as representing a true settlement system and is therefore looking for a single-period reality behind them,[48] it seems clear that the Persian period (and as explained above, the early Hellenistic period as well) is not an option. Eleven sites were not inhabited and eight sites were sparsely inhabited in the Persian period; together they represent almost half of the total number. Needless to say, in the case of a site that was investigated in only a single survey and which yielded a limited number of sherds the information may be less than complete. Yet, most sites mentioned above were thoroughly surveyed, many of them more than once, and yielded a meaningful quantity of finds. Hence the data seem to be reliable, especially when evaluated regarding the entire system of sites: a single negative result may be arbitrary, but a large number of sites with negative results for the same period carries a great deal of weight.

From the strictly archaeological point of view one is left with the late Iron II and the late Hellenistic periods. Only a single site was not inhabited in the late Iron II. But the identification of Ayyah is less secure than that of the other sites. Some late Iron II sites may have been sparsely inhabited in the final phase of the period; this can be seen in the case of two important sites that were thoroughly excavated—Bethel and Gezer.

Only a single site—Eshtaol—does not have a record of occupation for the late Hellenistic period. Eshtaol is located under the remains of the Arab village of Ishwaʿ. The survey conducted there by Lehmann et al.[49]

---

48. Even if the author is nostalgic, on the one hand, or utopian, on the other (meaning that the sites must not all be inhabited in one period—a possibility rightly suggested to me by Oded Lipschits), his perspective would likely reflect his own time and conditions. One may therefore search for a historical period in which the sites mentioned in these lists would have been relevant to the author.

49. Lehmann, Niemann, and Zwickel, "Zora und Eschtaol," fig. 2.

5. Genealogical Lists in 1 Chronicles 91

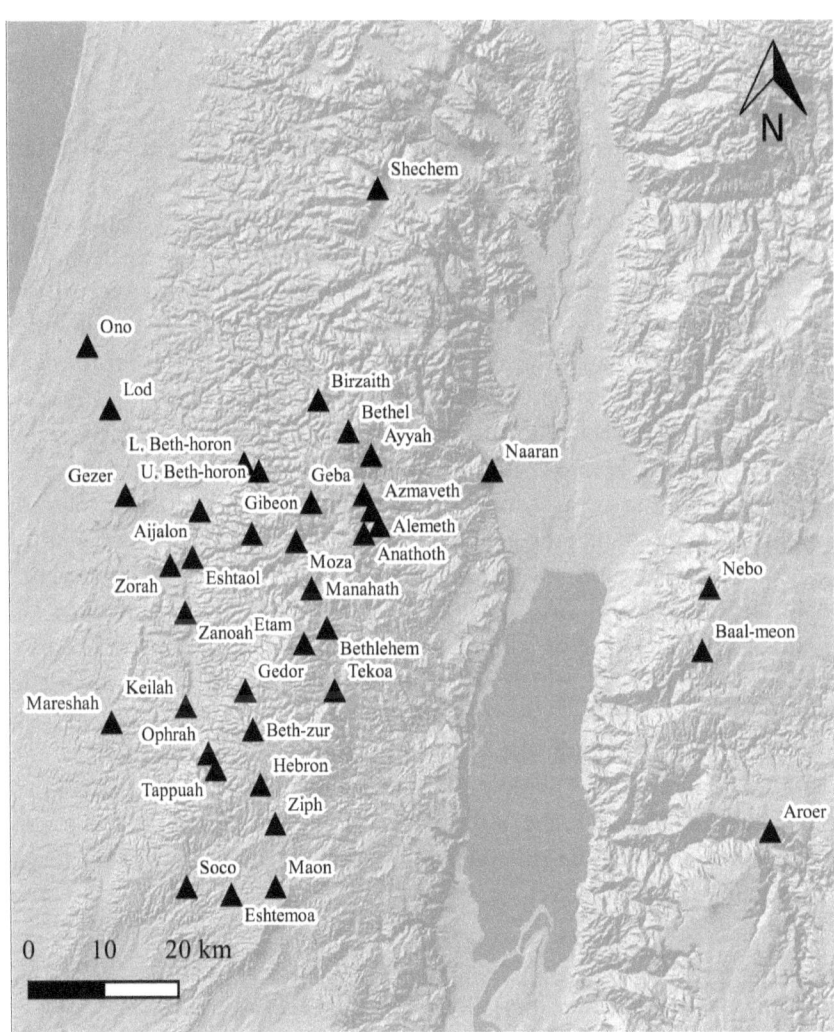

Figure 5.1. Places mentioned in the genealogies in 1 Chr 2–9

yielded only fifteen sherds, most of them from post-Byzantine periods.[50] Dagan states that "the survey yielded only a few remains, on the margin of the *moshav* [the Israeli settlement—I.F.] mainly on the southern slope."[51] The data for this site are therefore insufficient.

## 2. The Territorial Reality behind the Lists

In choosing between the late Iron II and the Hellenistic period, I am inclined to opt for the latter. Had the lists preserved a memory of the settlement situation in the late Iron II, one could have expected to find many more sites in the Shephelah, first and foremost among them Lachish,[52] as well a genuine reference to the Beer-sheba Valley (rather than a repetition of a list from Josh 19; see below), which was densely inhabited at that time. In any event, the territorial dispersal of the sites mentioned in the lists provides additional evidence for dating them.

Scholars who dealt with the genealogical lists noted that there are no details (at least not toponyms) for the northern tribes. The genealogies of Naphtali and Issachar[53] are short and provide almost no information; only the central highlands genealogy of Asher is given; and there is no genealogy for Zebulun. In the case of Manasseh the author reiterated the data on the sons and daughters of Manasseh which appears in Josh 17, and incorporated a list of famous places (Beth-shean, Taanach, Megiddo, and Dor—1 Chr 7:29), which he probably took from the Deuteronomistic History (Judg 1:27).

Regarding the south, the list of Simeon is probably taken from the book of Joshua (19:1–7).[54] In the case of Judah there are no data about the east (the Judean Desert and the area of Jericho-Dead Sea) and south (except for repeating the Simeon list from Josh 19); the information about the Shephelah is limited.

---

50. Lehmann, Niemann, and Zwickel, "Zora und Eschtaol," fig. 2.

51. Dagan, *Shephelah*, 77.

52. Lachish was the second most important Judahite site at that time; see also Ran Zadok, "On the Reliability of the Genealogical and Prosopographical Lists of the Israelites in the Old Testament," *TA* 25 (1998): 244.

53. And Dan? (e.g., Knoppers, *I Chronicles 1–9*, 453).

54. Rudolph, *Chronikbücher*, 38–39; Albrecht Alt, *Kleine Schriften zur Geschichte des Volkes Israel* Vol. II (Munich: C. H. Beck, 1953), 285; Nadav Na'aman, "The Inheritance of the Sons of Simeon," *ZDPV* 96 (1980): 136–52.

Detailed lists with names of towns are therefore given for Judah and Benjamin, for Ephraim, and for part of the territory of Reuben (see also, 1 Chr 9:3; fig. 5.1). It is also noteworthy that the genealogy of the return in 1 Chr 9:2-34 mentions repatriates from Judah, Benjamin, Ephraim, and Manasseh).[55] In Judah the list includes the highlands and part of the Shephelah (five sites—two in the eastern Shephelah, two in the northern Shephelah, and Mareshah). Except for Shechem, the list of Ephraim concentrates on the southern part of its inheritance. For Reuben the list mentions three places in the area of Madaba (the *Mishor*). The territory covered by the list stretches, therefore from Eshtemoa and Maon in the south to Bethel and Birzaith in the north, and to the Zorah-Keilah line in the west (with the addition of Mareshah), plus the area of Madaba in the east. *This territory* should be checked against the possible historical realities that may stand behind the genealogical lists.

The premise of this discussion is that rather than being nostalgic and/or utopian,[56] the genealogical lists represent a given settlement reality in the history of Judah/Yehud/Judea. This is true even if the author of the genealogies used different (chronologically layered?) materials, because he referred to settlements that still existed in his own day.[57] In other words, the distribution of the places mentioned in the core-area covered by the lists should represent the extent of the Jerusalem territorial entity at a given period of time.

Four possibilities should be checked: that the lists represent past memory—of the late Iron II; that they reflect the realities of the Persian period;[58] that they depict the situation in the early Hellenistic period; that they correspond to the reality of the late Hellenistic (Hasmonean) period.

---

55. Knoppers, *I Chronicles 1-9*, 264

56. Schweitzer, *Reading Utopia*, 31-75, and see n. 47 above. Had the list been utopian, one would have expected the author to fill the entire extent of the tribal system with information taken from the Deuteronomistic History.

57. See the discussion in Roddy L. Braun, "1 Chronicles 1-9 and the Reconstruction of the History of Israel," in *The Chronicler as Historian*, ed. M. Patrick Graham, Kenneth G. Hoglund, and Steven L. McKenzie, JSOTSup 238 (Sheffield: Sheffield Academic Press, 1997), 92-105; see also Hugh G. M. Williamson, "Sources and Redaction in the Chronicler's Genealogy of Judah," *JBL* 98 (1979): 351-59; Nadav Na'aman, "Sources and Redaction in the Chronicler's Genealogies of Asher and Ephraim," *JSOT* 49 (1991): 99-111.

58. This is the conventional theory; see, e.g., recently, Levin, "Chronicler's Audience"; Knoppers, *I Chronicles 1-9*, 253; Wright, "Remapping Yehud."

## 2.1. Late Iron II Reality Adapted for Postexilic Needs?

A brief scan is sufficient to show that the list does not represent the territorial reality of late Iron II Judah: (1) The Beer-sheba Valley (apart from a repetition of the Josh 19 Simeonite list) and the Judean Desert are missing in the south and east. (2) One would have expected many more sites in the Shephelah. (3) Central places in the Shephelah, mainly Lachish, the second most important site in Judah in late-monarchic times, do not appear.[59] (4) In the northwest the list includes the area of Gezer, Lod, and Ono, which had never been under Judahite domination.[60]

One could have argued that the list fits the days of Josiah, because of the inclusion of Benjamin and southern Ephraim around Bethel. But even in the late seventh century Judah did not control the Gezer-Lod area, not to mention that in the days of Josiah it stretched further west in the Shephelah.[61] One cannot eliminate the possibility that a memory of the reality in the Iron II had been adopted for postexilic needs. And this is precisely my premise: if this were the case, what would be the reality behind a situation in which only part of the Judahite kingdom's territory is listed?

## 2.2. Persian Period Yehud Reality?

This has been the conventional view.[62] Scholars reconstructed the borders of the province of Yehud according to two items of information: the geographical lists in the book of Ezra and Nehemiah, first and foremost among them the list of builders of Jerusalem's city wall in Neh 3; and the distribution of the Persian-period Yehud seal impressions.[63] In reality, the

---

59. See also, Zadok, "On the Reliability," 244.

60. Israel Finkelstein and Nadav Na'aman, "Shechem of the Amarna Period and the Rise of the Northern Kingdom of Israel," *IEJ* 55 (2005): 182–83.

61. See, e.g., Nadav Na'aman, "The Kingdom of Judah under Josiah," *TA* 18 (1991): 3–71.

62. See, e.g., recently, Levin, "Chronicler's Audience"; Knoppers, *I Chronicles 1–9*, 253; Wright, "Remapping Yehud."

63. Type 1–12 in David Vanderhooft and Oded Lipschits, "A New Typology of the Yehud Stamp Impressions," *TA* 34 (2007): 12–37; for summary of the different opinions, see, Charles E. Carter, *The Emergence of Yehud in the Persian Period: A Social and Demographic Study*, JSOTSup 294 (Sheffield: Sheffield Academic Press, 1999), 75–90; Oded Lipschits, *The Fall and Rise of Jerusalem: Judah under Babylonian Rule* (Winona Lake, IN: Eisenbrauns, 2005), 154–84.

5. Genealogical Lists in 1 Chronicles 95

main consideration has always been the biblical text; the distribution of the Yehud seal impressions covers only part of the area described in Neh 3, but this has not been thoroughly considered, mainly because most scholars have not questioned the Persian-period date of the geographical material in Nehemiah.

Nehemiah 3 speaks about the division of the territory ruled from Jerusalem into several districts (*pelekh*) and half districts (half *pelekh*). Five places are listed as headquarters in this administrative system: Jerusalem, Beth-haccherem, Mizpah, Beth-zur, and Keilah (fig. 3.1). Several scholars have suggested adding districts in the east (Jericho) and northwest (Gezer).[64] I agree with Lipschits,[65] that the province described in the list was divided into five units—those specifically referred to in the text. Accordingly, the territory described in Neh 3 extended from Beth-zur in the south to the area of Mizpah in the north (including the areas around these two sites), and from the Judean Desert in the east to Keilah in the west. The latter is the only extension into the Shephelah.

Yet the Neh 3 list cannot serve as a basis for reconstructing the borders of Yehud in the *Persian period*.

(1) Elsewhere I have argued that the description of the building of the city wall in Neh 3 does not fit what we know about the archaeology of Jerusalem in the Persian period.[66] While Neh 3 refers to a large city, which probably includes the southwestern hill and which was fortified by a major wall with many towers and gates, Persian-period Jerusalem was an *unfortified* village that extended over a very limited area in the central part of the "City of David" ridge. It seems that the description in Neh 3—which does not belong to the Nehemiah Memoir[67] and which was probably inserted into the text of Nehemiah[68]—if not utopian, may represent the reality of

---

64. For summaries of the different opinions, see Ephraim Stern, *Material Culture of the Land of the Bible in the Persian Period, 538–332 B.C.* (Warminster: Aris & Phillips, 1982), 247–49; Carter, *Emergence of Yehud*, 79–80; Lipschits, *Fall and Rise of Jerusalem*, 168–74.

65. Lipschits, *Fall and Rise of Jerusalem*, 168–74.

66. Finkelstein, "Jerusalem in the Persian (and Early Hellenistic) Period."

67. See, e.g., Charles C. Torrey, *Ezra Studies* (Chicago: University of Chicago Press, 1910), 225; Hugh G. M. Williamson, *Ezra, Nehemiah*, WBC 16 (Waco, TX: Word Books, 1985), 200; Joseph Blenkinsopp, *Ezra/Nehemia: A Commentary* (Philadelphia: Westminster, 1988), 231.

68. See, e.g., Charles C. Torrey, *The Composition and Historical Value of Ezra-*

the construction of the First Wall by the Hasmoneans in the second century BCE.[69]

(2) The archaeology of Beth-zur, mentioned as the headquarters of half a district (Neh 3:16), poses another problem. Based on a single locus (!), Stern adhered to the notion of significant activity at the site in the Persian period.[70] Reich[71] argued in the same vein according to an architectural analysis. But Funk, Paul and Nancy Lapp, and Carter showed that the site was very sparsely, in fact, insignificantly, inhabited in the Persian and early Hellenistic periods.[72] Funk noted that the "interpretation of the Persian-Hellenistic remains at Beth-zur is dependent in large measure on the extant literary references,"[73] meaning that it was written according to one's understanding of the text rather than the archaeological data. Indeed, the published material from the excavations includes only a limited number of finds—sherds, vessels, and coins—that can safely be dated to the Persian period, while most forms typical of the Persian-period repertoire are missing altogether. Hence, though archaeology may have revealed traces of some Persian-period activity at the site, it is clear that it was an important place only in the late Iron II and more so in the late Hellenistic period (see below for the latter period).

(3) Nor did Gibeon, which is also mentioned in Nehemiah (3:7), yield unambiguous Persian-period finds. Without delving into the debate over the dating of the Gibeon winery and inscriptions (late monarchic or sixth century[74]) one may observe that the *mwsh* seal impressions and wedge-shaped

---

*Nehemiah* (Giessen: Ricker, 1896), 37–38; Torrey, *Ezra Studies*, 249; Sigmund Mowinckel, *Studien zu dem Buche Ezra-Nehemia* (Oslo: Universitetsforlaget, 1964), 109–16.

69. Finkelstein, "Jerusalem in the Persian (and Early Hellenistic) Period"; Dieter Böhler explicitly puts the rebuilding of Jerusalem story in Nehemiah on a Hasmonean background—*Die heilige Stadt in Esdras α und Esra-Nehemia: Zwei Konzeptionen der Wiederherstellung Israels*, OBO 158 (Fribourg: Universitätsverlag, 1997), 382–97.

70. Ephraim Stern, *The Assyrian, Babylonian, and Persian Periods (732–332 B.C.E.)*, vol. 2 of *Archaeology of the Land of the Bible* (New York: Doubleday, 2001), 437–38; also Stern, *Material Culture of the Land of the Bible*, 36.

71. Ronny Reich, "The Beth-Zur Citadel II—A Persian Residency?," *TA* 19 (1992): 113–23.

72. Funk, "Beth-Zur," 261; Paul and Nancy Lapp, "Iron II," 70; P. Lapp, "Excavation of Field II," 29. Carter, *Emergence of Yehud*, 157.

73. Robert W. Funk, "The History of Beth-Zur with Reference to Its Defenses," in Sellers et al., *1957 Excavation at Beth-Zur*, 4–17.

74. For summaries of the debate, see Stern, *Assyrian, Babylonian, and Persian*

and reed-impressed sherds found at the site attest to a certain activity in the Babylonian or Babylonian/early Persian period.[75] According to Pritchard, there is "only scant evidence of occupation from the end of the sixth century until the beginning of the first century B.C.E." at Gibeon.[76] Yet, typical Persian-period pottery and Yehud seal impressions were not found.[77] Late Hellenistic pottery and coins are attested.

(4) Last but not least, the distribution of the Persian-period Yehud seal impressions[78] does not fit the territory described in Neh 3 (fig. 3.1). In the highlands, these seal impressions are concentrated in Jerusalem and its surroundings, including Ramat Rahel. Only six items were found in the highlands to the north of Jerusalem (the area of Mizpah), compared to seventeen in the City of David and seventy-nine at Ramat Rahel. No seal impression of this type was found south of Ramat Rahel (the area of Beth-zur). In the east, seal impressions of these types were found at Jericho and En-Gedi (six items)—a sensible reason for the inclusion of this area within the borders of Yehud. In the west they were found at Gezer and Tel Harasim in the western Shephelah (four items altogether), places clearly outside the borders of Yehud until the expansion of the Hasmonean state in the days of Jonathan and Simeon (see below). None was found in the many sites of the upper Shephelah.

Considering the problem of dating the reality behind Neh 3, and with no extrabiblical textual data for the Persian period, one can (should?) try to reconstruct the borders of Yehud *only* according to the distribution of the Persian-period seal impressions and the fragmentary textual data from somewhat later, the third and early second centuries BCE (see below). Accordingly, Yehud seems to have included mainly the area of Jerusalem, between Ramat Rahel and the City of David. It could have extended a bit further to the south, but Beth-zur seems to have been outside of Yehud. In

---

*Periods*, 32–33; Stern, *Material Culture of the Land of the Bible*, 433; Oded Lipschits, "The History of the Benjaminite Region under Babylonian Rule" [Hebrew], *Zion* 64 (1999): 287–91.

75. Stern, *Material Culture of the Land of the Bible*, 32–33; Stern, *Assyrian, Babylonian, and Persian Periods*, 433; Lipschits, *Fall and Rise of Jerusalem*, 243–45; James B. Pritchard, *Winery, Defenses and Soundings at Gibeon* (Philadelphia: University Museum, University of Pennsylvania, 1964), figs. 32:7, 48:17.

76. Pritchard, "Gibeon," 513.

77. For the latter, see Lipschits, *Fall and Rise of Jerusalem*, 180.

78. Groups 1–12 in Vanderhooft and Lipschits, "New Typology of the Yehud Stamp Impressions."

the north, the dearth of seal impressions from the area of Mizpah and Nebi Samuel[79] raises the question whether this area was an important part of fifth–fourth centuries BCE Yehud.[80] In the east, there was a possible extension to Jericho and En-Gedi. As for the southwest, in the time of the Zenon Papyri of the mid-third century BCE, Mareshah and Adoraim belonged to Idumea. The area of Lod and Gezer (which were Israelite rather than Judahite towns in the Iron II), and Ekron in the western Shephelah, were annexed to Judea only in the days of Jonathan and Simeon, in the 140s BCE. I therefore tend to agree with Carter that Persian-period Yehud did not extend to the Shephelah.[81]

It is clear, then, that the distribution of the places mentioned in the core of the genealogical lists in 1 Chr 2–9 (fig. 5.1) does not fit the territorial extension of Persian-period Yehud (fig. 3.1). On the one hand, the lists include places in four areas which were outside of the borders of Yehud: the Hebron and south-Hebron hills in the south; the area of Bethel-Birzaith in the north; the Shephelah in the west; and the Gezer-Lod-Ono area in the northwest. On the other hand, the genealogical lists do not include the area of En-Gedi, which was probably included in Yehud. Further, they do not mention Beth-haccherem, the supposed name of Ramat Rahel,[82] the most important archaeological site in the province of Yehud, which yielded the largest number of Persian-period Yehud seal impressions.[83] To sum-up, the borders of Yehud and the distribution of places in the core of the genealogical lists have very little in common. The genealogical lists do not reflect Persian-period Yehud realities.

---

79. There are only six items, which make 5.5 percent of the total of the Persian-period types, compared to thirty-two items, which make 11 percent of the later Types 13–14 in the work of Vanderhooft and Lipschits, "New Typology of the Yehud Stamp Impressions."

80. The List of Returnees in Ezra 2:1–67; Neh 7:6–68, which mentions places in this area, should probably be dated to the Hellenistic period—Finkelstein, "Archaeology and the List of Returnees," 7–16 (ch. 2 in this book).

81. Carter, *Emergence of Yehud*, 91–98.

82. Yohanan Aharoni, "Beth Haccherem," in *Archaeology and Old Testament Study*, ed. Winston D. Thomas (Oxford: Clarendon, 1967), 171–85.

83. Vanderhooft and Lipschits, "New Typology of the Yehud Stamp Impressions."

## 2.3. Early Hellenistic Situation?

Direct textual information for the Ptolemaic period is meager: the Zenon Papyri reveal that Mareshah in the Shephelah and Adoraim southwest of Hebron belonged to Idumea.

Turning to archaeology, the main concentrations of the Yehud seal impressions of Types 13–15, which seem to belong to the late-fourth and third centuries BCE,[84] are in Jerusalem and Ramat Rahel, Jericho and En-Gedi, and Mizpah and Nebi Samuel. Their distribution north of Jerusalem is especially noteworthy; in this area Impressions 13–14 grow from circa 5.5 percent of the total in the early group (Types 1–12, of the Persian period), to 11 percent in the period under discussion. This may indicate the growing importance of this area (expansion of Jewish population?) at that time.[85]

The borders of Judea in the first half of the second century BCE can be drawn according to several literary sources: the location of the battles between Judas Maccabeus and the Seleucids, the location of the fortresses built by Bacchides after the death of Judas, and other clues in 1 Maccabees (fig. 3.2).

The importance of the area to the north and northwest of Jerusalem as commanding the main approach to the city, and possibly as the frontier of expansion of Judea, is indicated by the fact that five of the eight battles of Judas Maccabeus took place here, three of them (Beth-horon, Adasa and Kafar Salama) along the Beth-horon–Gibeon Road. It is reasonable to assume that Judas Maccabeus encountered the Seleucid forces on the borders of Judea or close to them. The two battles in the south—at Beth-zur and Beth Zacharia (slightly to the north of Beth-zur)—should probably indicate the southern boundary of Judea. First Maccabees seems to point out that Beth-zur changed hands more than once during the wars,[86] which means that it was located on the southern border of Judea.

---

84. Vanderhooft and Lipschits, "New Typology of the Yehud Stamp Impressions."

85. For the theory that this happened following the Samaritan revolt against Alexander the Great, see Menahem Stern, *The Documents on the History of the Hasmonaean Revolt* [Hebrew] (Tel Aviv: Hakkibutz Hameuchad, 1965), 110; Aryeh Kasher, "Some Suggestions and Comments Concerning Alexander Macedon's Campaign in Palestine" [Hebrew], *Beit Miqra* 20 (1975): 187–208; against this idea, see, e.g., Albrecht Alt, "Zur Geschichte der Grenze zwischen Judäa und Samaria," *PJ* 31 (1935): 94–97.

86. Beth-zur had been fortified by Judas Maccabeus (1 Macc 4:61), held by Lysias

Locating the places fortified by Bacchides "in Judea" (1 Macc 9:50–52) is also essential for drawing its borders in the 160s BCE (fig. 3.2). The sites mentioned in the list are Jericho, Emmaus, Beth-horon, Bethel, Thamnatha, Pharathon, Tephon, Beth-zur, Gazara, and the Akra in Jerusalem. The location of most of these sites is self-evident. The places difficult to identify are Thamnatha, Pharathon, and Tephon.

Thamnatha and Pharathon were identified by Abel[87] with biblical Timnath-heres (Kh. Tibne in southwestern Samaria) and biblical Pirathon = the village of Far'ata west of Shechem). This proposal is difficult to accept as it locates both places outside of Judea.[88] I therefore follow Avi-Yonah and Roll, who identify Thamnatha with another Timna—probably Kh. Tibna southwest of Jerusalem, on a ridge sloping down into the Valley of Elah.[89] The problem with this identification is that an initial survey of the site apparently did not reveal Hellenistic sherds.[90]

Safrai and Na'aman located Pharathon in the village of Farkha near Nahal Shiloh, far from the boundaries of Judea.[91] Avi-Yonah sought Pharathon in Wadi Fara northeast of Jerusalem,[92] but there is no actual site

---

(1 Macc 6:7), fortified by Bacchides (1 Macc 9:52) besieged by Simeon (1 Macc 11:65) and fortified by him (1 Macc 14:33).

87. Felix-Marie Abel, *Les livres des Maccabées* (Paris: Librairie Lecoffre, 1949), 172.

88. Michael Avi-Yonah, *The Holy Land from the Persian to the Arab Conquests (536 B.C. to A.D. 640): A Historical Geography* (Grand Rapids: Baker, 1977), 53. For the same reason—keeping the sites "in Judea"—I would argue against Israel Roll, "Bacchides' Fortifications and the Arteries of Traffic to Jerusalem in the Hellenistic Period" [Hebrew], *ErIsr* 25 (1996): 511 and also Moshe Fischer, Israel Roll and Oren Tal, "Persian and Hellenistic Remains at Tel Yaoz," *TA* 35 (2008): 152–55, who suggested identifying Gazara on the coast rather than at Gezer. I find it difficult to agree to the idea that the term "in Judea" is anachronistic: Felix-Marie Abel, "Topographie des campagnes Machabéennes," *RB* 34 (1925): 202–8; Jonathan A. Goldstein, *1 Maccabees: A New Translation with Introduction and Commentary*, AB 41 (Garden City: Doubleday, 1976), 386.

89. Avi-Yonah, *Holy Land*, 53; Roll, "Fortifications and the Arteries," 512.

90. Amihai Mazar, "The Excavations of Khirbet Abu et-Twein and the System of Iron Age Fortresses in Judah" [Hebrew], *ErIsr* 15 (1981): 246.

91. Zeev Safrai, *Borders and Government in the Land of Israel in the Period of the Mishna and the Talmud* [Hebrew] (Tel Aviv: Hakkibutz Hameuchad, 1980), 61–62; Nadav Na'aman, "Pirathon and Ophrah," *BN* 50 (1989): 11–16.

92. Avi-Yonah, *Holy Land*, 53–54.

there that can be proposed for this identification. I have recently suggested locating it in Tell el-Ful.[93]

Tephon was identified with Tapuah south of Shechem,[94] the southern Tapuah, west of Hebron,[95] Beit Nattif near the Valley of Elah,[96] Tekoa,[97] and Kh. Bad-Faluh north of Tekoa.[98] The first identification should be dismissed, as it puts the fortress far from Judea.

Plotting these places (at least those securely identified) on a map (fig. 3.2), one gets a system that surrounds the core area of Judea: Jericho, Bethel and Beth-horon in the north, Gezer and Emmaus in the northwest, Timna near the Valley of Elah in the west, and Beth-zur and possibly Tephos/Tekoa in the south. Only the Akra is clearly located within the territory of Judea.

Second Maccabees (12:38) also tells us that in the west, Adullam was probably in the territory of Judea, while Gezer belonged to Ashdod until it was conquered by Simeon. Ekron and the area of Lod were annexed to Judea only in the time of Jonathan (below).

Turning again to archaeology, we find that Types 16 and 17 of the Yehud seal impressions[99] and the *yrslm* seal impressions date to the second century BCE, first and foremost because of their distribution in the southwestern hill of Jerusalem, which was not inhabited between the early sixth and second centuries BCE.[100] A more accurate date is difficult to establish; the following arguments should be taken into consideration.

(1) Their relatively modest number of seal impressions there, compared to their number in the City of David,[101] seems to indicate that they

---

93. Israel Finkelstein, "Tell el-Ful Revisited: The Assyrian and Hellenistic Periods (With a New Identification)," *PEQ* 143 (2011): 106–18.

94. Abel, *Les Livres des Maccabées*, 173.

95. Abraham Kahana, *Hasfarim Hahitzoniim II* [Hebrew] (Tel Aviv: Masada, 1960), 142, n. 50.

96. Christa Möller and Gotz Schmitt, *Siedlungen Palästinas nach Flavius Josephus* (Wiesbaden: Reichert, 1976), 36–37; Gershon Galil, "Pirathon, Parathon and Timnatha," *ZDPV* 109 (1993): 49–53.

97. Avi-Yonah, *Holy Land*, 54.

98. Roll, "Fortifications and the Arteries," 513.

99. The paleo-Hebrew Yehud impressions—Vanderhooft and Lipschits, "New Typology of the Yehud Stamp Impressions," 29–30.

100. Ronny Reich, "Local Seal Impressions of the Hellenistic Period," in Geva, *Jewish Quarter Excavations in the Old City of Jerusalem II*, 256–62.

101. There are twenty-seven in the southwestern hill compared to fifty-nine in the

went out of use in the early days of the southwestern quarter; otherwise their number there would be expected to be much higher.

(2) No seal impression of these types was found at Bethel in the north and Beth-zur in the south. The same holds true for Lod and the entire area of the three toparchies annexed to Judea in the days of Jonathan, and for Joppa. Only one *yrslm* seal impression is known from the Shephelah (found at Azekah).

It seems, then, that Types 16 and 17 and the *yrslm* seal impressions date to the first half of the second century BCE, before the meaningful expansion of Judea. Their relatively strong appearance at Gezer (five Yehud items and two *yrslm* impressions), which was annexed to Judea in the days of Simeon, may be explained as evidence for its strong commercial links to Judea.

According to these sources—textual and archaeological—Judea of the first half of the second century BCE stretches from the area of Beth-zur, or just north of it, to Mizpah and from the Judean Desert to the eastern Shephelah. This seems to mean that relative to Yehud of the Persian period, Judea of the early Hellenistic period expanded in two directions: in the west to the upper Shephelah and possibly in the north. This territory still does not correspond to the distribution of places in the core of the genealogical lists, mainly because the latter include sites in the Hebron and south-Hebron hills and in the area of Gezer-Lod-Ono.

## 2.4. Hasmonean Reality?

In the 140s BCE, the Hasmonean state began expanding to the north, west, and east. The three toparchies to the north of Judea—Lod, Ephraim (Apheraema), and Ramathaim (1 Macc 11:34)—and the area of Ekron (1 Macc 10:89) were handed over to Judea in the days of Jonathan,[102] who, in addition, seems to have annexed the Jewish Peraea in Transjordan.[103] Gezer

---

City of David for Types 16 and 17 (Vanderhooft and Lipschits, "New Typology of the Yehud Stamp Impressions," 29–30); ten compared to twenty-two respectively for the *yrslm* seal impressions (Reich, "Local Seal Impressions," 259).

102. See, e.g., Zecharia Kallai, *The Northern Boundaries of Judah* [Hebrew] (Jerusalem: Magnes, 1960), 99–106; Avi-Yonah, *Holy Land*, 47, 55–57; Joshua J. Schwartz, *Lod (Lydda): Israel from Its Origins through the Byzantine Period, 5600 B.C.E.–640 C.E.*, BARIS 571 (Oxford: BAR, 1991), 50–51.

103. Avi-Yonah, *Holy Land*, 57.

and Joppa were then taken by Simeon (1 Macc 13:43, 48; 14:5).[104] Judea now stretched from Beth-zur in the south to Nahal Shiloh in the north; and from the Judean Desert and the Peraea in the east to beyond Ekron and Gezer in the west, and to Joppa in the northwest.

The next step in the expansion of Judea came in the days of John Hyrcanus (134–104 BCE), with the conquest of Madaba in Transjordan, the conquest and destruction of Shechem and the Samaritan temple on Mount Gerizim; and the conquest of Idumea, which included Adoraim (and the Hebron and south Hebron hills) and Mareshah. The later days of John Hyrcanus (about two decades later), saw the conquest of Samaria, with a possible extension into the Jezreel Valley.[105]

The Hasmonean expansion was seen as a legitimate reconquest of the territory of biblical Israel, an ideology best represented in the words put by the author of 1 Maccabees (probably composed in the days of John Hyrcanus or immediately thereafter) in the mouth of Simeon: "we have neither taken any other man's land, nor do we hold dominion over other people's territory, but only over the inheritance of our fathers. On the contrary, for a certain time it was unjustly held by our enemies, but we, seizing the opportunity, hold fast the inheritance of our fathers" (1 Macc 15:33).

The distribution of places in the core area of the genealogical lists perfectly fits the days of John Hyrcanus. It depicts the nucleus of the Hasmonean state (from Beth-zur to Mizpah) plus the expansion in the days of Jonathan to the three toparchies in the north and northwest (Birzaith, Lod, Ono in the lists); the expansion in the days of Simeon to Gezer;[106] and the expansion in the days of John Hyrcanus to Mareshah,[107]

---

104. Avi-Yonah, *Holy Land*, 58–59.

105. On the territorial expansion in the days of John Hyrcanus, see, e.g., Joseph Klausner, "John Hyrcanus I," in *The Hellenistic Age*, vol. 6 of *The World History of the Jewish People*, ed. Abraham Shalit (New Brunswick: Rutgers University, 1972), 211–21; Uriel Rappaport, "The Hasmonean State (160–37 B.C.E.)" [Hebrew], in *The History of Eretz Israel: The Hellenistic Period and the Hasmonean State (332–37 B.C.E.)*, ed. Menahem Stern (Jerusalem: Yad Ben-Zvi, 1981), 3:193–273; Aryeh Kasher, "The Hasmonean Kingdom" [Hebrew], in *The Hasmonean State: The History of the Hasmoneans during the Hellenistic Period*, ed. Uriel Rappaport and Israel Ronen (Jerusalem: Yad Ben-Zvi, 1993), 243; Tessa Rajak, "The Jews under Hasmonean Rule," *CAH* IX (1994): 287–96.

106. The references to a place named Gath in 1 Chr 7:21; 1 Chr 8:13, located in the lowlands, also seem to relate to this westward expansion of Judea.

107. On the latter pointing to the postexilic date of the lists, see Zadok, "On the

to other areas of Idumea (the Hebron hills),[108] to the area of Shechem, and to the area of Madaba (Baal-meon, Nebo, and Aroer in the list—1 Chr 5:8). At that moment in history the Hasmonean state ruled the entire area depicted in the core of the lists (appearance of towns): from the south Hebron hills in the south to Shechem in the north; to Marisa, Gezer, Lod, and Ono in the west; and possibly to the area of Madaba in the east.

### 3. Discussion

The genealogical lists probably meant to legitimize Jewish rule over this area, part of which was inhabited by a large gentile population, by giving it ancient Israelite tribal pedigree. This seems to be in line with several Hasmonean pseudepigraphic compositions—the book of Jubilees, which was written in the days of John Hyrcanus and possibly the Testament of the Twelve Patriarchs—which looked at the Bible in order to explain and legitimize the gradual territorial expansion of Judea in the second century BCE.[109] These books legitimized the Hasmonean conquests and addressed problems related to the relationship with non-Jews who lived in the new territories.[110] Jubilees used biblical materials in order to legitimize the inclusion of foreign groups into Judaism,[111] and the genealogies in Chronicles, too, do not reject the inclusion of foreigner groups[112] and foreign individuals through mixed marriages.[113] According to this scheme, the

---

Reliability," 244; for numismatic evidence indicating the importance of the town in the days of John Hyrcanus, see Kloner, *Maresha Excavations*, 5.

108. The author took the towns of Simeon from Josh 19 as he had no knowledge of the area further to the south, that is, the Beer-sheba Valley.

109. See, e.g., Doron Mendels, *The Land of Israel as a Political Concept in Hasmonean Literature*, TSAJ 15 (Tübingen: Mohr, 1987). For a survey of opinions regarding the date of the book of Jubilees, see James C. VanderKam, *The Book of Jubilees* (Sheffield: Sheffield Academic Press, 2001), 17–21.

110. VanderKam, *Jubilees*, 17–21; Doron Mendels, *The Rise and Fall of Jewish Nationalism* (New York: Doubleday, 1992), 81–99.

111. Mendels, *Land of Israel*, 60, 67.

112. Gary N. Knoppers, "Intermarriage, Social Complexity, and Ethnic Diversity in the Genealogy of Judah," *JBL* 120 (2001): 15–30.

113. Williamson, *1 and 2 Chronicles*, 38; Knoppers, "Intermarriage." For the incorporation of "new-Jews" in the Hasmonean elite, see, e.g., Seth Schwartz, "Israel

genealogical lists were composed in the late second century BCE, in the middle of the reign of John Hyrcanus I.

The inclusion—in general outline, without mentioning towns—of Issachar, Naphtali, and north Transjordanian tribes (1) may be seen as reflecting the ideology of the Hasmoneans and their future aspirations to conclude the conquest of the territories of the twelve tribes of Israel (or great United Monarchy) as percieved in the early days of John Hyrcanus; (2) may reflect the end-days of his rule, when Samaria and the Jezreel Valley (Scythopolis) were annexed to the Hasmonean state (note that Jubilees puts Jacob in the area of Scythopolis, Dothaim (= Dothan and Akrabbim); or (3) may represent the time of Judah Aristobulus (104–103 BCE), when the annexation of much of this area to the Hasmonean state had been fulfilled (and hence the mention of Manassite towns in the Jezreel Valley?). Whether the absence of genealogies for Zebulun and Dan can be judged against this background is difficult to say.

The books of Chronicles describe the constant, gradual expansion of Judah, with the goal of restoration of the Davidic boundaries.[114] It is tempting to argue that this scheme, too, was influenced by the constant, gradual expansion of the Hasmonean state. Yet, such a claim would force a second century BCE dating of Chronicles, which most scholars would see as somewhat too late a date.

### 4. Summary

Assuming that the distribution of the sites menionted in the lists of genealogies in 1 Chr 2–9 reflects a given, genuine moment in history, their date can be varified according to the archaeology of these sites, and their distribution compared to what we know about the borders of Judah/Yehud/Judea in the late Iron II, Persian, and Hellenstic periods. The only period that fits both criteria is that of the Hasmonean rule in the second half of the second century BCE.

---

and the Nations Roundabout: 1 Maccabees and the Hasmonean Expansion," *JJS* 42 (1991): 16–38.

114. Sara Japhet, *The Ideology of the Book of Chronicles and Its Place in Biblical Thought*, BEATAJ 9 (Frankfurt am Main: Lang, 1997), 355–56.

## Addendum

### New Data Regarding Sites

Recent excavations at Hebron (Tell er-Rumeideh) revealed evidence of Iron IIB–C and late Hellenistic (Hasmonean) activity, but no finds from the Persian period.[115]

The first season of excavations at the site of Kiriath-jearim (2017) confirmed the results of past explorations of the site: Strong occupation in the Iron IIB–C, weak activity in the Persian and early Hellenistic periods and significant activity in the late Hellenistic period.[116]

There is one change regarding the identification of the sites mentioned in the genealogies: I would now identify Pharathon with Ophrah (= et-Taiyibeh), which means a פרע > עפר metathesis.[117] Note that in 2 Chr 13:19 (seemingly close in date to 1 Maccabees) Ophrah appears as Ephron—probably closer to Pharathon.[118]

### The Book of Chronicles and the Genealogies

When I wrote the original article on the genealogies, I was perhaps a bit too cautious regarding Hasmonean material in Chronicles (the end of the discussion subsection above). A few years later I wrote a broader essay on Chronicles, in which I proposed that the descriptions of the expansion of Judah in 2 Chronicles was composed in order to legitimize the expansion of the Hasmonean state.[119] The three articles—on the genealogies, the Rehoboam forts, and Chronicles—should be read together (chs. 5–7).

In a recent article, Oeming challenged my dating of the genealogies to the second century BCE based mainly on three points:[120]

---

115. Emanuel Eisenberg and David Ben-Shlomo, *The Tel Hevron 2014 Excavations: Final Report* (Ariel University Institute of Archaeology Monograph Series Number 1 (Ariel: Ariel University, 2017), 13–14, 441–42.

116. Israel Finkelstein et al., "Excavations at Kiriath-Jearim Near Jerusalem, 2017: Preliminary Report," *Semitica* 60 (2018): 31–83.

117. I wish to thank Benjamin Sass and Ran Zadok for helping me with this issue.

118. Israel Finkelstein, "Major Saviors, Minor Judges: The Historical Background of the Northern Accounts in the Book of Judges," *JSOT* 41 (2017): 440–41.

119. Israel Finkelstein, "The Expansion of Judah in II Chronicles: Territorial Legitimation for the Hasmoneans?," *ZAW* 127 (2015): 669–95.

120. Manfred Oeming, "Rethinking the Origins of Israel: 1 Chronicles 1–9 in the

## 5. Genealogical Lists in 1 Chronicles

- Oeming objects to my (ostensible—see below) dating of the list to around 120 BCE and argues that "a precise date such as 120 BCE is impossible to establish by archaeological tools."[121]
- He doubts the ability of archaeological surveys to provide reliable information about the settlement history of sites.
- Oeming argues that the genealogical lists in 1 Chronicles have more than one layer and that the "assumption that they reflect the historical reality of a single moment in time is not convincing."[122]

These arguments do not withstand scrutiny.

(1) Nowhere in the original article (or above) do I fix an exact date for the genealogies in 120 BCE. This is a windmill created by Oeming, who then proceeds to fight it.

(2) A survey of a given site may indeed provide less than the desirably accurate results when compared to later excavations at the same place. Yet, when results in a large group of sites are consistent, it is difficult to argue that the same period was missed in all of them. In this regard, note that pottery of the Persian period (e.g., bases and rims of mortaria bowls and basket handles of storage jars) are easy to distinguish in surveys.

(3) The most important observation in my analysis of the archaeological finds in the sites mentioned in the genealogies addresses those sites that were not inhabited or were weakly inhabited in the Persian (and probably early Hellenistic) period. Here Oeming failed to get to the heart of the matter. First, among the eleven sites that provided negative evidence, seven were thoroughly *excavated* (rather than surveyed: Hebron, Gibeon, Moza, Bethel, Ayyah, Aroer, and Nebo). Of the four other sites, three produced a large number of sherds collected in surveys, which diminishes the possibility of error. Of the seven sites that produced weak results for the Persian period, five were thoroughly excavated (Mareshah, Beth-zur, Kiriath-jearim, Gezer, and Shechem). The results are

---

Light of Archaeology," in *Rethinking Israel: Studies in the History and Archaeology of Ancient Israel in Honor of Israel Finkelstein*, ed. Oded Lipschits, Yuval Gadot, and Matthew J. Adams (Winona Lake, IN: Eisenbrauns, 2017), 303–18.

121. Oeming, "Rethinking the Origins of Israel," 308, also 307, 309.
122. Oeming, "Rethinking the Origins of Israel," 315.

therefore robust regardless of the question of accuracy of survey work.
(4) The assumption that the genealogical lists represent several layers from different periods is as uncertain as the one cited by Oeming, and this is exactly the aim of this work: to deploy archaeology as a way to escape circular reasoning in text analysis.

# 6
# Rehoboam's Fortified Cities (2 Chr 11:5-12)

## 1. Introduction

A list of cities ostensibly fortified by Rehoboam appears in 2 Chr 11:5-12,[1] with no parallel in the book of Kings. Many scholars have dealt with this short account, in efforts to establish its date, geographical setting, and place in the Chronicler's description of the reign of Rehoboam.[2] Regarding chronology, researchers have suggested dating the list to the time of Rehoboam, as related in the text,[3] or to a later date in the history of Judah:

---

1. I do not intend to deal with the question of whether verses 5a and 10b-12 belong to the original list; see further, e.g., Volkmar Fritz, "The 'List of Rehoboam's Fortresses' in 2 Chr 11:5-12—A Document from the Time of Josiah," *ErIsr* 15 (1981): 46\*-53\*.
2. E.g., Gustav Beyer, "Beiträge zur Territorialgeschichte von Südwestpalästina im Altertum: 1. Festungssystem Rehabeams," *ZDPV* 54 (1931): 113-34; Mordechai Gichon, "The System of Fortifications in the Kingdom of Judah," in *The Military History of the Land of Israel in Biblical Times* [Hebrew], ed. Jacob Liver (Tel Aviv: Maarachot, 1964), 410-25; Zechariah Kallai, "The Kingdom of Rehoboam" [Hebrew], *ErIsr* 10 (1971): 245-54; Fritz, "List of Rehoboam's Fortresses"; Nadav Na'aman, "Hezekiah's Fortified Cities and the *LMLK* Stamps," *BASOR* 261(1986): 5-21.
3. Beyer, "Beiträge zur Territorialgeschichte"; Wilhelm Rudolph, *Chronikbücher*, HAT 1 (Tubingen: Mohr Siebeck, 1955), 227-30; Gichon, "System of Fortifications"; Peter Welten, *Die Königs-Stempel: Ein Beitrag zur Militarpolitik Judas unter Hiskia und Josia*, Abhandlungen des Deutschen Palästina-Vereins (Wiesbaden: Harrassowitz, 1969), 167-71; Kallai, "Kingdom of Rehoboam"; Yohanan Aharoni, *The Land of the Bible: A Historical Geography* (Philadelphia: Westminster, 1979), 330-33; Maxwell J. Miller, "Rehoboam's Cities of Defense and the Levitical City List," in *Archaeology and Biblical Interpretation: Essays in Memory of D. Glenn Rose*, ed. Leo G. Perdue, Lawrence E. Toombs, and Gary Lance Johnson (Atlanta: John Knox, 1987), 273-86; Sara Japhet, *I and II Chronicles: A Commentary* (London: SCM, 1993), 666; T. R. Hobbs, "The 'Fortresses of Rehoboam': Another Look," in *Uncovering Ancient Stones, Essays*

the days of Hezekiah[4] or Josiah.[5] Regarding the geographical background, scholars have attempted to understand the function of the towns mentioned in the list in relation to the main roads leading to the heartland of Judah[6] and have struggled to explain why the northern border of the kingdom was left unprotected.

Without addressing the tantalizing question of the historical reliability of materials in Chronicles that are not mentioned in Kings,[7] it seems to

---

in *Memory of H. Neil Richardson*, ed. Lewis M. Hopfe (Winona Lake, IN: Eisenbrauns, 1994), 41–64. Scholars argued whether the fortresses were built in anticipation of—or as a result of—the Shishak campaign—see summary in Hobbs, "Fortresses of Rehoboam," 42–43.

4. Na'aman, "Hezekiah's Fortified Cities."

5. Ehrhard Junge, *Der Wiederaufbau des Heerwesens des Reiches Juda unter Josia*, BWANT 23 (Stuttgart: Kohlhammer, 1937), 75–80; Albrecht Alt, "Festungen und Levitenorte im Lande Juda," *Kleine Schriften zur Geschichte des Volkes Israel* (Munich: Beck, 1953), 2:306–15; Fritz, "List of Rehoboam's Fortresses." Hermann proposed that the system of Rehoboam fortresses "never existed as a comprehensive entity" and that "the Chronicler may have adopted the system and ascribed its 'basic pattern' as a Judaean defensive system to Rehoboam" (Siegfried Hermann, "The So-called 'Fortress System of Rehoboam', 2 Chron. 11:5-12: Theoretical Considerations," *ErIsr* 20 [1989], 76* and 75* respectively).

6. E.g., Beyer, "Beiträge zur Territorialgeschichte"; Gichon, "System of Fortifications." Hobbs ("Fortresses of Rehoboam") suggested that Rehoboam's goal was not to protect the roads leading to Judah, but to enable an efficient control of Judah after the secession of the North.

7. For a positive attitude, see Martin Noth, *The Chronicler's History*, JSOTSup 50 (Sheffield: Sheffield Academic Press, 1987), 59–60; Baruch Halpern, "Sacred History and Ideology: Chronicles' Thematic Structure—Identification of an Earlier Source," in *The Creation of Sacred Literature: Composition and Redaction of the Biblical Text*, ed. Richard E. Friedman, Near Eastern Studies 22 (Berkeley: University of California, 1981), 35–54; Sara Japhet, "The Historical Reliability of Chronicles: The History of the Problem and Its Place in Biblical Research," *JSOT* 33 (1985): 83–107; Anson F. Rainey, "The Chronicles of the Kings of Judah: A Source Used by the Chronicler," in *The Chronicler as Historian*, ed. M. Patrick Graham, Kenneth G. Hoglund, and Steven L. McKenzie, JSNTSup 238 (Sheffield: Sheffield Academic Press, 1997), 30–72; Andrew G. Vaughn, *Theology, History, and Archaeology in the Chronicler's Account of Hezekiah*, ABS 4 (Atlanta: Scholars Press, 1999). For a negative approach, which I tend to accept, see, e.g., Peter Welten, *Geschichte und Geschichtsdarstellung in den Chronikbüchern*, WMANT 42 (Neukirchen-Vluyn: Neukirchener Verlag, 1973), 195–96; Robert S. North, "Does Archaeology Prove Chronicle's Sources?," in *A Light unto My Path: Studies in Honor of J. M. Meyers*, ed. Howard N. Bream, Ralph Daniel Heim, and Carey A. Moore, Gettysburg Theological Studies 4 (Philadelphia:

me that the list of Rehoboam's fortresses does not fit any Iron II reality and that it should be understood against the background of the Chronicler's or a later Chronicles redactor's time.

2. The Identification of Soco and Gath

Most of the places mentioned in the list are well known (fig. 6.1), and there is no need to repeat the details of their identification here.[8] Only two are somewhat ambiguous.

(1) *Soco*. This could be either of the two sites in Judah/Judea that bear this name—the first in the southern Hebron hills (Khirbet Shuweikeh between es-Samuʿ and edh-Dhahiriya) or the second in the Shephelah (Khirbet ʿAbbad in the Valley of Elah). The former is situated much to the south of all other sites in the list and is not located on any important road; the latter is therefore preferable: together with Azekah and Adullam it is located on an important artery leading to the highlands of Judah.

(2) *Gath*. Fritz,[9] Hermann,[10] and Naʾaman[11] equated the Gath of 2 Chr 11:8 with Gath of the Philistines, identified with Tell es-Safi.[12] Yet, the site is situated somewhat to the west of the line that stretches from Lachish to Azekah and Zorah, in a location that hardly fits the reality of the kingdom of Judah. This is certainly true until the destruction of Gath in the late ninth century BCE.[13] Sargon II mentions the conquest of Gath in the course of his campaign against Ashdod, and even if the city was annexed by Hezekiah (see Mic 1:10),[14] the annexation was short-lived, on the eve

---

Temple University Press, 1974), 375–401; Patrick M. Graham, *The Utilization of 1 and 2 Chronicles in the Reconstruction of Israelite History in the Nineteenth Century*, SBLDS 116 (Atlanta: Scholars Press, 1990), 93–249; Ehud Ben Zvi, "The Chronicler as a Historian: Building Texts," in Graham, Hoglund, and McKenzie, *Chronicler as Historian*, 132–49.

8. See, e.g., Aharoni, *Land of the Bible*, 330–33; Naʾaman, "Hezekiah's Fortified Cities"; Miller, "Rehoboam's Cities"; Hermann, "Fortress System."

9. Fritz "List of Rehoboam's Fortresses," 47.

10. Hermann, "Fortress System," 72.

11. Naʾaman, "Hezekiah's Fortified Cities."

12. Anson F. Rainey, "The Identification of Philistine Gath: A Problem in Source Analysis for Historical Geography," *ErIsr* 12 (1975): 63\*–76\*.

13. Aren M. Maeir, "The Historical Background and Dating of Amos VI 2: An Archaeological Perspective from Tell Es-Safi/Gath," *VT* 54 (2004): 319–34.

14. I would side with Siegfried Mittmann ("Hiskia und die Philister," *JNSL* 16

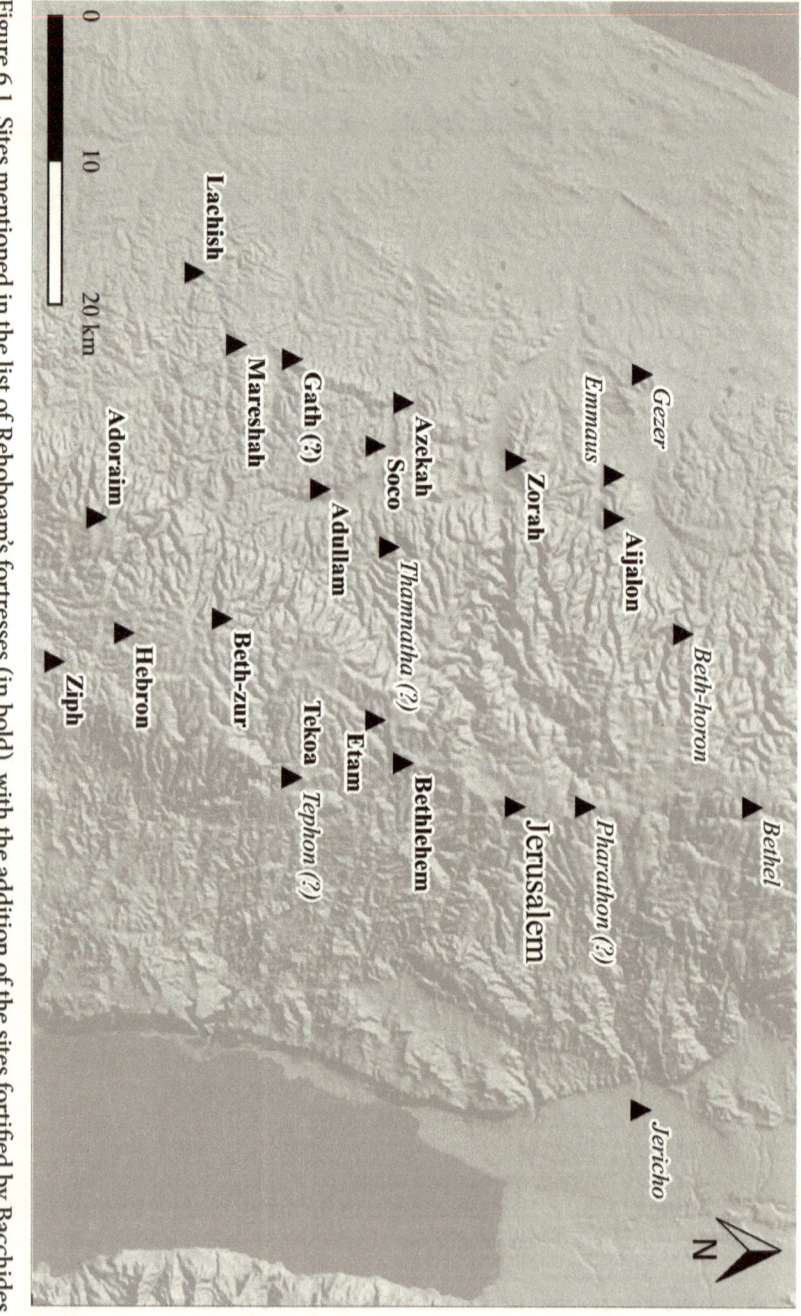

Figure 6.1. Sites mentioned in the list of Rehoboam's fortresses (in bold), with the addition of the sites fortified by Bacchides according to 1 Macc 9 (in italics). Question mark denotes sites whose identification is not secure

of the Sennacherib campaign. In the seventh century, Gath is not included in the list of Judahite towns in Josh 15.[15]

Aharoni suggested reading 2 Chr 11:8 Moresheth-gath: "the original text may have been 'Adullam, Moresheth-gath, Mareshah, etc.', from which 'Moresheth' accidentally fell out due to its similarity to 'Mareshah' near by."[16] Na'aman[17] noted, with a parallel from an Amarna letter (EA 335:17) and the Hebrew Bible (Jer 26:18; Mic 1:1), that the name Moresheth-gath would have been shortened to Moresheth rather than Gath. Weighting the two possibilities, I tend to side with those equating Gath of 2 Chr 11:8 with Moresheth-gath and possibly identifying it in Tell Judeideh north of Mareshah.

### 3. Does 2 Chr 11:5–12 Depict an Iron Age Reality?

Those who argue that the Chronicler could have used old sources that do not appear in Kings and try to find an Iron II reality behind the list of Rehoboam's fortresses face numerous geographical and archaeological problems.

### 3.1. No Tenth-Century BCE Fortifications in Judah

Dating the list to the time of Rehoboam raises a chronological problem. Radiocarbon determinations of a large number of samples from many sites and strata in Israel have shown that Rehoboam's reign in the second half of the tenth century falls close to the transition from the late Iron I to

---

[1990]: 98–99) and Nadav Na'aman ("Hezekiah and the Kings of Assyria," *TA* 21 [1994]: 235–54), identifying the "royal city of the Philistines" in the Azekah Inscription of Sennacherib with Ekron, rather than with Gath (for the latter possibility, see recently Alexander Zukerman and Itzhak Shai, "The Royal City of the Philistines in the 'Azekah Inscription' and the History of Gath in the Eighth Century B.C.E.," *UF* 38 [2006]: 1–50).

15. Opinions differ on how to view the material culture of late eighth century BCE Tell es-Safi—Raz Kletter, "Pots and Polities: Material Remains of Late Iron Age Judah in Relation to Its Political Borders," *BASOR* 314 (1999): 19–54; Zukerman and Shai, "Royal City."

16. Aharoni, *Land of the Bible*, 380, n. 28; also Kallai, "Kingdom of Rehoboam," 248–49; Miller, "Rehoboam's Cities," 276.

17. Na'aman, "Hezekiah's Fortified Cities," 5–6.

the Iron IIA.[18] The first fortifications that can safely be affiliated with the kingdom of Judah in both the Shephelah and the Beer-sheba Valley were built in the *late* Iron IIA, now securely dated to the ninth century BCE.[19] Especially telling is the situation at Lachish, which is mentioned in the list:[20] the site was fortified for the first time in the late Iron IIA,[21] in the mid- to late ninth century BCE.[22] It is also noteworthy that some of the sites mentioned in the list, which have been excavated, did not yield late Iron I and/or early Iron IIA finds, or produced negligible finds from this time-range.[23]

---

18. Ilan Sharon, Ayelet Gilboa, Timothy A. J. Jull, and Elisabetta Boaretto, "Report on the First Stage of the Iron Age Dating Project in Israel: Supporting a Low Chronology," *Radiocarbon* 49 (2007): 1–46; Israel Finkelstein, and Eli Piasetzky, "Radiocarbon-Dated Destruction Layers: A Skeleton for Iron Age Chronology in the Levant," *OJA* 28 (2009): 255–274; Israel Finkelstein and Eli Piasetzky, "The Iron I/IIA Transition in the Levant: A New Perspective," *Radiocarbon* 52 (2010): 1667–80, contra Amihai Mazar, and Christopher Bronk Ramsey, "$^{14}$C Dates and the Iron Age Chronology of Israel: A Response," *Radiocarbon* 50 (2008): 159–80.

19. Probably not early in that century—Israel Finkelstein, "The Rise of Jerusalem and Judah: The Missing Link," *Levant* 33 (2001): 105–15; Alexander Fantalkin, and Israel Finkelstein, "The Sheshonq I Campaign and the Eighth Century B.C.E. Earthquake—More on the Archaeology and History of the South in the Iron I–IIA," *TA* 33 (2006): 18–42; for the absolute date, see Israel Finkelstein, and Eli Piasetzky, "Radiocarbon Dating the Iron Age in the Levant: A Bayesian Model for Six Ceramic Phases and Six Transitions," *Antiquity* 84 (2010): 374–85. Yosef Garfinkel and Saar Ganor (*Excavation Report 2007-2008*, vol. 1 of *Khirbet Qeiyafa* [Jerusalem: Israel Exploration Society, 2009]) have now dated a fortification system that was discovered in Khirbet Qeiyafa in the western Valley of Elah to the tenth century BCE. Yet, the date of this fortification system is debatable (e.g., Yehudah Dagan, "Khirbet Qeiyafa in the Judean Shephelah: Some Considerations," *TA* 36 [2009]: 68–81) and in any event, in the tenth century BCE, the site must have been located in the territory of nearby Gath.

20. Na'aman, "Hezekiah's Fortified Cities," 6; David Ussishkin, "A Synopsis of the Stratigraphical, Chronological and Historical Issues," in *The Renewed Archaeological Excavations at Lachish (1973–1994)*, by David Ussishkin; Monograph Series of the Institute of Archaeology Tel Aviv University 22 (Tel Aviv: Institute of Archaeology, 2004), 77–78.

21. Ussishkin, "Synopsis," 76, 78–83.

22. Finkelstein and Piasetzky, "Radiocarbon Dating the Iron Age in the Levant."

23. For Beth-zur, see Ovid R. Sellers et al., *The 1957 Excavation at Beth-Zur*, AASOR 38 (Cambridge: American Schools of Oriental Research, 1968), 8; for Mareshah, see Amos Kloner, *Maresha Excavations Final Report I: Subterranean Complexes 21, 44, 70*, IAA Reports 17 (Jerusalem: Israel Antiquities Authority, 2003), 5; for Azekah, Oded Lipschits, personal communication; see table 1.

## 3.2. No Sites in the North

An outstanding feature of the list is that no fortification is mentioned along the northern boundary of the kingdom. Aharoni's explanation[24] that this was due to "Rehoboam's constant desire to expand in this direction" resulted from his acceptance of the historicity of a vast and powerful United Monarchy. But in any event, Judah was less powerful than Israel and hence was vulnerable to attacks from the north. Na'aman[25] proposed that the Chronicler omitted any reference to fortifications in the north in order to adhere to his ideology of gradual annexation of the territories to the north of Jerusalem by the Judahite kings.[26] But if this had been the case, why did he repeat the story from 1 Kings about the building of Mizpah and Geba by Asa (2 Chr 16:6)?

Leaving the northern border unfortified was not an option for the kingdom of Judah.[27] Several scholars have argued that the king behind the list integrated in his defense system sites that had been fortified in the past: Rehoboam could have included Levitical cities built during the time of the United Monarchy,[28] and Josiah could have incorporated towns fortified by Manasseh after the Sennacherib campaign.[29] Yet: (1) the list of Levitic cities—whatever its function and original scheme—dates to late monarchic times[30] if not later;[31] (2) Asa's reign falls in the early Iron IIA—a period with no trace of fortification in Judah; (3) the Assyrian adminis-

---

24. Aharoni, *Land of the Bible*, 330.
25. Na'aman, "Hezekiah's Fortified Cities," 10.
26. Sara Japhet, *The Ideology of the Book of Chronicles and Its Place in Biblical Thought*, BEATAJ 9 (Frankfurt am Main: Lang, 1997), 355–56.
27. Hugh G. M. Williamson's explanation (*1 and 2 Chronicles* [Grand Rapids: Eerdmans, 1982], 241) that there was no suitable site to the north of Jerusalem is unacceptable in view of commanding sites such as Nebi Samuel and Tell el-Ful.
28. Kallai, "Kingdom of Rehoboam"; for a similar line of thought, see Karl Elliger, "Studien aus dem Deutschen Evang. Institut für Altertumswissenschaft des Heiligen Landes. 44. Die Heimat des Propheten Micha," *ZDPV* 57 (1934): 108–9, 149–50 for Asa.
29. Junge, *Wiederaufbau*, 76–78.
30. E.g., Alt, "Festungen und Levitenorte"; Nadav Na'aman, *Borders and Districts in Biblical Historiography* (Jerusalem: Simor, 1986), 203–36.
31. Ehud Ben Zvi, "The List of the Levitical Cities," *JSOT* 54 (1992): 77–106; for those who still accept the historicity of a great United Monarchy, it should be obvious that there was no reason for its kings to fortify cities so close to Jerusalem in the north.

tration at Samaria would not allow Manasseh to fortify towns (of a vassal kingdom) bordering on their territory.

During Josiah's reign, Judah expanded to the north, at least as far as Bethel. This is supported by the list of towns of Judah in Josh 15, which dates to the late seventh century BCE,[32] and by the distribution of typical items of late Iron II Judahite material culture.[33] Had the list depicted the reality of the days of Josiah, one would have expected towns in the newly taken territories in the north to be included in it.

3.3. No Sites in the Beer-sheba Valley

In addition to the difficulties posed by the area north of Jerusalem, those who dated the list to the late Iron II (the reign of Hezekiah or Josiah), faced a problem regarding the southernmost sites mentioned in it. The Beer-sheba Valley was an important region in the kingdom of Judah. Archaeology shows that this was so starting with the construction of the late Iron IIA Stratum V at Beer-sheba and the fort of Stratum XI at Arad in the second half of the ninth century.[34] The importance of the Beer-sheba Valley grew when Judah played an important role in the Assyrian economy as a vassal kingdom, controlling the northern terminus of the main Arabian trade route that passed in the valley on the way to the Mediterranean ports. In the time of Josiah, the Beer-sheba Valley was densely settled, as reflected in the list of Negeb towns in Josh 15. Yet, no fortified town in the Beer-sheba Valley[35] appears in the list of Rehoboam's fortresses. Na'aman's explanation, that this was due to the fact that "they lay outside the expected

---

32. Albrecht Alt, "Judas Gaue unter Josia," *PJ* 21 (1925): 100–16; Nadav Na'aman, "The Kingdom of Judah under Josiah," *TA* 18 (1991): 3–71.

33. Kletter, "Pots and Polities."

34. For relative chronology, see Zeev Herzog and Lily Singer-Avitz, "Redefining the Centre: The Emergence of State in Judah," *TA* 31 (2004): 209–44; for absolute chronology, see Finkelstein and Piasetzky, "Radiocarbon Dating the Iron Age in the Levant"; for the territorial affiliation, see Fantalkin and Finkelstein, "Sheshonq I Campaign."

35. For instance, Beer-sheba, Arad, Ramat-negeb (= Tel Ira—André Lemaire, *Les ostraca hébreux de l'époque royale israélite* [PhD thesis; Paris: Universite de Paris, 1973], 361), Qinah (= Kh. Uza—Itzhaq Beit-Arieh, *Horvat 'Uza and Horvat Radum: Two Fortresses in the Biblical Negev*, MSIA 25 [Tel Aviv: Institute of Archaeology], 2007, 1, 4).

Assyrian line of approach,"[36] diminishes the sophistication of the Assyrian military machine and is in any case contradicted by the fact that Assyria inflicted a major blow on the Beer-sheba Valley in the late eighth century BCE, with the destruction of Beer-sheba II and Arad VIII.

3.4. Problems with Specific Sites

The town of Mizpah, to the north of Jerusalem, was an important Judahite stronghold. First Kings 15:22 relates that Mizpah was fortified by King Asa, but there is good reason to believe that story reflects the reality of a somewhat later phase in the history of the kingdom.[37] In any event, an impressive fortification existed at the site no later than the late eighth century BCE. Mizpah produced a large number of *LMLK* seal impressions,[38] which is another indication of its importance at that time. Its absence from the 2 Chr 11 list is therefore telling.

Beth-shemesh was an important Judahite city in the Shephelah in the late eighth century BCE; it yielded many *LMLK* seal impressions as well as evidence for a flourishing olive-oil industry.[39] If the list represented the time of Hezekiah, one would expect Beth-shemesh to be included in it.[40] Na'aman[41] argued that the distribution of the *LMLK* seal impressions of the late eighth century BCE corresponds to the 2 Chr 11:5–12 list, including the fact that only a few impressions have been found in the Beer-sheba Valley. This is not so because six of the nine sites that yielded the largest number of *LMLK* seal impressions[42] are not included in the

---

36. Na'aman, "Hezekiah's Fortified Cities," 13.
37. E.g., Haya Katz, "A Note on the Date of the 'Great Wall' of Tell en-Nasbeh," *TA* 25 (1998): 131–33.
38. Vaughn, *Theology*, 166.
39. Shlomo Bunimovitz and Zvi Lederman, "The Archaeology of Border Communities: Renewed Excavations at Tel Beth-shemesh, Part 1: The Iron Age," *NEA* 72 (2009): 136–39; Israel Finkelstein and Nadav Na'aman, "The Judahite Shephelah in the Late Eighth and Early Seventh Centuries B.C.E.," *TA* 31 (2004): 60–79.
40. Libnah was besieged by Sennacherib (2 Kgs 19:8), and therefore its absence from the list also contradicts its dating to the time of Hezekiah (Na'aman, "Hezekiah's Fortified Cities," 11).
41. Na'aman, "Hezekiah's Fortified Cities."
42. Ramat Rahel, Gibeon, Mizpah, Beth-shemesh, Gezer, and Kh. el-Burj (= Beeroth—Shmuel Yeivin, "The Benjaminite Settlement in the Western Part of their Territory," *IEJ* 21 [1971]: 141–54).

list;[43] in fact, of those sites that yielded a large number of *LMLK* seal impressions, only one third appear in the list.[44]

Finally, Aijalon (2 Chr 11:10) was probably located in the territory of the northern kingdom rather than Judah.

To sum up this section, it seems clear that the list of fortified towns in 2 Chr 11:5–12 does not represent an Iron Age reality, neither of the days of Rehoboam nor the days of Hezekiah or Josiah.

### 4. 2 Chr 11:5–12 and the Hasmonean State

Assuming that the list in 2 Chr 11:5–12 depicts a given reality in the history of Judah/Judea,[45] several clues seems to point to the Hasmonean (late Hellenistic) period.

### 4.1. Adoraim, Mareshah, and Beth-zur

Two of the towns in the list—Adoraim and Mareshah (Marisa)—are mentioned in the Zenon Papyri of the mid-third century BCE as administrative centers in Idumea. The prominence of Mareshah in the third and early second centuries BCE is revealed by archaeological discoveries,[46] including the recently published Heliodoros Inscription.[47] In fact, though inhabited previously, Mareshah became a significant city only in the Hellenistic period. A century later the two towns—Adoraim and Mareshah—are mentioned in the same breath as having been conquered by John Hyrcanus I (Josephus, *A.J.* 13.257). The mention of Adoraim in the list of 2 Chr 11 is especially telling since it does not appear elsewhere in the Hebrew Bible—not even in the detailed list of Judahite towns in Josh 15. This list repre-

---

43. Vaugn, *Theology*, 166.
44. Yosef Garfinkel, "2 Chr 11:5–10 Fortified Cities List and the *Lmlk* Stamps—Reply to Nadav Na'aman," *BASOR* 271 (1988): 69–73.
45. One could argue that the list represents a combination of past memories, realities from the time of the author, and future hopes. Yet, if this were the case, one would have expected a different array, with forts further to the south (which would include the Beer-sheba Valley), possibly a line further to the west, and maybe a line in the north.
46. Kloner, *Maresha Excavations*.
47. Hannah Cotton, and Michael Wörrle, "Seleukos IV to Heliodoros, A New Dossier of Royal Correspondence from Israel," *ZPE* 159 (2007): 191–205; Yuval Goren, "Scientific Examination of a Seleucid Limestone Stele," *ZPE* 159 (2007): 206–16.

sents the settlement pattern of the late seventh century BCE,[48] and includes many settlements in the vicinity of Adoraim. One more site that appears in the 2 Chr 11 list—Etam—appears in the Hebrew Bible only in Chronicles.

Beth-zur was a highly important stronghold on the southern boundary of Judea during the Hasmonean revolt; a major battle was fought there, and 1 Maccabees seems to indicate that it switched hands more than once during the wars.[49] Archaeological excavations conducted at the site indicate its importance in the late Hellenistic period.[50] Though it was inhabited in the late Iron II, Beth-zur is not mentioned as an important town in any late-monarchic biblical text.

4.2. The Line in the South

The southern line of fortifications listed in 2 Chr 11 passes between Ziph and Adoraim. This line (which, as I have already indicated above, does not suit any Iron II reality) fits the southern fringe of the Hasmonean state after the takeover of Idumea by John Hyrcanus (Josephus, *A.J.* 13.257–258). Indeed, none of the major sites located south of this line—Eshtemoh, Juttah, Jattir, and Maon—are mentioned in texts describing the Hasmonean period.

4.3. The North

The Hasmonean period provides an answer to why the area north of Jerusalem is not mentioned in the 2 Chr 11 list. At the end of the Hasmonean revolt, the Seleucid general Bacchides fortified a group of sites around the core area of Judea. Of the eight sites mentioned (1 Macc 9:50–52, excluding the Akra in Jerusalem), six are located to the north of Jerusalem: Jericho, Bethel, Beth-horon, Emmaus, Gazara (= Gezer),[51] and Pharathon.[52] These fortifications were most likely taken over by the Hasmoneans in the

---

48. Alt, "Judas Gaue unter Josia"; Na'aman, "Kingdom of Judah."

49. Beth-zur had been fortified by Judas Maccabeus (1 Macc 4:61), held by Lysias (1 Macc 6:7), fortified by Bacchides (1 Macc 9:52), besieged by Simeon (1 Macc 11:65), and fortified by him (1 Macc 14:33).

50. Sellers et al., *1957 Excavation at Beth-Zur*, 8–17.

51. Contra Moshe Fischer, Israel Roll, and Oren Tal, "Persian and Hellenistic Remains at Tel Yaoz," *TA* 35 (2008): 123–63.

52. Probably in the area of Wadi Fara—Michael Avi-Yonah, *The Holy Land from the Persian to the Arab Conquests (536 B.C. to A.D. 640): A Historical Geography* (Grand Rapids: Baker, 1977), 53–54.

days of Jonathan. Although with the annexation of the three toparchies in his days the border of the Hasmonean state shifted somewhat to the north, the only effective way to protect the northern approach to Jerusalem was in Bacchides' line of fortifications, which blocked the roads from the west (Gazara, Emmaus, and Beth-horon), north (Bethel), and east (Jericho and possibly Pharathon). The Bacchides fortresses could have been incorporated into the Hasmonean system and this may have been the reason for the lack of a northern line in the 2 Chr 11 list.

## 4.4. Relationship to Other Postexilic Literary Works

In regard of the textual evidence, two points are noteworthy:
1. Most of the sites listed in 2 Chr 11:5–12 (except for Adoraim, Soco, and Gath), are mentioned in the books of Ezra and Nehemiah and in other places in Chronicles;
2. Seven or eight of the sites appear in sources describing the Hasmonean era (table 6.1).

Table 6.1. The sites listed in 2 Chr 11:5–12, reference to them in other textual sources, and bibliography for their Hellenistic remains

| Site and ref. to Hellenistic occupation | In sources describing the Hasmonean era | In Ezra and Nehemiah lists; in the genealogies in Chronicles |
|---|---|---|
| Bethlehem[53] | — | + |
| Etam[54] | Copper Scroll V, 1–9; Josephus, A.J. 8.186? | + |
| Tekoa[55] | 1 Macc 9:33 [Tephon]? 50; Josephus, A.J. 13.15 | + |
| Beth-zur[56] | See, e.g., n. 49 in this chapter | + |

---

53. Avi Ofer, *The Highland of Judah during the Biblical Period* [Hebrew] (PhD thesis, Tel Aviv University, 1993), IIA:13.

54. Moshe Kochavi, "The Land of Judah" [Hebrew], in *Judaea, Samaria and the Golan, Archaeological Survey 1967–1968*, ed. Moshe Kochavi (Jerusalem: Carta, 1972), 42; Ofer, *Highland of Judah*, IIA:13.

55. Ofer, *Highland of Judah*, IIA:28.

56. Israel Finkelstein, "Archaeology of the List of Returnees in the Books of Ezra and Nehemiah," *PEQ* 140 (2008): 7–16.

| Site and ref. to Hellenistic occupation | In sources describing the Hasmonean era | In Ezra and Nehemiah lists; in the genealogies in Chronicles |
|---|---|---|
| Soco[57] | — | + |
| Adullam[58] | 2 Macc 12:38 | + |
| Gath[59] | — | ? (depending on identification) |
| Mareshah[60] | See text of article | + |
| Ziph[61] | — But note Aristobulias nearby[62] | + |
| Adoraim[63] | See text of article | — |
| Lachish[64] | — | + |
| Azekah[65] | — | + |
| Zorah[66] | — | + |
| Aijalon[67] | — | + |
| Hebron[68] | 1 Macc 5:65; Josephus, *A.J.* 12.353 | + |

57. In sherds' box stored in the Israel Antiquities Authority. I am grateful to Yehuda Dagan for showing me the material from Khirbet ʿAbbad (Soco) and Khirbet esh-Sheikh Madkur (Adullam).
58. Possibly a single sherd in box in the storehouses of Israel Antiquities Authority.
59. Magen Broshi, "Judeideh, Tell," *NEAEHL* 3 (1993): 837–38.
60. Kloner, *Maresha Excavations*, 9–30.
61. Kochavi, "Land of Judah," 68; Ofer, *Highland of Judah*, IIA:44.
62. Avi-Yonah, *Holy Land*, 74.
63. Kochavi, "Land of Judah," 62–63.
64. Ussishkin, "Synopsis," 95–97.
65. Yehuda Dagan, "Tel Azekah: A New Look at the Site and Its 'Judean' Fortress," in *The Fire Signals of Lachish: Studies in the Archaeology and History of Israel in the Late Bronze Age, Iron Age and Persian Period in Honor of David Ussishkin*, ed. Israel Finkelstein and Nadav Naʾaman (Winona Lake, IN: Eisenbrauns, 2009), 71–86.
66. Raveh, Bunimovitz, and Lederman personal communication. I am grateful to Rami Raveh, Shlomo Bunimovitz and Zvi Lederman for sharing this information with me.
67. Ram Gophna and Yosef Porat, "The Land of Ephraim and Manasseh" [Hebrew], in Kochavi, *Judaea, Samaria and the Golan*, 236.
68. Avi Ofer, "Hebron," *NEAEHL* 2 (1993), 609; Ofer, *Highland of Judah*, IIA:30;

## 4.5. Hellenistic Fortifications in the Excavated Sites

All sites mentioned in the list were inhabited in the Hellenistic period (table 6.1). The five that have been excavated (assuming that Gath is identified with Tell Judeideh)[69] yielded interesting results for the Hellenistic period.

*Beth-zur* was not fortified in the Iron II.[70] Reich's suggestion,[71] that Citadel II dates to the Persian period, cannot be accepted in view of the meager Persian-period finds at the site.[72] A large fortress with several construction phases and an outer fortification dates to the Hellenistic period, including Hasmonean times.[73] Attempts to assign the different phases to Hasmonean figures are unconvincing.

*Gath*: An impressive fortification system with towers and gates was uncovered at Tell Judeideh.[74] It was probably built in the Hellenistic period.[75] The layout of a solid wall and internal buttresses resemble that of the Hasmonean wall in Jerusalem.[76] A fortified tower was built in the center of the mound in the Hellenistic (possibly late Hellenistic) period.[77]

---

Emanuel Eisenberg and Alla Nagorski, "Tel Hevron (er-Rumeidi)," *Hadashot Arkheologiot/ESI* 114 (2002): 91–92; no data under modern city.

69. Tell Rumeideh, the site of Bronze and Iron Age Hebron was also excavated, but the main Hellenistic settlement was probably located in the valley, under the modern town.

70. Sellers et al., *1957 Excavation at Beth-Zur*, 8; Robert W. Funk, "Beth-Zur," *NEAEHL* 1 (1993): 261.

71. Ronny Reich, "The Beth-Zur Citadel II—A Persian Residency?," *TA* 19 (1992): 113–23.

72. Israel Finkelstein, "Jerusalem in the Persian (and Early Hellenistic) Periods and the Wall of Nehemiah," *JSOT* 32 (2008): 501–20. Charles E. Carter, *The Emergence of Yehud in the Persian Period: A Social and Demographic Study*, JSOTSup 294 (Sheffield: Sheffield Academic Press, 1999), 154–57.

73. Sellers et al., *1957 Excavation at Beth-Zur*, 17; Oren Tal, *The Archaeology of Hellenistic Palestine: Between Tradition and Renewal* [Hebrew] (Jerusalem: Bialik Institute, 2006), 150–52.

74. Frederick J. Bliss and Stewart R. A. Macalister, *Excavations in Palestine during the Years 1898-1900* (London: Palestine Exploration Fund, 1902), 45–47.

75. Bliss and Macalister, *Excavations in Palestine*, 50; Shimon Gibson, "The Tell ej-Judeideh (Tel Goded) Excavations: A Re-appraisal Based on Archival Records in the Palestine Exploration Funds," *TA* 21 (1994): 213; 230–31. Tell Judeideh was inhabited in the Iron II, but it did not yield evidence for a fortification system dating to this period.

76. Gibson, "Tell ej-Judeideh," 213.

77. Gibson, "Tell ej-Judeideh," 231. Only a few Hellenistic finds were retrieved at

*Mareshah*[78] had reached its peak prosperity in the third and second centuries BCE, when it was the most important town in Idumea;[79] it was probably destroyed in the late second century BCE. The stamped Greek amphorae found at the site date to the third and second centuries BCE. Of the sixty-one coins found in the excavations of Bliss and Macalister in 1900, twenty-five belonged to John Hyrcanus I. Only a few finds can be safely dated to the first century BCE. Recent excavations in the northwest tower indicate that the massive Hellenistic fortifications of the upper town display two stages. The first dates to the early Hellenistic period, while the second has been dated by Kloner[80] to the first half of the second century, and by Tal[81] to the time of the Hasmoneans. The large number of John Hyrcanus I coins may support the latter assumption. Kloner[82] suggested that a Hasmonean garrison was established at Mareshah. He dated the destruction of the town to 112/111 BCE (the later days of John Hyrcanus), while Tal dated it to 40 BCE.[83]

*Lachish* was fortified during the Iron II (Levels IV–II). Level I revealed three phases that cover the Persian and Hellenistic periods. Its main elements are the Residency, the Solar Shrine, and a city wall. Ussishkin[84] argued that they had been built together in the second phase, still within the Persian period, and continued in use until the second century BCE. Fantalkin and Tal[85] proposed that the Solar Shrine was built in the Hellenistic period, when the Residency had already been abandoned. A large number of Ptolemaic and Seleucid coins, but only one Hasmonean coin (of Alexander Jannaeus), have been found at Lachish.[86] It is difficult, then,

---

Tell es-Safi (Gath of the Philistines, the other contender for the location of Gath of the list), pointing to a meager settlement (Aren Maeir, personal communication).

78. Kloner, *Maresha Excavations*, 5–16.
79. On its history, see Kloner, *Maresha Excavations*, 5–7.
80. Kloner, *Maresha Excavations*, 13.
81. Tal, *Archaeology of Hellenistic Palestine*, 28.
82. Kloner, *Maresha Excavations*, 5.
83. Tal, *Archaeology of Hellenistic Palestine*, 28.
84. Ussishkin, "Synopsis," 95–97.
85. Alexander Fantalkin and Oren Tal, "The Persian and Hellenistic Pottery of Level I," in *The Renewed Archaeological Excavations at Lachish (1973–1994)*, by David Ussishkin, MSIA 22 (Tel Aviv: Institute of Archaeology, 2004), 2174–94.
86. Olga Tufnell, *Lachish III: The Iron Age*, The Wellcome Archaeological Research Expedition to the Near East Publications 1 (London: Oxford University Press, 1953), 412–13.

to accurately date the construction of the city wall of Level I (late Persian or Hellenistic), but it seems to have served until sometime in the second century BCE.

*Azekah*: A massive rectangular fortress with six towers was uncovered in the highest sector of the site.[87] The excavators identified two stages of construction, which they dated to the days of Rehoboam and the Hellenistic period respectively.[88] Dagan[89] has now convincingly shown that the fortress should be attributed to the Hellenistic period.

To sum up this section, all five sites mentioned in the list of Rehoboam fortresses that have been excavated were fortified in the Hellenistic period. Though the exact date of construction of some of these fortifications is difficult to establish, at all five sites the fortification seems to have been in use in the second century BCE.

## 5. Discussion

As already stated, I assume that the list in 2 Chr 11:5–12 is not utopian; that is, it depicts a real historical situation. In attempting to identify a specific period in the history of the Hasmonean state that may stand behind the list, one needs to consider the following points: (1) as suggested above, the system of fortresses should probably represent a post-Bacchides reality; (2) the list includes Adoraim and Mareshah, which were conquered by John Hyrcanus I; (3) the conquests of Samaria in the later days of John Hyrcanus and the continuing expansion of the Hasmoneans in the days of Alexander Jannaeus made the lines described in the list obsolete. It is reasonable to assume therefore that the list represents the days of John Hyrcanus, after the conquest of Idumea.

An event in the early days of John Hyrcanus's reign must have demonstrated the urgent need to protect the borders of Judah and the roads leading to Jerusalem. I refer to the swift military campaign of Antiochus VII Sidetes in 134 BCE (the year John Hyrcanus came to power). With no obstacles in his path, Antiochus VII invaded Judea, effectively conquered it, laid siege to Jerusalem, and imposed a tax on the Hasmoneans. Only upon Antiochus's death in 129 BCE could the Hasmoneans break the Seleucid yoke and begin a new phase of territorial expansion. It therefore

---

87. Bliss and Macalister, *Excavations in Palestine*, 12–27, Pls. 2–3.
88. Bliss and Macalister, *Excavations in Palestine*, 23.
89. Dagan, "Tel Azekah."

makes sense that after 129 BCE the Hasmoneans were concerned with the fortification of Judea, mainly its western approaches.

Needless to say, this does not mean that all sites mentioned in 2 Chr 11:5–12 were fortified by John Hyrcanus. The need to fortify Judea—as recalled in this text—reflects the realities of his time. Some of the sites mentioned in the list could have been fortified by him, in other places the Hasmoneans could have inherited sites fortified before their rule; and at some of the sites the quick pace of expansion of the Hasmonean state could have made a fortification plan obsolete.

Elsewhere, I recently suggested identifying a Hasmonean reality behind the lists of genealogies in 1 Chr 2–9.[90] My observations—there and here—do not call for dating the entire work of the Chronicler to the late second century BCE. The genealogies could have been added to an existing work,[91] and it seems possible that 2 Chr 11:5–11 too is a later addition to the main text of Chronicles. If one removes the seven verses, the text reads fluently both thematically and structurally as follows:[92]

> 2 But the word of the LORD came to Shemaiah the man of God: 3 "Say to Rehoboam the son of Solomon king of Judah, and to all Israel in Judah and Benjamin, 4 'Thus says the LORD, You shall not go up or fight against your brethren. Return every man to his home, for this thing is from me.'" So they hearkened to the word of the LORD, and returned and did not go against Jeroboam. 13 And the priests and the Levites that were in all Israel resorted to him from all places where they lived. 14 For the Levites left their common lands and their holdings and came to Judah and Jerusalem, because Jeroboam and his sons cast them out from serving as priests of the LORD, 15 and he appointed his own priests for the high places, and for the satyrs, and for the calves which he had made. 16 And those who had set their hearts to seek the LORD God of Israel came after them from all the tribes of Israel to Jerusalem to sacrifice to the LORD, the God of their fathers.

---

90. Israel Finkelstein, "The Historical Reality behind the Genealogical Lists in 1 Chronicles," *JBL* 131 (2012): 65–83.

91. For instance, Adam C. Welch, *The Work of the Chronicler: Its Purpose and Date* (London: Milford, 1939), 81–96; Rudolph, *Chronikbücher*, viii; Noth, *Chronicler's History*, 36–42.

92. Note that 2 Chr 11:1–4 is matched by a parallel passage in 1 Kgs 12:21–24.

The question remains, why would a late second-century BCE redactor choose to affiliate a Hasmonean reality with—of all Judahite monarchs—Rehoboam? Had the redactor been looking for a foreign campaign of a northern power on Judah and its capital, with salvation but heavy taxation paid by a Jerusalem ruler (to compare to the campaign of Antiochus VII Sidetes), the most obvious choice would have been Sennacherib's campaign on Hezekiah. Was this a warning aimed at the future but based on the past, pronouncing that even a set of mighty fortresses offers no safeguard from devastation by enemy (Shishak) if the ruler does not follow in the ways of the God of Israel?

## Addendum

### Khirbet Qeiyafa

The Khirbet Qeiyafa casemate fortification (mentioned in n. 19 above) has now proven to date to the tenth century BCE,[93] most probably to the middle of that century.[94] The territorial affiliation of the site is disputed: The excavators see Khirbet Qeiyafa as belonging to Judah,[95] while others associate it with an early Iron Age territorial entity that survived in the Shephelah[96] or with an early north Israelite formation that was centered north of Jerusalem.[97] The latter assertion is based, among other considerations, on the fact that so far fortifications of this early date in the Iron Age are known only in the Gibeon plateau and southern Transjordan.

---

93. Yosef Garfinkel et al., "King David's City at Khirbet Qeiyafa: Results of the Second Radiocarbon Dating Project," *Radiocarbon* 57 (2015): 881–90.

94. Israel Finkelstein and Eli Piasetzky, "Radiocarbon Dating Khirbet Qeiyafa and the Iron I–IIA Phases in the Shephelah: Methodological Comments and a Bayesian Model," *Radiocarbon* 57 (2015): 891–907; Alexander Fantalkin and Israel Finkelstein, "The Date of Abandonment and Territorial Affiliation of Khirbet Qeiyafa: An Update," *TA* 44 (2017): 53–60.

95. Garfinkel et al., "King David's City," with reference to previous publications.

96. Nadav Na'aman, "Khirbet Qeiyafa in Context," *UF* 42 (2010): 497–526; Na'aman, "Was Khirbet Qeiyafa a Judahite City? The Case Against It," *JHS* 17 (2017): art. 7; Ido Koch, "The Geopolitical Organization of the Judean Shephelah during the Iron Age I–IIA (1150–800 B.C.E.)" [Hebrew], *Cathedra* 143 (2012): 45–64.

97. Israel Finkelstein and Alexander Fantalkin, "Khirbet Qeiyafa: An Unsensational Archaeological and Historical Interpretation," *TA* 39 (2012): 38–63; Fantalkin and Finkelstein, "Date of Abandonment."

## The Archaeology of Sites Mentioned in the Rehoboam List

Two sites mentioned in the Rehoboam List supply fresh evidence on the Hellenistic period. At Azekah, the renewed excavations have revealed Hellenistic remains beyond the area of the fortress.[98] Excavations at Hebron (Tell er-Rumeideh) have provided evidence of late Hellenistic (Hasmonean) activity.[99] A recent survey of Khirbet ʿAbbad, the site of biblical Soco, has revealed evidence of strong activity in the Iron IIB–C, weak presence in the Persian period and a new phase of strong activity in the Hellenistic period.[100]

## Other Issues

- For note 31: Itzhak Lee now dates the list of Levitical towns to the Hellenistic period.[101]
- Uncertainties regarding the chronology of Judah in the Iron Age have diminished thanks to a growing number of radiocarbon results from sites in the Shephelah.[102]
- In view of my study of the book of Chronicles (ch. 8), carried out a few years after the article on the Rehoboam forts was published, it is not mandatory to date the list of fortifications separately, later than the rest of the Rehoboam account in 2 Chronicles.

---

98. Oded Lipschits, Yuval Gadot and Manfred Oeming, "Tel Azekah 113 Years After: Preliminary Evaluation of the Renewed Excavations at the Site," *NEA* 75 (2012): 196–206.

99. Emanuel Eisenberg and David Ben-Shlomo, *The Tel Hevron 2014 Excavations: Final Report* (Ariel University Institute of Archaeology Monograph Series Number 1; Ariel: Ariel University, 2017), 13–14, 441–42.

100. Yoav Tzur, *The History of the Settlement at Tel Socho in Light of Archaeological Survey* [Hebrew] (MA thesis, Tel Aviv: Tel Aviv University).

101. Itzhak Lee-Sak, "The Lists of Levitical Cities (Joshua 21, 1 Chronicles 6) and the Propagandistic Map for the Hasmonean Territorial Expansion," *JBL* 136 (2017): 783–800.

102. Finkelstein and Piasetzky, "Radiocarbon Dating Khirbet Qeiyafa."

# 7
# The Expansion of Judah in 2 Chronicles

## 1. Introduction

The land of Israel and territorial gains and losses are major themes in Chronicles. The period of David and Solomon is conceived as the ideal rule of Jerusalem over the entire area inhabited by the Hebrews. After the "division" of the monarchy, 2 Chronicles pays much attention to the gradual territorial growth of Judah, aimed at restoring Jerusalem's rule over the entire land of Israel.[1] This expansion—undertaken during the reign of a few monarchs—is described in several sections that do not appear in the books of Kings.

Scholars have been divided on the historical reliability of these "unparallel" texts. Some have argued that the author had access to old sources which had not been available to the Deuteronomistic Historian/s or were omitted by him/them,[2] while others have dismissed the historical validity of the unparallel descriptions.[3] Three factors seem to support the view that the unparallel accounts were indeed written with no access to old materials.

---

1. E.g., Hugh G. M. Williamson, *Israel in the Books of Chronicles* (Cambridge: Cambridge University, 1977), 100; Sara Japhet, *The Ideology of the Book of Chronicles and Its Place in Biblical Thought*, BEATAJ 9 (Frankfurt: Lang, 1997), 298–99, 355–56.

2. E.g., Baruch Halpern, "Sacred History and Ideology: Chronicles' Thematic Structure—Identification of an Earlier Source," in *The Creation of Sacred Literature: Composition and Redaction of the Biblical Text*, ed. Richard E. Friedman, Near Eastern Studies 22 (Berkeley: University of California, 1981), 35–54; Hugh G. M. Williamson, *1 and 2 Chronicles* (Grand Rapids: Eerdmans, 1982), 20, 250–54; Sara Japhet, "The Historical Reliability of Chronicles: The History of the Problem and Its Place in Biblical Research," *JSOT* 33 (1985), 83–107; Japhet, *I and II Chronicles: A Commentary* (London: SCM, 1993), 18, 666, 688; Robb A. Young, *Hezekiah in History and Tradition*, VTSup 155 (Leiden: Brill, 2012), 231–33, 254–55.

3. For instance, Charles C. Torrey, "The Chronicler as Editor and as Independent

(1) Both the gradual expansion of the borders of Judah during its early days and the full territorial extension in the days of Hezekiah, after the collapse of the Northern Kingdom, do not fit the territory described in Kings and the reality that emerges from extrabiblical tests and archaeological research.

(2) There is no evidence for scribal activity in Israel and Judah before the late ninth century and no indication for complex texts before the early eighth century (and at that time mainly in Israel[4]); hence contra to, for example, Williamson[5] and Japhet[6] there were probably no original accounts from the days of the early kings of Judah.

(3) Today's tendency to date Chronicles in the late Persian or early Hellenistic periods (below) casts doubt on the probability of access to centuries-old materials which do not appear in Kings.

Evidently, if these accounts were written with no access to genuine early materials, the author must have done so in order to advance his own territorial ideology. There are two possibilities: either his descriptions are utopic,[7] or he wrote against the background of realities of his own time. I would side with the latter view, which was phrased long ago by Robert H. Kennett: "it is most important that we should ask the question whether the Chronicler's account of a particular event was sheer imagination or was based upon something which he himself had seen or had heard

---

Narrator," *AJSL* 25 (1908), 157–73; Peter Welten, *Geschichte und Geschichtsdarstellung in den Chronikbüchern*, WMANT 42 (Neukirchen-Vluyn: Neukirchener Verlag, 1973), 195–96; Ehud Ben Zvi, "The Chronicler as a Historian: Building Texts," in *The Chronicler as Historian*, ed. M. Patrick Graham, Kenneth G. Hoglund, and Steven L. McKenzie, JSNTSup 238 (Sheffield: Sheffield Academic Press, 1997), 132–49; Steven L. McKenzie, *1–2 Chronicles* (Nashville: Abingdon, 2004), 42–43; on the material omitted and added, see Steven L. McKenzie, *The Chronicler's Use of the Deuteronomistic History*, HSM 33 (Atlanta: Scholars Press, 1984).

4. Israel Finkelstein and Benjamin Sass, "The West Semitic Alphabetic Inscriptions, Late Bronze II to Iron IIA: Archeological Context, Distribution and Chronology," *HeBAI* 2 (2013): 149–220.

5. Williamson, *1 and 2 Chronicles*, 20.

6. Japhet, *I and II Chronicles*, 18–19.

7. Steven J. Schweitzer, *Reading Utopia in Chronicles*, LHBOTS 442 (New York: T&T Clark, 2007); Mark J. Boda, "Gazing through the Cloud of Incense: Davidic Dynasty and Temple Community in the Chronicler's Perspective," in *Chronicling the Chronicler: The Book of Chronicles and Early Second Temple Historiography*, ed. Paul S. Evans and Tyler F. Williams (Winona Lake, IN: Eisenbrauns, 2013), 242.

described by eye-witnesses."[8] Indeed, the unparallel accounts give geographical details which include toponyms that do not play an important role in earlier biblical records but are significant in Hellenistic texts. In these accounts—especially in the evaluation of the religious behavior of the given monarchs (a theme connected to territorial gains and losses)— the author challenges the authority of Kings; one should assume that only severe geopolitical, religious, and cultural conditions, such as the pressure of Hellenism on Jewish life, would allow such a move.

If this is so, the possibilities for the historical background of the author's approach to the expansion of Judah are limited. The geographical extent of the conquests of Judah as described in the unparallel accounts does not fit the Persian or early Hellenistic periods. In those days Yehud/ Judea was limited to the core area of Jerusalem and the highlands around it; had an insignificant population; and had no practical concerns for the coastal plain, Samaria, Idumea, and Transjordan.[9] Yehud and early Judea had no power to carry out military campaigns and as far as we know there was no threat to their inhabitants from their neighbors.[10]

This is the reason why, when discussing the date of Chronicles, several scholars focused on the Hasmonean period.[11] Most of these researchers pointed to the early days of the Maccabees. But once the spotlight is placed on the second century BCE, its second half, and especially the days of John Hyrcanus, including points of resemblance between Chronicles and

---

8. Robert H. Kennett, *Old Testament Essays* (Cambridge: Cambridge University Press, 1928), 129.

9. For the demography and expansion of Yehud/Judea, see Israel Finkelstein, "The Territorial Extent and Demography of Yehud/Judea in the Persian and Early Hellenistic Periods," *RB* 117 (2010): 39–54 (ch. 3 in this book).

10. The specific list of adversaries of Yehud in the book of Nehemiah should be read against a Hellenistic background —Israel Finkelstein, "Nehemiah's Adversaries: A Hasmonaean Reality?," *Transeu* 47 (2015): 47–55 (ch. 4 in this book).

11. Kennett, *Old Testament Essays*, 130–31; Adolphe Lods, *Israel: From Its Beginning to the Middle of the Eight Century* (New York: Knopf, 1932), 14; Peter R. Ackroyd, "Criteria for the Maccabean Dating of Old Testament Literature," *VT* 3 (1953): 113–32; Kurt Galling, *Die Bücher der Chronik, Esra, Nehemia*, ATD 12 (Göttingen: Vandenhoeck & Ruprecht, 1954); Martin Noth, *The Chronicler's History*, JSOTSup 50 (Sheffield: Sheffield Academic Press, 1987), 73; Georg Steins, *Die Chronik als kanonisches Abschlussphänomen: Studien zur Entstehung und Theologie von 1/2 Chronik*, BBB 93 (Weinheim: Beltz Athenaum, 1995), 491–99; Steins, "Zur Datierung der Chronik: Ein neuer methodischer Ansatz," *ZAW* 109 (1997): 84–92; Reinhard G. Kratz, *The Composition of the Narrative Books of the Old Testament* (London: T&T Clark, 2005), 44, 91.

1 Maccabees (written in the days of Hyrcanus[12] or slightly later[13]), come to mind. The crucial question is whether the material from the second century should be considered as additions or late redactions[14] or if the book was written in Hasmonean times.

In what follows, I wish to suggest that the descriptions in 2 Chronicles of the gradual growth of Judah from the days of Rehoboam to the reign of Hezekiah were written against the background of the expansion of the Hasmoneans, with the actual compilation in the days of John Hyrcanus.[15] I will try to show how each of the conquests achieved by Judah finds expression in the history of the Hasmoneans as described in 1 Maccabees and in Josephus's *Antiquities*.

But first, I need to ask: is a date as late as the second half of the second century BCE for texts in Chronicles possible?

Excursus 1: The Lowest Possible Date for Chronicles

The date of Chronicles is disputed, with a range of theories that extends from the sixth to the second centuries BCE.[16] Most scholars today advocate a date in the fourth or third century BCE.[17] At the same time, several

---

12. Uriel Rappaport, *The First Book of Maccabees: Introduction, Hebrew Translation, and Commentary* [Hebrew] (Jerusalem: Yad Ben Zvi, 2004), 60–61 and bibliography. Note that similarities between Chronicles and 1 Maccabees are significant from the perspective of ideology regardless of the question of historicity of the accounts in the latter.

13. E.g., Jonathan A. Goldstein, *1 Maccabees: A New Translation with Introduction and Commentary* (Garden City: Doubleday, 1976), 63–64.

14. E.g., Wilhelm Boussett, *Die Religion des Judentums im späthellenistischen Zeitalter*, HNT 21 (Tübingen: Mohr, 1926), 10; Lods, *Israel*, 14; Noth, *Chronicler's History*, 73; Kratz, *Composition of the Narrative Books*, 91–92.

15. As far as I can judge the only modern scholar who opted (in passing) for this late date is Kennett, *Old Testament Essays*, 130–31; and see Spinoza, who asserted that the books of Chronicles were composed "long after Ezra, perhaps even after Judas Maccabeus had restored the Temple" (Baruch Spinoza, *Theological-Political Treaties* [Cambridge: Cambridge University], 144).

16. Recent summaries in Gary N. Knoppers, *I Chronicles 1–9: A New Translation with Introduction and Commentary* (New York: Doubleday, 2003), 101–17; McKenzie, *1–2 Chronicles*, 29–33; Isaac Kalimi, *An Ancient Israelite Historian: Studies in the Chronicler, His Time, Place and Writing*, SSN 46 (Assen: Royal Van Gorcum, 2005).

17. E.g., Thomas Willi, *Chronik* (Göttingen: Vandenhoeck & Ruprecht, 1972), 190; Welten, *Geschichte*; Peter R. Ackroyd, *I and II Chronicles, Ezra, Nehemiah* (London: SCM, 1973), 25–27; Williamson, *1 and 2 Chronicles*, 16; Noth, *Chronicler's History*,

## 7. The Expansion of Judah in 2 Chronicles

scholars (from Spinoza to Noth and Kratz) have pointed to the closeness between the ideology and needs of Chronicles and the Hasmonean period. These two directions have created a "tension" regarding the understanding of Chronicles and brought about constrained "solutions," for example, Kellermann,[18] who noticed Hasmonean ideology in Chronicles but continued to support an earlier date, arguing that the author anticipated events to come.

So how low can one go? The essential arguments for the *latest* possible dating of Chronicles[19] are as follows.

(1) The historian Eupolemus, who ostensibly lived in the mid-second century, composed a book that was probably titled *On the Kings of Judea*. He relied on nonparallel material in Chronicles; moreover, there are cases in which Eupolemus seems to prefer 2 Chronicles over 1 Kings.[20] Note, for instance, that: Eupolemus views the reason for David not constructing the temple in the same way as 1 Chr 22:8; similar to Chronicles, he omits the revolt of Adonijah; and like Chronicles, he says that the builders of the temple were *gerim*. On the broader scope, there are the questions of the date of translation of Chronicles to Greek[21] and whether a text of Chronicles was found in Qumran.

(2) For his description of King David, Ben Sira 47:8–10, who worked in the early second century BCE, depended on 1 Chr 15:16–21, 16:4–42, and 25:1–31.

(3) Dan 1:2, regarding the exile of Jehoiakim to Babylon, is a citation of 2 Chr 36:7 (not mentioned in Kings). Daniel was composed no later than the 160s BCE.

(4) Chronicles does not express Hellenistic influence.

---

73; Manfred Oeming, *Das wahre Israel: Die "genealogische Vorhalle" 1 Chronik 1–9*, BWANT 8 (Stuttgart: Kohlhammer, 1990), 44–45; Japhet, *I and II Chronicles*, 27–28; Kratz, *Composition of the Narrative Books*, 91.

18. Ulrich Kellermann, "Anmerkungen zum Verständnis der Tora in den chronistischen Schriften," *BN* 42 (1988): 49–92.

19. E.g., Williamson, *1 and 2 Chronicles*, 15; Knoppers, *I Chronicles*, 105–11; Kalimi, *Ancient Israelite Historian*, 49–51; Ralph W. Klein, *1 Chronicles: A Commentary* (Minneapolis: Fortress, 2006), 13.

20. Isaac Kalimi, "History of Interpretation the Book of Chronicles in Jewish Tradition from Daniel to Spinoza," *RB* 105 (1998): 15–17; Ehud Ben Zvi, *History, Literature and Theology in the Book of Chronicles* (London: Equinox, 2006), 255.

21. Summary in Japhet, *I and II Chronicles*, 30; Knoppers, *I Chronicles*, 55–65.

These observations seem to mean that Chronicles must have already existed in the early second century or circa 200 BCE.

Zooming-in on these ostensible clues, one discovers that not one of them is compelling.

1. A series of problems haunts the Eupolemus case.[22]
1.1. The argument depends on identifying Eupolemus the author with Eupolemus, son of John, son of Accos, who was sent by Judas Maccabeus as an emissary to Rome in 161–160 BCE (1 Macc 8:17; 2 Macc 4:11; Josephus, *A.J.* 12.415);[23] but this is far from having been proven.
1.2. In the writings of Eupolemus one may identify two authors: Eupolemus and Pseudo-Eupolemus; the references which are found in writings of Eusebius and Clement of Alexandria may be assigned to the latter. Disassociating Eupolemus from the Eupolemus of Judas Maccabeus leaves no reason to date the latter earlier than circa 100 BCE.
1.3. We have no idea of the original content of Eupolemus and the way his work had been transmitted; six passages from his writings survived in the works of Eusebius and Clement of Alexandria, who ostensibly found them in the writings of Alexander Polyhistor (85–35 BCE). In other words, had the two individuals called Eupolemus been the same person and had there been a dependency of Eupolemus on Chronicles, it could have been inserted many years after his time.
1.4. There is no clear-cut connection between Eupelomus and Chronicles, and it is not easy to decide what text served as his model[24] and who depends on what. The theme of the Kings of Judah and the method of rewriting the past in the light of contemporary realities were popular in second century Jewish texts;[25] for

---

22. Frank Clancy, "Eupolemus the Chronographer and 141 B.C.E.," *SJOT* 23 (2009): 274–81.

23. Ben Zion Wacholder, *Eupolemus: A Study of Judaeo-Greek Literature*, Monographs of the Hebrew Union College 3 (Cincinnati: Hebrew Union College, 1974), 4.

24. Steins, *Chronik*, 491–92.

25. Doron Mendels, *The Land of Israel as a Political Concept in Hasmonean Literature: Recourse to History in Second Century B.C. Claims to the Holy Land*, TSAJ 15 (Tübingen: Mohr, 1987).

instance, Eupolemus describes David's conquests with a notion of the adversaries of Judea in his own days;[26] that is, both address their own needs according to the great kingdom of the past.

2. Ben Sira's ideas in 47:8–10 could have been taken from Ezra (3:10) and Nehemiah (12:24) rather than from Chronicles. Or, the appearance of the same theme may show that it was popular in Second Temple literature, which is especially true for King David. Both Ben Sira and Chronicles could have been based on a widespread tradition concerning the role of David in the organization of the temple cult.[27] Hence there is no unequivocal relationship between Ben Sira and Chronicles, nor is there indication that Ben Sira knew Chronicles.[28] Also, Ben Sira was probably composed in several stages, and the work which we possess is not the original; rather it has additions dated to the first century BCE;[29] moreover, Corley[30] sees the Praise of the Ancestors, which includes 47:8–10, as "the last supplement for the book's final edition."[31]

3. The relationship between Dan 1:2 and 2 Chr 36:7 is far from clear and both could have been taken from the same second century BCE tradition.

4. The lack of Hellenistic influence is no argument. The ideology of the author/s of Chronicles could have led him/them to intention-

---

26. Mendels, *Land of Israel*, 35–36.
27. Steins, *Chronik*, 492–93.
28. Noth, *Chronicler's History*, 166; Ben Zvi, *History, Literature and Theology*, 253.
29. Giuseppe Bellia, "An Historico-Anthropological Reading of the Work of Ben Sira," in *The Wisdom of Ben Sira: Studies on Tradition, Redaction, and Theology*, ed. Angelo Passaro and Giuseppe Bellia, DCLS 1 (Berlin: de Gruyter, 2008), 52.
30. Jeremy Corley, "Searching for Structure and Redaction in Ben Sira: An Investigation of Beginnings and Endings," in Passaro and Bellia, *Wisdom of Ben Sira*, 45.
31. For absolute dates, see Angelo Passaro and Giuseppe Bellia, "Sirach, or Metamorphosis of the Sage," in Passaro and Bellia, *Wisdom of Ben Sira*, 356; for a summary of structure and redactions in Ben Sira, see Johannes Marböck, "Structure and Redaction History in the Book of Ben Sira Review and Proposals," in *The Book of Ben Sira in Modern Research*, ed. Pancratius Cornelis Beentjes, BZAW 255 (Berlin: de Gruyter, 1997), 61–79.

ally erase every such trace.[32] After all, the Hasmoneans were great promoters of Hebrew.[33]

Now, apart from territorial ideology, and similarities to 1 Maccabees (below), other considerations seem to point to the late date of Chronicles (or large parts of it).

1. Chronicles belongs to the genre of "Rewritten (or Reworked) Bible," which was popular in the second century BCE (for instance Jubilees, Qumran Reworked Pentateuch).[34]
2. The concept of David and Solomon representing the ideal unity of all Israel which does not exist in the "present" and needs to be fulfilled in the future (see below) is typical of early second century Jewish literature.[35]

---

32. Kay Peltonen, "A Jigsaw Without a Model? The Date of Chronicles," in *Did Moses Speak Attic? Jewish Historiography and Scripture in the Hellenistic Period*, ed. Lester L. Grabbe, JSOTSup 317 (Sheffield: Sheffield Academic Press, 2001), 238; note Rainer Albertz, *A History of Israelite Religion in the Old Testament* (Louisville: Westminster, 1994), 555 and Steins, *Chronik*, 498, who describe Chronicles as "deliberately a-Hellenistic." Doron Mendels called my attention to the fact that other Jewish works of the time, such as Jubilees and even 1 Maccabees, do not depict an explicit Hellenistic background.

33. For other arguments, see Knoppers, *I Chronicles*, 102–3.

34. E.g., George J. Brooke, "The Books of Chronicles and the Scrolls from Qumran," in *Reflection and Refraction: Studies in Biblical Historiography in Honour of A. Graeme Auld*, ed. Robert Rezetko, Timothy H. Lim, and W. Brian Aucker, VTSup 113 (Leiden: Brill, 2007), 35–48; for this genre, see also, e.g., Michael Segal, *The Book of Jubilees: Rewritten Bible, Redaction, Ideology and Theology* (JSJSup 117; Leiden: Brill, 2007); Sidnie W. Crawford, *Rewriting Scripture in Second Temple Times* (Grand Rapids: Eerdmans, 2008); Reinhard G. Kratz, "Rewriting Torah in the Hebrew Bible and the Dead Sea Scrolls," in *Wisdom and Torah: The Reception of "Torah" in the Wisdom Literature of the Second Temple Period*, ed. Bernd U. Schipper and D. Andrew Teeter, JSJSup 163 (Leiden: Brill, 2013), 273–92; various articles in József Zsengellér, ed., *Rewritten Bible after Fifty Years: Texts, Terms, or Techniques? A Last Dialogue with Geza Vermes*, JSJSup 166 (Leiden: Brill, 2014); for Chronicles as a Rewritten Bible, see Ralph W. Klein, *2 Chronicles: A Commentary* (Minneapolis: Fortress, 2012), 4–5. I am grateful to Konrad Schmid, who drew my attention to this idea.

35. I am grateful to Doron Mendels, who mentioned this to me.

3. Scholars asserted that the book of Chronicles includes a polemic against the Samaritans,[36] while others rejected this notion.[37] Suffice it to say that the ideology behind Abijah's speech (2 Chr 13), which leaves the door open for the people of Samaria to rejoin the nation—and the ensuing defeat of the north—should be read against the background of the relationship with the Samaritans. The same is true for Hezekiah's call to the people of Ephraim and Manasseh to join the celebration of Passover in Jerusalem (2 Chr 30), and their derision of his emissaries (v. 10). This fits the situation in the second century BCE, the time of the break between Judaism and the Samaritans,[38] when the Mount Gerizim temple threatened to overshadow Jerusalem,[39] and the following clash with the Hasmoneans. Propaganda against the Samaritans can be found in other second century literary works.[40] Still, with the conquest of the area of Shechem and Samaria the Hasmoneans needed to find a way to incorporate the Samaritans into their expanding state.

4. The meticulous organization of the priests and other groups in Chronicles[41] fits a well-organized cult system and a significant population. If not utopic, this best fits the Hasmonean state. The population of Persian-period Yehud was limited (circa 12,000 souls), while after the territorial expansion of the Hasmoneans

---

36. E.g., Charles C. Torrey, *Ezra Studies* (Chicago: University of Chicago Press, 1910), 154–55; Galling, *Bücher der Chronik*, 14–15; Wilhelm Rudolph, *Chronikbücher*, HAT 1 (Tübingen: Mohr, 1955), viii–ix; recently Albertz, *History of Israelite Religion*, 554.

37. Willi, *Chronik*, 190–93; Roddy L. Braun, "A Reconsideration of the Chronicler's Attitude toward the North," *JBL* 96 (1977): 59–62; Williamson, *Israel in the Books of Chronicles*, 84; Japhet, *Ideology of the Book of Chronicles*, 325–34; on the Samaritan issue, see summary in Peltonen, "Jigsaw without a Model."

38. Stefan Schorch, "The Construction of Samaritan Identity from the Inside and from the Outside," in *Between Cooperation and Hostility: Multiple Identities in Ancient Judaism and the Interaction with Foreign Powers*, ed. Rainer Albertz and Jakob Wöhrle, JAJSup 11 (Göttingen: Vandenhoeck & Ruprecht, 2013), 136–38.

39. On the excavations and comparison between the temples, see Yitzhak Magen, Haggai Misgav, and Levana Tsfania, *The Aramaic, Hebrew and Samaritan Inscriptions*, vol. 1 of *Mount Gerizim Excavations* (Jerusalem: Israel Antiquities Authority, 2004), 1–13; Yitzhak Magen, *A Temple City*, vol. 2 of *Mount Gerizim Excavations* (Jerusalem: Israel Antiquities Authority, 2008), 141–64.

40. Mendels, *Land of Israel*, 110.

41. Sara Japhet, "The Supposed Common Authorship of Chronicles and Ezra-Nehemiah Investigated Anew," *VT* 18 (1968): 332–72; Japhet, *I and II Chronicles*, 26.

the inhabitants of Judea can be estimated at up to 100,000 individuals.[42] The depleted population of Jerusalem in the Persian and Ptolemaic periods and the dramatic growth of the city in the late Hellenistic period should also be taken into consideration.[43]

5. Mattathias the Hasmonean was a priest of the Joarib (Jehoiarib) family that is placed in the opening of the list of priestly families in 1 Chr 24:7; in other biblical references this family is listed second or lower.[44]

6. It is possible that Chronicles is not represented in Qumran. According to some scholars,[45] there is one fragment there, a few words long, that if restored correctly can be identified with 2 Chr 29:1–3. Others doubt this identification.[46]

To summarize the dating issue, it seems to me that there is no decisive argument that would prevent dating at least parts of Chronicles in the late second century BCE. I would therefore side with Japhet, that the "date and provenance of Chronicles must thus be determined mostly on the basis of

---

42. Finkelstein, "Territorial Extent and Demography of Yehud."

43. Israel Finkelstein, "Jerusalem in the Persian (and Early Hellenistic) Period and the Wall of Nehemiah," *JSOT* 32 (2008): 501–20 (ch. 1 in this book); Hillel Geva, "Jerusalem's Population in Antiquity: A Minimalist View," *TA* 41 (2014): 131–60.

44. Ackroyd, "Criteria for the Maccabean Dating," 126; Steins, *Chronik*, 498; Knoppers, *I Chronicles*, 107.

45. E.g., Kalimi, *History of Interpretation*, 19–21; Julio T. Barrera, "118.4Qchr," in *Qumran Cave 4.XI: Psalms to Chronicles*, ed. Eugene Ulrich et al., DJD 16 (Oxford: Clarendon, 2000), 295–97; Eugene Ulrich, ed., *The Biblical Qumran Scrolls: Transcriptions and Textual Variants*, VTSup 134 (Leiden: Brill, 2010), 778.

46. Jens B. Kofoed, *Text and History: Historiography and the Study of the Biblical Text* (Winona Lake, IN: Eisenbrauns, 2005), 35; Ben Zvi, *History, Literature and Theology*, 252; Brooke, "Books of Chronicles," 38–40; Hanne von Weissenberg, "'Canon' and Identity at Qumran: An Overview and Challenges for Future Research," in *Scripture in Transition: Essays on Septuagint, Hebrew Bible, and Dead Sea Scrolls in Honour of Raija Sollamo*, ed. Anssi Voitila and Jutta Jokiranta, JSJSup 126 (Leiden: Brill, 2008), 635. Welten's discussion of 2 Chr 26:15 (*Geschichte und Geschichtsdarstellung*, 111–14) is irrelevant for the question deliberated here; even if the reference is to catapults, they were known starting in the fourth century (e.g., Klein, *1 Chronicles*, 15; see detailed discussion in Francesco Bianchi and Gabriele Rossoni, "L'armée d'Ozias [2 Ch 26, 11–15] entre fiction et réalité: Une esquisse philologique et historique," *Transeu* 13 [1997]: 21–37).

general considerations."[47] Chronicles portrays several such "general considerations," among them the theocratic stance of the text, the attitude to the North, the cultic role of David and Solomon, and the territorial ideology of the author/s. The question is, which of them can help to identify the time of composition. I would opt for the latter; evidently, references to territory come with a map—real or imagined—which may be critical for disclosing the historical settings behind the author/s.

## 2. The Expansion of Judah According to Chronicles in Relation to the History of the Hasmoneans

The spotlight should focus on the account of six kings about whom 2 Chronicles adds material that does not appear in Kings. They are Rehoboam, Abijah, Asa, Jehoshaphat, Uzziah, and Hezekiah.

### 2.1. A Preliminary Note: David and Solomon

The founding figures of the dynasty, described in Samuel and Kings as ruling over a United Monarchy which covered the later territories of all Israel—all tribes and the kingdoms of Israel and Judah combined—were of the utmost importance to the author/s of Chronicles.[48] Reaching these ideal borders—from Dan to Beer-sheba—was an ultimate goal. The author makes sure to "adapt" the concept to the realities of his time: On the one hand he erases the memory of David as the ruler of only Judah at the beginning of his career.[49] On the other hand he eliminates the Samuel-Kings' detailed references to the territorial extent of the United Monarchy —the Joab census and the land of Cabul affair.

David is important as a symbol of a pious warrior and founder of the dynasty, the king who established the rule over the entire land.[50] Both

---

47. Japhet, *I and II Chronicles*, 25.
48. On the concept of "all Israel" in Chronicles, see Japhet, *Ideology of the Book of Chronicles*, 264–70, 285–90; see also Jacob L. Wright, "David, King of Judah (Not Israel)," The Bible and Interpretation, 2014, https://tinyurl.com/SBL2637a.
49. Wright, "David, King of Judah."
50. Still, at least one of David's wars is used for practical reasons: 1 Chronicles adds Madaba as the location of the war against the Ammonites and their supporters (compare 1 Chr 19:7 to 2 Sam 10); Ammon and Madaba played an important role in the expansion of the Hasmoneans (1 Macc 9:35–42; Josephus, *A.J.* 13.255 and, for Alexander Janneus, *A.J.* 13.397).

David and Solomon, the founders of the temple cult, are stripped of sins and wrong-doings. It is noteworthy that the author of Chronicles criticizes even Hezekiah, his hero (below), and Josiah, the most righteous king of Judah according to Kings; he does this possibly in order to diminish their stature somewhat in comparison to David (and Solomon) whom he adores.

## 2.2. Rehoboam

The account of Rehoboam is a twisting story—one of the more complicated in Chronicles.[51] In Kings Rehoboam is depicted negatively. Chronicles evaluates his first three years positively. In these years he ruled over Judah and Benjamin (2 Chr 11:12, 23), where he constructed fifteen fortified towns. Priests and Levites from "all Israel" left their homes and came to Judah and Jerusalem, meaning that the pious population from all Israel gathered there. But later Rehoboam "forsook the law of the Lord" (2 Chr 12:1) and was punished by the military campaign of Pharaoh Shishak. He then "humbled himself" and by doing so saved Judah from destruction (v. 12).

The fifteen towns that were fortified cover the area from Adoraim and Ziph in the south to Ayalon in the north, and from the Lachish-Azekah line in the Shephelah in the west to Tekoa in the east. I have dealt with this list elsewhere[52] and have shown that:

1. It does not fit any Iron II geographical or historical reality; especially note that the fortification project excludes both the north and south of Iron Age Judah.
2. Three sites mentioned in the list—Adoraim, Mareshah, and Beth-zur—were prominent places in the Hellenistic period.
3. The line in the south fits the southern fringe of the Hasmonean state after the takeover of Idumea by John Hyrcanus (Josephus, *A.J.* 13.257–258).
4. Seven or eight of the fifteen sites appear in sources describing the Hasmonean era.

---

51. See, e.g., Williamson, *1 and 2 Chronicles*, 238–50; Gary N. Knoppers, "Rehoboam in Chronicles: Villain or Victim?," *JBL* 109 (1990): 423–40; Japhet, *I and II Chronicles*, 682–84.

52. Israel Finkelstein, "Rehoboam's Fortresses Cities (II Chr 11, 5–12): A Hasmonean Reality?," *ZAW* 123 (2011): 92–107 (ch. 6 in this book).

5. All sites in the list were inhabited in the Hellenistic period. The five that have been excavated yielded evidence for Hellenistic period fortifications; though the exact date of construction of some of these defenses is difficult to establish, at all five sites the fortification seems to have been in use in the second century BCE.

I concluded that the text about Rehoboam's fortified cities should be understood against the background of Hasmonean times. An event in the year when John Hyrcanus came to power must have demonstrated the urgent need to protect the borders of Judea and the roads leading to Jerusalem. I refer to the swift military campaign of Antiochus VII Sidetes in 134 BCE. With no obstacles in his path, Antiochus invaded Judea, effectively conquered it, laid siege to Jerusalem and imposed a tax on the Hasmoneans (Josephus, *A.J.* 13.236–248; more below).

The description in Chronicles of the core territory of Judah (the tribal areas of Judah and Benjamin) during the reign of its first king after the secession of the North is the starting point for the gradual expansion of the kingdom, that is, for the story of how the kings of Judah tried to territorially "reconstruct" the golden age of the United Monarchy. This territory is somewhat similar to the core area of the Hasmoneans before the beginning of their territorial expansion. Yet, at that time Judea's southern border was at Beth-zur,[53] and in the west it had not yet expanded into the Shephelah, so why add the areas of Idumea and Mareshah? It seems to me that the author, who knew the geographical-history of Judah/Judea well, included them in order to avoid giving the impression that the core territory of First Temple Judah omitted the area of Hebron and the Upper Shephelah.

This core territory is where the story begins—both for Hasmonean Judea and for the author of 2 Chronicles' description of the expansion of Judah.

### 2.3. Abijah

The second king of Judah is given eight verses in 1 Kgs 15 and twenty-three in 2 Chr 13. He is described negatively in Kings, and favorably in Chronicles; Abijam of Kings is given a Yahawistic name—Abijah—in Chronicles.

---

53. Beth-zur had been fortified by Judas Maccabeus (1 Macc 4:61), held by Lysias (1 Macc 6:7), and fortified by Bacchides (1 Macc 9:52; later it was besieged by Simeon [1 Macc 11:65] and fortified again by him [1 Macc 14:7, 33]).

Why did the author turn the evaluation in Kings upside down and render Abijah good? And from where did he take the story (with very specific geographical background) about the war against the North? I suggest that the author needed to demonstrate that the expansion of Judah, especially the beginning of conquests in the territory of Israel, started immediately with the rule of its second king. Since territorial gains can be granted only to pious kings, the author was forced to describe Abijah positively.[54]

The account in Chronicles concentrates on the war between Abijah and Jeroboam and the speech delivered by the king of Judah at Mount Zemaraim. Israel seems to be given a chance to repent and join the nation; when Jeroboam (not the people of Israel) refuses, Israel is crushed. This happens despite the fact that Jeroboam's forces were twice as massive as Abijah's, because the Judahites "relied upon the Lord, the God of their fathers" (2 Chr 13:15–18). As a result of this victory, Abijah took from Jeroboam "Bethel with its villages and Jeshanah with its villages and Ephron [or Ephraim] with its villages" (v. 19).

The geography of this confrontation (Abijah seems to deliver the speech to the Israelites from a lookout on the northern border of Judah) and the name of the place (from *tzameret* = tree-top), indicate that Zemaraim should be identified in a high spot overlooking great distances to the north. In the book of Joshua (18:22) Zemaraim appears in the eastern district of Benjamin. The best (and only?) place to fit these descriptions is the site of Ras et-Tahune in el-Bireh,[55] located on a commanding hill overlooking the Ephraimite territories of the Northern Kingdom.[56] As for Abijah's conquests, Bethel is well known. Jeshanah should probably be identified in

---

54. On various aspects of the portrayal of Abijah in Chronicles, see, e.g., Ralph W. Klein, "Abijah's Campaign against the North (II Chr 13)—What Were the Chronicler's Sources?," *ZAW* 95 (1983): 210–17; David G. Deboys, "History and Theology in the Chronicler's Portrayal of Abijah," *Bib* 71 (1990): 48–62; Gwilym H. Jones, "From Abijam to Abijah," *ZAW* 106 (1994): 420–34. The author then faced a theological problem that he himself had created: if Abijah was good, how is it that he ruled for only three years? This may be the reason for the enigmatic summary (2 Chr 13:22), possibly hinting that there is more to tell about him, and for the fact that Abijah does not get a summary evaluation.

55. Zecharia Kallai, "The Land of Benjamin and Mt. Ephraim" [Hebrew], in *Judaea, Samaria and the Golan: Archaeological Survey 1967–1968*, ed. Mosheh Kochavi (Jerusalem: Carta, 1972), 178.

56. Israel Finkelstein, Zvi Lederman, and Shlomo Bunimovitz, *Highlands of Many Cultures: The Southern Samaria Survey, the Sites*, MSIA 14 (Tel Aviv: Tel Aviv Univer-

Burj el-Lisaneh circa 5 km northwest of Bethel[57] and Ephron (= Ophrah), also located in the eastern district of Benjamin (Josh 18:23), is to be placed in et-Taiyibeh, circa 6 km northeast of Bethel.

First Maccabees 11:34 says that in the days of Jonathan, in the 140s BCE, three toparchies were taken from Samaria and handed over to Judea— Lod, Ephraim (Apheraema), and Ramathaim. Lod and Ramathaim (the latter probably to be identified in the village of Rantis, 22 km northwest of modern Ramallah) are located to the northwest of the area discussed here, but Ephraim is the same place (Ephron = Ophrah = et-Taiyibeh) that is mentioned in 2 Chr 13:19.

According to the author of 2 Chronicles, then, Abijah started the expansion of Judah, taking over from Jeroboam territory around and north of Bethel. The same area was given by Demetrius to Jonathan—the first Hasmonean ruler after Judas.

2.4. Asa

Chronicles describes the first thirty-five years of Asa's rule (2 Chr 14:19)— until the war with Baasha of Israel—favorably. Asa is blessed with construction of fortified cities in Judah (2 Chr 14:6), conquered towns in the hill country of Ephraim and "gathered all Judah and Benjamin, and those from Ephraim, Manasseh and Simeon ... for great numbers had deserted to him from Israel when they saw that the Lord his God was with him" (2 Chr 15:9-10). The last few years of Asa's reign are described negatively. In order to explain the fact that a good king faced the invasion of an enemy (Baasha) the Chronicler blames him for calling on Ben-hadad of Damascus for help rather than trusting in YHWH. And in order to explain how a good king fell ill, he blames Asa for punishing the prophet who criticized his call on Ben-hadad (2 Chr 16:7-12).[58]

The most important unparallel event during the good-behavior years is the invasion of Judah by Zerah the Cushite with an army of a million men—in this case too, a force more than double that of Judah. Asa met

---

sity Institute of Archaeology, 1997), 512-13. The lack of Hellenistic sherds in the two surveys conducted there may be the result of severe erosion and modern urbanization.

57. William F. Albright, "New Identifications of Ancient Towns," *BASOR* 9 (1923): 7-8; Finkelstein, Lederman, and Bunimovitz, *Highlands of Many Cultures*, 573-77.

58. On Asa in Chronicles, see Williamson, *1 and 2 Chronicles*, 255-77; Japhet, *I and II Chronicles*, 701-41.

him at Mareshah and the battle took place "in the valley of Zephathah at Mareshah," usually read with the LXX "in the valley north (Hebrew = zaphona) of Mareshah." Asa called on YHWH for help and God routed Zerah's army. The king of Judah then "pursued them as far as Gerar" (2 Chr 14:9–13). What we have here, then, is an invasion of Judah from the west up to Mareshah in the Upper Shephelah, a great victory, and a pursuit from Mareshah to the southwest, all the way to Gerar.

Who was Zerah the Cushite, why is Mareshah the focal point and not nearby Lachish—the most important Judahite city in the Shephelah in the Iron Age, and what is the role of Gerar in this story? Here too attention should be given to 1 Maccabees. The area referred to in 2 Chronicles was the scene of several Hasmonean confrontations. First Maccabees 10:77–86 describes a clash and a chase of the invaders to the west in the days of Jonathan. First Maccabees 15:40–41, 16:1–10 describes the invasion of Cendebeus up to Jamnia (Jabneh) in the days of Simeon. A battle took place and the invading army was defeated and pursued all the way to Ashdod. Note that Mareshah was the most important city in Idumea and was conquered by John Hyrcanus (Josephus, *A.J.* 13.257), and that Gerar is mentioned in 2 Macc 13:25 as a southern administration border spot on the coastal plain.

Asa continues, therefore, Abijah's expansion in the north, this time into towns in the hill country of Ephraim (also 2 Chr 17:2). He also defends the western border of Judah and chases his enemy to the southwest, events which resemble clashes that took place in the same area in the days of the early Hasmoneans.

### 2.5. Jehoshaphat

When describing the days of Jehoshaphat, the author of 2 Chronicles faced a problem—Jehoshaphat cooperated with the despised Ahab. He does not ignore this matter; rather, he emphasizes the great piety of the king of Judah (2 Chr 19:2–3). As a good king, Jehoshaphat is blessed with both building activities of fortresses and storage cities in Judah and territorial gains.[59]

---

59. On Jehoshaphat in Chronicles, see, e.g., Gary N. Knoppers, "Reform and Regression: The Chronicler's Presentation of Jehoshaphat," *Bib* 72 (1991): 500–524; Kim Strübind, *Tradition als Interpretation in der Chronik: König Josaphat als Paradigma chronistischer Hermeneutik und Theologie*, BZAW 201 (Berlin: de Gruyter,

The author deals with the relationship of Judah with all its neighbors (2 Chr 17:10). In the north Jehoshaphat puts garrisons in the hill country towns of Ephraim that his father Asa had taken from Israel (2 Chr 17:2, 19:4). In the south, his power reaches Beer-sheba (19:4; no reference is made to the story in 1 Kgs 22:49, that Jehoshaphat was active in Ezion-geber—the Chronicler is not concerned with the far south, way beyond Judea of his time). The Arabs in the desert and the Philistines in the west bring presents to Jehoshaphat (v. 11). In the east, YHWH defeats the Moabites and Ammonites who invaded Judah (2 Chr 20). Jehoshaphat, then, consolidates Judah's grip on the territory that he inherited from his father. Only in the south does he rule over an area that is not specifically mentioned in 2 Chronicles as belonging to Judah before him.

The land of the Philistines appears several times in 1 Maccabees in relation to the territory beyond Mareshah and Ashdod (e.g., 5:66, 68). Wars in Ammon and Moab are an important issue for the Hasmoneans (for Jazer in Ammon, e.g., 1 Macc 5:8). The wilderness of Tekoa—mentioned in relation to the war against Ammon and Moab—appears in 1 Macc 9:33 regarding a confrontation with Bacchides, which involves a group from Madaba (9:36).[60] And beyond these details, the expression "round about" Judah (Hebrew = *sevivot*; Greek κύκλῳ Ιουδα) for the enemies of the kingdom (2 Chr 17:10) is echoed in 1 Maccabees (3:25, 5:1, 12:53).[61]

## 2.6. Uzziah

According to the author of 2 Chronicles, in the days of Uzziah Judah reached its maximal territory *before* the collapse of the Northern Kingdom. Uzziah fought against the Philistines, "broke down" the walls of Gath, Jabneh, and Ashdod and built cities in the territory of Ashdod "and

---

1991); Ralph W. Klein, "Reflections on Historiography in the Account of Jehoshaphat," in *Pomegranates and Golden Bells: Studies in Biblical, Jewish, and Near Eastern Ritual, Law, and Literature in Honor of Jacob Milgrom*, ed. David P. Wright, David Noel Freedman, and Avi Hurvitz (Winona Lake, IN: Eisenbrauns, 1995), 643–57; Steven L. McKenzie, "The Trouble with King Jehoshaphat," in *Reflection and Refraction: Studies in Biblical Historiography in Honour of A. Graeme Auld*, ed. Robert Rezetko, Timothy H. Lim and W. Brian Aucker, VTSup 113 (Leiden: Brill, 2007), 299–314; the special attention given by 2 Chronicles to this king is beyond the scope of the discussion here.

60. For the idea that the story reflects a third century BCE event, see Martin Noth, "Eine palästinische Lokalüberlieferung in 2 Chr. 20," *ZDPV* 67 (1945): 45–71.

61. For the theme of storage cities (2 Chr 17:12), note 1 Macc 14:10.

elsewhere among the Philistines." God helped him against the Philistines, the Arabs and the Meunites (2 Chr 26:6-7, possibly an elaboration on 2 Kgs 18:8 [for Hezekiah]), and the Ammonites paid him tribute. Obviously, the territory of Uzziah in Chronicles covers areas in Philistia that had never been ruled by Iron Age Judah. It is also noteworthy that Uzziah built towers in Jerusalem and "in the wilderness, and hewed out many cisterns" (vv. 9-10). In order to explain why Uzziah contracted leprosy, the Chronicler associates him with a cultic offense in his later years (v. 16).

These descriptions also recall the reality of the days of the Hasmoneans, who time and again clashed with Jamnia (= Jabneh—1 Macc 4:15; 5:58; 10:69; 15:40) and Ashdod (4:15; 5:68; 10:76-84; 11:4; 16:10). These places had probably been conquered by John Hyrcanus, because when Alexander Jannaeus came to power they already belonged to Judea.[62] Within Judea the Hasmoneans constructed the First Wall (with towers) in Jerusalem and palaces/forts with elaborate water systems in the Judean Desert (compare 2 Chr 26:9-10).

2.7. Hezekiah

In Chronicles, Hezekiah is the most important king after David and Solomon.[63] Hezekiah is essential for the author's description of the expansion of Judah because he ruled immediately after the fall of the Northern Kingdom. He is the first to go into the heartland of Israel; he invited "all Israel and Judah" from Dan to Beer-sheba (all tribes of Israel west of the Jordan except Naphtali are mentioned) to come celebrate the Passover in Jerusalem (2 Chr 30:1, 5). But the author makes a distinction between these areas and territories where all Israel actually "broke in pieces the pillars and hewed down the Asherim and broke down the high places and the

---

62. Michael Avi-Yonah, *The Holy Land from the Persian to the Arab Conquests (536 B.C. to A.D. 640): A Historical Geography* (Grand Rapids: Baker, 1977), 64, based on Josephus, *A.J.* 13.324.

63. Williamson, *1 and 2 Chronicles*, 350; Japhet, *I and II Chronicles*, 912; on Hezekiah in Chronicles, e.g., Williamson, *Israel in the Books of Chronicles*, 119-25; August H. Konkel, *Hezekiah in Biblical Tradition* (Ann Arbor: University Microfilms International, 1989), 217-82; Mark A. Throntveit, "The Relationship of Hezekiah to David and Solomon in the Books of Chronicles," in *The Chronicler as Theologian: Essays in Honor of Ralph W. Klein*, ed. M. Patrick Graham, Steven L. McKenzie, and Gary N. Knoppers, JSOTSup 271 (London: T&T Clark, 2003), 105-21; Young, *Hezekiah in History and Tradition*, 195-283.

altars." In the latter, only Judah, Benjamin, Ephraim, and Manasseh are mentioned. It seems, then, that the territories of "all Israel" are divided into two: (1) Claim for the entire territory of Israel and Judah combined, from Dan to Beer-sheba, which also includes the tribes of the Galilee. (2) Land actually ruled by Hezekiah; the land of Manasseh—the area of Shechem and further to the north in the hill country—is added to what had already been ruled by Uzziah. It seems, then, that the Galilee is not yet in the hands of a king who rules from Jerusalem. The latter—the territory of Judah, Benjamin, Ephraim, and Manasseh—is the maximal Judahite territory described in 2 Chronicles; the pious Josiah goes to war at Megiddo, but there is no mention of his rule over territories in the Galilee.

Hezekiah is the hero of 2 Chronicles, some say the new Solomon,[64] if not the new David,[65] overshadowing the great Josiah of the Deuteronomistic History. It seems to me that John Hyrcanus, in whose days 1 Maccabees was seemingly composed,[66] is equated with him. Hyrcanus was the Hasmonean ruler who conquered Shechem (Josephus, *A.J.* 13.255) and Samaria (*A.J.* 13.281), and destroyed the Samaritan temple on Mount Gerizim (*A.J.* 13.155–256, 281). Hezekiah of Chronicles and John Hyrcanus therefore ruled over the same territory west of the Jordan, most significantly the entire central hill country.[67] It is noteworthy that another Hasmonean text—the Testaments of the Twelve Patriarchs, which probably dates to the later days of John Hyrcanus—also makes a distinction between the tribal areas which were in the hands of the Hasmoneans and the tribes of the Galilee.[68] Also note the two references to God's triumph over Sennacherib in 1 Macc 7:41 and 2 Macc 8:19 in relation to the Hasmonean victory over Nicanor. The days of Hezekiah seem to demonstrate the ability of the God of Israel to defeat a great world power. This may possibly have been written against the background of the struggle with Antiochus VII Sidetes: both foreign armies—the Assyrian and the Seleucid—laid siege

---

64. E.g., Klein, *2 Chronicles*, 10. Williamson (*1 and 2 Chronicles*, 366) thinks that in the time of Hezekiah Judah of Chronicles reached the extent of the kingdom in the days of Solomon. Yet, in Kings Solomon reigns over (almost) the entire land of Israel, including the northern valleys and the Galilee, areas not ruled by Hezekiah of Chronicles.

65. E.g., Young, *Hezekiah in History and Tradition*, 282.

66. Rappaport, *First Book of Maccabees*, 60–61 with references to earlier literature.

67. For Hyrcanus, see Avi Yonah, *Holy Land*, 63–67; map in Yohanan Aharoni and Michael Avi-Yonah, *The Macmillan Bible Atlas* (New York: Macmillan, 1993), 156.

68. Mendels, *Land of Israel*, 95–96.

to Jerusalem; "victory" was achieved with the help of YHWH and both foreign monarchs died unexpectedly after their campaign to Judah/Judea.

To summarize, the Chronicler's description of the territory of Judah in the time of Hezekiah draws the lines for the Hasmonean conquests until the later days of John Hyrcanus (except for Madaba, and Gezer and Jaffa, which will be discussed below). The fact that no king of Judah—not even Josiah—is credited with the conquest of the northern valleys and the Galilee (to achieve the ideal goal of reconstructing the kingdom of David and Solomon) may be revealing, hinting that Chronicles reflects the expansion of the Hasmoneans before the days of Aristobolus and Alexander Jannaeus.

## 2.8. Other Kings: Good and Bad

The descriptions in 2 Chronicles discussed here raise two questions:

1. Why is the expansion of Judah which is not recounted in Kings credited to the above-mentioned monarchs, two of whom are negatively evaluated in the Deuteronomistic History? And why much of the expansion is ascribed to the first four kings of Judah?
2. Why are other kings not "given" territorial gains, especially those evaluated positively in Kings (Jehoash, Amaziah, Jotham and Josiah)?

In order to answer these questions, let me briefly summarize the author's territorial attitude to each of the Judahite kings.

Of the early four kings, Rehoboam was the first after the "division" of the United Monarchy, so 2 Chronicles needed to mark the core area of the kingdom before it started re-expanding. Regarding Abijah, the author took advantage of the mention in Kings that he was at war with the despised Jeroboam in order to show that Judah had begun expanding into Israelite territory without delay. To that end he needed to evaluate Abijah positively. Expansion continued in the days of the next two "good" kings. Asa was attacked by Israel and hence was given territory there—towns in the hill country of Ephraim. Jehoshaphat was active in territory taken by his father in the north and was attacked (and saved by YHWH) in the east.

It comes as no surprise that the three monarchs related to the Omrides—Jehoram, Ahaziah, and Athaliah—are judged severely and evidently their reign is not blessed by territorial gains. The opposite is true—

Jehoram suffers attacks on all sides of his kingdom—even more so than is related in Kings (2 Chr 21:16-17).

Jehoash and Amaziah—described as pious monarchs in Kings—pose a riddle. The author of 2 Chronicles diminishes their stature and does not grant them territorial gains. According to him Jehoash did good only during the days of the high priest Jehoiada (note the difference between 2 Kgs 12:3 ["all his [Jehoash's] days"] and 2 Chr 24:2 ["all the days of Jehoiada"]). Since he was attacked by Aram and paid tribute from the treasures of the temple (a fact which is omitted in Chronicles), and because he did not die peacefully, the author had to lessen his piety (2 Chr 24:17-22; though much of the blame is put on the "princes of Judah"). Amaziah could not be granted conquests because he was defeated by Israel and taken captive, Jerusalem was attacked and its walls breached, and treasures were taken from the temple. Second Chronicles, then, obliges Amaziah to sin (2 Chr 25:14-16); the vague reference to a regiment from Ephraim that attacked Judah (v. 13) may be connected to this story.[69]

The expansion of Judah before the fall of the Northern Kingdom ends with Uzziah—the last pious king before 720 who also ruled for many years—a symbol of piety (though he is criticized in 2 Chr 26:16 in order to explain his leprosy). Since the expansion into Manasseh is left to Hezekiah—after the fall of the North—Jotham is not given territorial gains despite his devotion (though he too receives tribute from Ammon—2 Chr 27:5). Ahaz is all bad, like the kings related to the Omrides before him, and is punished in Chronicles beyond the attacks by Aram and Israel and Tiglath-pileser III (2 Chr 28:17-19).

Hezekiah, the hero of the Chronicler, achieves the full expansion of Judah in the highlands—all the way north to the Manasseh hill country, that is, Shechem and Samaria included. Amon and Manasseh are judged negatively, but the latter is made to repent in order to explain his fifty-five year-long reign.[70]

---

69. On Amaziah in Chronicles, see Ehud Ben Zvi, "A House of Treasures: The Account of Amaziah in 2 Chronicles 25—Observations and Implications," *SJOT* 22 (2008): 63-85.

70. On Manasseh in Chronicles, see Philippe Abadie, "From the Impious Manasseh (2 Kings 21) to the Convert Manasseh (2 Chronicles 33)," in Graham, McKenzie, and Knoppers *Chronicler as Theologian*, 89-104; Brian E. Kelly, "Manasseh in the Books of Kings and Chronicles (2 Kings 21:1-18; 2 Chron 33:1-20)," in *Windows into Old Testament History: Evidence, Argument, and the Crisis of "Biblical Israel,"* ed.

Josiah is less important to the author of 2 Chronicles than to the Deuteronomistic Historian, and much of the text repeats the acts of Hezekiah.[71] Josiah is almost entirely pious, with a minor criticism that he did not consult YHWH before going to war at Megiddo; this was essential in order to explain how such a good king was killed by a foreign monarch. No territorial conquests are mentioned in his days, because it was essential for the author to show that Judah expanded into the land of the Northern Kingdom immediately after its demise. But when speaking about the cleansing of the high places, 2 Kings' "cities of Samaria" (23:19) are replaced by the "cities of Manasseh, Ephraim, and Simeon, and as far as Naphtali" (2 Chr 34:6). The original could have been Manasseh and Ephraim with Simeon and Naphtali added; or the four were there from the outset, to comply with the utopic ideal of Judahite rule from Beersheba to Dan.

3. The Territorial Aspects of the Genealogies in 1 Chronicles 2–9

The territorial ideology in Chronicles and the extent of the Hasmonean state brings to mind the genealogical lists in 1 Chr 2–9. I have discussed this issue elsewhere,[72] so I will restrict myself here to a brief summary. Most scholars agree that the genealogical lists form an independent block, a kind of introduction to history. Opinions differ, however, on whether they belong to the work of the Chronicler,[73] or if they were added after the main substance of the book had already been formulated.[74] While

---

V. Philips Long, David W. Baker, and Gordan J. Wenham (Grand Rapids: Eerdmans, 2002), 131–46. Repentance of a wicked king is a theme repeated in second century literature—especially noteworthy is 1 Macc 6 (see also 2 Macc 9—I am grateful to Doron Mendels for calling my attention to this reference).

71. Williamson, *1 and 2 Chronicles*, 396; on Josiah in Chronicles, see Ehud Ben Zvi, "Observations on Josiah's Account in Chronicles and Implications for Reconstructing the Worldview of the Chronicler," in *Essays on Ancient Israel in Its Near Eastern Context: A Tribute to Nadav Na'aman*, ed. Yairah Amit, Ehud Ben Zvi, Israel Finkelstein, and Oded Lipschits (Winona Lake: Eisenbrauns, 2006), 89–106 and bibliography.

72. Israel Finkelstein, "The Historical Reality behind the Genealogical Lists in 1 Chronicles," *JBL* 131 (2012): 65–83 (ch. 5 in this article).

73. E.g., Marshall D. Johnson, *The Purpose of the Biblical Genealogies*, SNTSMS 8 (Cambridge: Cambridge University, 1969), 47–55; Oeming, *Das wahre Israel*.

74. E.g., Frank M. Cross, "A Reconstruction of the Judean Restoration," *JBL* 94 (1975): 4–18; Noth, *Chronicler's History*, 36–42.

researchers associated the genealogies with the Davidic territorial ideal expressed in Chronicles, the actual territory described in the list, represented by names of towns, covers an area which stretches from Eshtemoa and Maon in the south to Bethel, Birzaith and Shechem in the north, and from Mareshah, Gezer, and Lod in the west to the area of Madaba in the east. In tribal terms, this area represents Judah, Benjamin, Ephraim, Manasseh (Shechem), and part of the territory of Reuben (fig. 5.1; see also 1 Chr 9:3). It is also noteworthy that the genealogy of the return in 1 Chr 9:2–34 mentions repatriates from Judah, Benjamin, Ephraim, and Manasseh.[75] This territory is supplemented by tribal areas (to differ from lists of towns). The genealogies of Naphtali and Issachar (and Dan?)[76] are short and provide almost no information; only the central highlands genealogy of Asher is given, and there is no genealogy for Zebulun. In the case of Manasseh the author reiterated the data on the sons and daughters of Manasseh which appears in Josh 17, and incorporated a list of famous places (1 Chr 7:29), which he probably took from the Deuteronomistic History (Jud 1:27). The list of Simeon is probably taken from Joshua (19:1–7).[77]

The area delineated by detailed genealogies is therefore somewhat similar to the territory of Judah in the time of Hezekiah as described in Chronicles, and similar to the territory of Hasmonean Judea in the later days of John Hyrcanus, including his expansion to the south (Idumea), north (Shechem and Samaria), west (including Mareshah, Gezer conquered by Simeon, and Lod given to Jonathan)[78] and east (Madaba). Issachar, Naphtali, and the north Transjordanian tribes are mentioned only in general outline, without referring to towns. This may be seen as reflecting the future aspirations of the Hasmoneans to conclude the conquest of the territories of the twelve tribes of Israel (or the great United Monarchy) as perceived in the days of John Hyrcanus; or may portray the time immediately thereafter, when the annexation of much of this area to the Hasmo-

---

75. Knoppers, *I Chronicles*, 264.
76. Knoppers, *I Chronicles*, 453.
77. E.g., Rudolph, *Chronikbücher*, 38–39; Albrecht Alt, *Kleine Schriften zur Geschichte des Volkes Israel*, vol. 2 (Munich: Beck, 1953), 285. The author did this as he had no knowledge of the area further to the south, that is, the Beer-sheba Valley.
78. The references to a place named Gath, located in the lowlands (1 Chr 7:21; 1 Chr 8:13), also seem to relate to this westward expansion of Judea.

nean state had been fulfilled (and this would then explain the listing of Manassite towns in the Jezreel Valley).

## 4. Hasmonean Need for Legitimacy

Even if the genealogical lists may once have been a separate literary unit from the rest of Chronicles (as argued by many), they represent the same ideology of territorial legitimation of the Hasmonean state. One speaks about places settled by the tribes of Israel and the other deals with areas conquered and then ruled by the kings of Judah.

The genealogical lists probably meant to legitimize Jewish rule over areas transferred to- or conquered by- the Hasmoneans, which were inhabited by a large gentile population, by giving them ancient Israelite tribal pedigree. This seems to be in line with several Hasmonean pseudepigraphic compositions. I refer to the book of Jubilees, which may have been written in the days of John Hyrcanus and possibly the Testament of the Twelve Patriarchs, which looked at the Bible in order to legitimize the Hasmonean conquests and addressed problems related to the relationship with non-Jews who lived in the new territories.[79] Jubilees used biblical material in order to validate the inclusion of foreign groups into Judaism,[80] and the genealogies in Chronicles too do not reject the inclusion of groups of foreigners[81] as well as foreign individuals who are related to Judah/Judea through mixed marriages.[82]

Regarding their conquests, the Hasmoneans' need for territorial legitimacy is perfectly expressed toward the end of 1 Maccabees. Antiochus VII sends an emissary to Simeon, who says:

> You hold control of Joppa and Gazara and the citadel in Jerusalem; they are cities of my kingdom. You have devastated their territory, you have done great damage in the land, and you have taken possession of many

---

79. Mendels, *Land of Israel*; Mendels, *The Rise and Fall of Jewish Nationalism* (New York: Doubleday, 1992), 81–99.
80. Mendels, *Land of Israel*, 60, 67.
81. Gary N. Knoppers, "Intermarriage, Social Complexity, and Ethnic Diversity in the Genealogy of Judah," *JBL* 120 (2001): 15–30.
82. Williamson, *1 and 2 Chronicles*, 38; Knoppers, "Intermarriage"; for the incorporation of "new-Jews" in the Hasmonean elite, see, e.g., Seth Schwartz, "Israel and the Nations Roundabout: 1 Maccabees and the Hasmonean Expansion," *JJS* 42 (1991): 16–38.

places in my kingdom. Now then, hand over the cities which you have seized ... or else give me for them five hundred talents of silver.... Otherwise we will come and conquer you. (1 Macc 15:28-31)

Simeon's answer to Antiochus is the culmination of the Hasmonean territorial ideology:

We have neither taken foreign land nor seized foreign property, but only the inheritance of our fathers, which at one time had been unjustly taken by our enemies. Now that we have the opportunity, we are firmly holding the inheritance of our fathers. (1 Macc 15:33-34)

But this is not all. Simeon continues, to make a distinction between the "inheritance of our fathers" and Jaffa and Gezer, which had been conquered by Simeon (1 Macc 14:5, 7), taken back by Sidetes, and retaken by the Hasmoneans (Josephus, *A.J.* 13.261):

As for Joppa and Gazara, which you demand, they were causing great damage among the people and to our land; for them we will give a hundred talents. (1 Macc 15:35)

In other words, while the "inheritance of our fathers," which was conquered according to this line of thinking twice—by the kings of Judah and by the Hasmoneans—is not negotiable, Jaffa and Gezer are only a matter of security and can therefore be paid for. It is noteworthy (and probably not a coincidence), that Jaffa and Gezer are not mentioned as part of Judah in 2 Chronicles (Gezer does appear in the genealogies).

Though it exists in other parts of the Bible, a related central theme in Chronicles which is paralleled in 1 Maccabees is the notion that victories of the few against the many can be secured only with the help of the God of Israel. As shown above, in Chronicles this is reiterated time and again. The book of Maccabees recounts the reaction of the people when seeing the army of Seron approaching them as follows:

They said to Judas, "How can we, few as we are, fight against so great and strong a multitude?..." Judas replied ... "It is not on the size of the army that victory in battle depends, but strength comes from Heaven. They come against us in great pride and lawlessness to destroy us ... but we fight for our lives and our laws. He himself will crush them before us. (1 Macc 3:17-22)

This theme is repeated in relation to other battles of Judas (1 Macc 4:10–11; 4:30–33; 7:41 [where Judas evokes the victory of YHWH over Sennacherib]). Perhaps it is not a coincidence that the two battles that were fought without a preliminary prayer—Beth-zechariah and Elasa—ended in disaster, including the death of Eleazar and Judas.

Mendels asserted that the Jews had no fixed ideas regarding the borders of the Hasmonean state. "Borders could be broadened or shrunk, and many events from the past could be brought forward to justify them.... Their dreams and speculations were based on the Hebrew Bible.... The literature could refer to the Promised Land, the borders of David and Solomon, and those of other kings as well. *They could embellish on other territorial variations and refer to the borders described in the Books of Chronicles, which were significantly different from parallel descriptions in Samuel and Kings.*"[83] In the second century BCE the Jews "used their *own* traditional material to justify their actions during the process of the conquest of Palestine."[84]

Most illuminating is the meticulous work of Mendels on Hasmonean texts regarding the concept of the land of Israel.[85] Mendels demonstrates that in the early second century "Ben Sira is not yet preoccupied with the question of ruler and sovereignty over the Land,"[86] and I would add—a question which is so central to Chronicles and 1 Maccabees. Slightly later, in the 120s BCE, the book of Jubilees "constitutes a typical example of how people were living their Bible anew, and how they transferred their own reality into their history."[87] Looking back at their history "the Jews could justify their present conquests more easily."[88] Still slightly later, in the 110s BCE, the Testament of the Twelve Patriarchs alludes to the wars and conquests of the Hasmoneans (John Hyrcanus in particular); the Testament of Judah especially "goes out of its way to give the Jewish wars on Eretz Israel an archaic scenery."[89] According to this analysis too, then, the reality described in 2 Chronicles best fits the end-days of John Hyrcanus.

---

83. Mendels, *Rise and Fall*, 96, my emphasis—I.F.
84. Mendels, *Rise and Fall*, 99.
85. Mendels, *Land of Israel*.
86. Mendels, *Land of Israel*, 16.
87. Mendels, *Land of Israel*, 59. For review of the possible dates of Jubilees, see James C. VanderKam, *The Book of Jubilees* (Sheffield: Sheffield Academic Press, 2001), 17–21.
88. Mendels, *Land of Israel*, 60.
89. Mendels, *Land of Israel*, 98.

Scholars noticed the closeness between Chronicles and the Hellenistic period, even Hasmonean times, mainly regarding the threat posed at that time to Judaism. Kellermann suggested that the Chronicler's criticism of cult behavior and the attitude of the kings of Judah to the torah matched cultic changes in Jerusalem and Judea during the Hasmonean revolt.[90] He noted the similarities between Chronicles and the books of Maccabees. Yet, instead of proposing a late date for Chronicles, he opted for the conventional wisdom in the early third century and proposed that the Chronicler anticipated events to come, in the days of Antiochus IV![91] Kegler noticed that the historical background in Chronicles is that of a threat posed to Jewish identity by foreign cults and identified this threat with the emergence of Hellenism;[92] more specifically, he seems to point to the conflict with the Seleucid Empire in the second century. Steins, too,[93] associated Chronicles with the severe religious and cultural crisis caused by the pressure of Hellenism.[94] Steins noted that Chronicles and Maccabees reflect a similar historical situation and dated the former to early Hasmonean times.[95]

Noth's observation is revealing: "it would hardly be advisable to date Chr. significantly later than about 200 BC.... For the additions, however, and in particular for the numerous supplements to the genealogies ... the Maccabean period should be seriously considered. It was at that time that there was a renewed interest in the twelve tribes of Israel."[96] Noth's cautious words evoke an important question: does the territorial ideology of 2 Chronicles and the genealogies require dating the entire body of Chronicles to the late second century BCE?

---

90. Kellermann, "Anmerkungen zum Verständnis der Tora."

91. Somewhat similarly Albertz (*History of Israelite Religion*, 555) asserts that: "We can see the national restitution of Judah under the Hasmonaeans in the second century as being remote political effect of Chronicles."

92. Jürgen Kegler, "Prophetengestalten im Deuteronomistischen Geschichtswerk und in den Chronikbüchern: Ein Beitrag zur Kompositions- und Redaktionsgeschichte der Chronikbücher," *ZAW* 105 (1993): 481–97.

93. Steins, *Chronik*, 495.

94. Welten (*Geschichte*, 195–206) interpreted Chronicles against the background of threats to the cult community in Jerusalem by opponents on all sides, but sought the background in the third century BCE, which provides no attestation for such a situation.

95. Especially, Steins, *Chronik*, 491–99.

96. *Chronicler's History*, 73.

Excursus 2: A Chronicler or Chroniclers?

Evidently, my proposal to date the unparallel texts in 2 Chronicles to the late second century BCE does not necessarily imply that the entire work of 1–2 Chronicles belongs to the same time. In other words, it is possible that the Hasmonean layer was added to a preexisting text from, for example, the third century BCE. There may be several clues for such an "early Chronicles."[97] First and foremost, this would explain why the book was included in the biblical canon while other Hasmonean texts which hint at territorial legitimation, such as Jubilees, were excluded. And among other issues, it would also explain the attitude of the author to David and Solomon as builders of the temple more than sovereign monarchs, which seems unfit for the time of the Hasmoneans.

Other arguments make it difficult to argue for such an old, early Hellenistic Chronicles. The unparallel texts in 2 Chronicles are long and complex; they make a big part of the text. These are no mere redactions—take them out and what is left is basically a repetition of Kings; in this case, what is the reason for composing Chronicles? Also, in order to argue for at least two major layers in Chronicles, one needs to demonstrate some literary, stylistic, theological, or language differences between the blocks. It seems to me that such (significant) differences cannot be easily identified in Chronicles.[98] From the perspective of strictly historical logic I could understand a reason to see 1 Chr 10–2 Chr 9 as one (early?) block telling the story of the ideal United Monarchy from a utopic perspective and 2 Chr 10–36 as another (late) block based on Hasmonean realities (both possibly depicting several layers). But again, I doubt if such a separation can be demonstrated. Finally, there remains the question: Is there real evidence—historical, literary, or other—for an old Chronicles that was composed in the early Hellenistic period? I am not competent to judge and hence leave it to the reader to decide.

---

97. I am grateful to Thomas Römer and Konrad Schmid for calling my attention to these points.

98. For the question of unity of Chronicles, see, e.g., Japhet, *I and II Chronicles*, 4–7; Williamson, *1 and 2 Chronicles*, 12–17; Steven L. McKenzie, "The Chronicler as Redactor," in *The Chronicler as Author*, ed. M. Patrick Graham and Steven L. McKenzie, JSOTSup 263 (Sheffield: Sheffield Academic Press, 1999), 70–90.

## 5. Conclusion

One of the central themes in the sections in Chronicles that do not appear in Kings is gradual expansion of the kingdom of Judah as a result of wars won with the help of YHWH. Because of the great similarity to the process of expansion of Judea in the days of the Hasmoneans—including reference to similar locations and use of comparable expressions—it is reasonable to suggest that one of the aims for the compilation of (at least) 2 Chronicles was to provide legitimacy for the Hasmonean conquests.

In 2 Chronicles Judah in the days of Hezekiah (the author's hero, apparently an image of John Hyrcanus) stretched from the Beer-sheba Valley to the Samaria highlands, possibly with some influence in Ammon east of the Jordan. Judah controlled Philistia, including the cities of Gath, Jabneh, and Ashdod. This is the territory ruled by the Hasmoneans in the later days of John Hyrcanus, that is, after the conquests of Idumea in the south and Samaria in the north: from south of Adoraim to Samaria and beyond in the north and from Madaba in the east to the border of Jamnia and Ashdod in the west. In this Chronicles should be seen as belonging to the genre of Hasmonean works—mainly 1 Maccabees, Jubilees, and the Testament of the Twelve Patriarchs—which look to the Bible in order to legitimize realities of the time.

This means that Chronicles (at least 2 Chr 10–36) was written (or significantly expanded) in the late second century BCE. The implications of this proposal for broader questions in biblical research are beyond the scope of this article; I would just say that it may resolve the question of why Chronicles—and not other contemporary works—found its way into the Masoretic canon: it is the ultimate summary of the past, which connects to the present with a view to the future.

## Addendum

In a recent article, Knoppers opposes my interpretation of the unparallel accounts in 2 Chronicles as representing legitimacy for Hasmonean territorial expansion.[99] There is no point in debating Knoppers's view, as it

---

99. Gary N. Knoppers, "Israel or Judah? The Shifting Body Politic and Collective Identity in Chronicles," in *Rethinking Israel: Studies in the History and Archaeology of Ancient Israel in Honor of Israel Finkelstein*, ed. Oded Lipschits, Yuval Gadot, and Matthew J. Adams (Winona Lake, IN: Eisenbrauns, 2017), 173–88.

repeats the conventional wisdom regarding the date of the author and his goals: "in advancing a large vision of Israel in his depiction of the Judahite monarchy ... the writer assumes something of the conditions of his own day in the late Persian/Early Hellenistic period in which some Israelites reside in Judah, some in Samaria, and some outside what they consider to be the traditional land of Israel.... In writing about the past, the Chronicler encourages his fellow Israelites in Judah, Samaria, and elsewhere to support the Jerusalem temple and to observe torah rites."[100] The chapter above speaks for itself against this theory; in fact, it was originally written to counter this traditional theory on 2 Chronicles.

---

100. Knoppers, "Israel or Judah?," 185.

# Conclusions

The geographical setting portrayed by the texts discussed in this book and the archaeology of the sites mentioned in them reflect realities in the second half of the second century BCE—in Hasmonean times. The literary genre of these materials and the ideology behind them also fit Hasmonean literature.[1] The main conclusions of the seven chapters are as follows.

**Nehemiah's Wall:** There are no Persian or early Hellenistic fortifications in Jerusalem to fit the Neh 3 description of a city wall with numerous gates and towers surrounding a large city. Furthermore, the depleted population of Yehud could not have supported a major construction effort such as the one Neh 3 describes. The Persian and early Hellenistic settlement must have been restricted to the old tell on the Temple Mount. The account in Neh 3 seems to fit the Hasmonean construction of the First Wall of Jerusalem, probably in a later phase of the second century BCE. But the general reference to the deplorable situation of Jerusalem and the need to repair the wall in the Nehemiah Memoir, without details of towers and gates, is part of the old core-text of the book.

**The list of returnees** (Ezra 2:1–67; Neh 7:6–68): The geographical extent behind the list goes beyond the distribution of the Persian-period Yehud seal impressions—the only reliable evidence for delineating the extent of the province at that time. Moreover, five of the fifteen identifiable sites that appear in the list were uninhabited in the Persian period and an additional six were sparsely populated, while all sites were inhabited in the late Hellenistic period, most of them providing evidence for strong

---

1. Another issue to explore is the theme of foreign wives in Ezra and Nehemiah. If one is looking for non-Judahite/Yehudite/Judean women (to differ from the decedents of the remainees), the only reality behind this concern can be found when the Hasmoneans started expanding from their core area with its homogenous population to the north and west, into regions inhabited by gentiles; but this theme is beyond the scope of the present book.

settlement activity at that time. In addition, important Persian-period places are not mentioned in the list. All this leads me to suggest that the list of returnees depicts Hasmonean realities in the second century BCE.

**Nehemiah's adversaries:** The theme of adversaries presents a case somewhat similar to that of the wall of Jerusalem. The idea of nameless opponents appears in the old Nehemiah Memoir, but the specific list of enemies belongs to a late layer in the book. The named adversaries do not refer to specific, single-period historical figures; rather, they portray the situation of enemies "roundabout," which fits the Hasmonean period. The reference to the Ashdodites is especially telling: Ashdod was far from Yehud and of no concern to the inhabitants of the province, while it plays an important role in 1 Maccabees as an enemy of Hasmonean Judea.

**The genealogies:** Eleven of the thirty-six identifiable places mentioned in the genealogical lists in 1 Chr 2–9 were not inhabited in the Persian period and an additional eight were sparsely settled. Assuming that the geographical background behind the genealogies represents a given phase in history (meaning that it is not invented or utopic), the only period which fits their territorial setting and the archaeology of the sites mentioned in them is that of the Hasmoneans. The genealogical lists were probably intended to legitimize Jewish rule over the territory mentioned in them, part of which was inhabited by a large gentile population, by giving it ancient Israelite tribal pedigree. This seems to be in line with several Hasmonean pseudepigraphic compositions, which looked to the Bible in order to explain and legitimize the gradual territorial expansion of Judea in the second century BCE.

**Rehoboam's fortified towns:** The distribution of towns fortified by Rehoboam (2 Chr 11:5–12) does not fit any period in the history of Iron Age Judah; rather, it adheres to the situation in Judea in the early days of John Hyrcanus. Sites mentioned in the list that have been excavated, have indeed revealed Hellenistic fortifications. The idea behind the text could have been a warning aimed at the future but based on the past, pronouncing that even a set of mighty fortresses offers no safeguard from devastation by enemy if the ruler does not follow in the ways of the God of Israel.

**Expansion of Judah in 2 Chronicles:** The "unparralel" accounts in 2 Chronicles (that is, texts which do not appear in Kings) describe the gradual expansion of the kingdom of Judah. These descriptions do not fit the territorial and geopolitical realities of the Iron Age. The great similarity to the process of expansion of Judea in the days of the Hasmoneans—including reference to similar locations and use of comparable expressions—makes it reasonable to suggest that 2 Chronicles aimed at providing legitimacy for the Hasmonean conquests. In 2 Chronicles the maximal borders of Judah stretch from the Beer-sheba Valley to the Samaria highlands, possibly with some influence in Ammon east of the Jordan. Judah controls Philistia, including the cities of Gath, Jabneh, and Ashdod. This is the territory ruled by the Hasmoneans in the later days of John Hyrcanus, after the conquests of Idumea in the south and Samaria in the north. Here too one finds similarities to several Hasmonean pseudepigraphic compositions, which looked to the Bible for legitimization of the Hasmonean expansion. Scholarly arguments against the possibility of dating at least part of Chronicles to the second half of the second century BCE are not founded on solid ground.

All this raises a broader question regarding the literary history of Ezra, Nehemiah, and Chronicles: were these books composed in Hasmonean times, or were the parts discussed in this study inserted into older texts?

A related question is the volume of scribal activity in Judah-Yehud-Judea. As is well known, scribal activity in Judah began to expand in the late eighth century and reached its peak in the (late) seventh century BCE. Most corpora of ostraca—Arad, Lachish, Uza, Malhata, Kadesh-barnea—belong to the latter period. The spread of literacy is also attested in the proliferation of seals and seal-impressions, including bullae. Algorithmic comparison of characters in the Arad ostraca, carried out by the digital epigraphy group at Tel Aviv University (which I direct together with Eli Piasetzky), demonstrates the proliferation of literacy into all echelons of the Judahite administration.[2] The seventh century BCE is therefore the moment when Judah becomes what one can describe as a "writing society," also beyond the circles of temple and palace in the capital. This was probably an outcome of the century when Judah was dominated by Assyria and was incorporated into the sphere of Assyrian global-economy, administration and culture.

In the Babylonian and Persian periods, Hebrew writing disappears from the archaeological record. The southern highlands show almost no evidence of Hebrew inscriptions that can be dated to these periods. In fact, the only (meager) evidence comes from the few YHD coins which date to the fourth century BCE, and coins can hardly attest to widespread

---

2. Shira Faigenbaum-Golovin et al., "Algorithmic Handwriting Analysis of Judahite Military Correspondence Sheds Light on Composition of Biblical Texts," *Proceedings of the National Academy of Sciences* 113 (2016): 4664–69.

scribal activity. This means that not a single inscription has been found for the period between 586 and circa 350 BCE—not an ostracon nor a seal, not a seal impression nor a bulla! This can hardly be a coincidence. I am not suggesting, of course, that the knowledge of writing Hebrew vanished; but scribal activity declined—and significantly so—until the next surge in writing in the second century BCE. This should come as no surprise: the destruction of Judah brought about the collapse of the kingdom's bureaucracy and deportation of many of the educated intelligentsia—the literati; the remainees in the land were hardly capable of producing written documents.

This should serve as a warning sign to those who tend to place much biblical material in Persian-period Yehud. My humble advice on this matter is twofold: first, to try dating as much material as possible to periods in the history of Judah/Judea that demonstrate widespread scribal activity and literacy in all media and all forms of inscriptions, that is, the latest phase of the Iron Age and late Hellenistic period after circa 200 BCE. My second recommendation: in the centuries between circa 600 and 200 BCE, especially the Babylonian and Persian periods, to place the compilation of as much material as possible in Babylonia.[3]

At the same time, I accept that there must have been some continuity of literary activity in Yehud; one can imagine, for instance, a secluded, educated priestly group near the temple. But even this is not an elegant solution, since evidence for activity on the Temple Mount in the Persian period is meager,[4] and as I would expect that some evidence for this situation would have leaked to daily life.

Considering all arguments, and with the data at hand, the solution that I would advocate is to date parts of the books dealt with in this volume to the late Persian or early Hellenistic periods and other parts to Hasmonean times. In the former, I can think, for example, of the Nehemiah Memoir and the description of an ideal United Monarchy in 1 Chr 10–2 Chr 9.

---

3. For instance, Rainer Albertz, *Israel in Exile: The History and Literature of the Sixth Century B.C.E.*, SBLStBL 3 (Atlanta: Society of Biblical Literature, 2003).

4. Itzhak Dvira (Zweig), Gal Zigdon, and Lara Shilov, "Secondary Refuse Aggregates from the First and Second Temple Periods on the Eastern Slope of the Temple Mount" [Hebrew], *NSJ* 17 (2011): 68; Gabriel Barkay and Yitzhak Zweig, "The Temple Mount Debris Sifting Project: Preliminary Report" [Hebrew], *NSJ* 11 (2006): 222; personal communication from Eilat Mazar regarding the "Ophel" excavations (south of al-Aqsa Mosque).

Finally, there is a lesson in all this, which by now is well known in the study of ancient Israel in the Iron Age but is less acknowledged in research of the Persian and early Hellenistic periods. I refer to the importance of archaeology in disentangling the discussion from circular argumentations by revealing the background behind biblical texts and the need to incorporate this evidence, despite the fact that at times it is mainly negative, and even if it threatens to shatter conventional wisdom.

# Bibliography

Abadie, Philippe. "From the Impious Manasseh (2 Kings 21) to the Convert Manasseh (2 Chronicles 33)." Pages 89–104 in *The Chronicler as Theologian: Essays in Honor of Ralph W. Klein*. Edited by M. Patrick Graham, Steven L. McKenzie, and Gary N. Knoppers. JSOTSup 271. London: T&T Clark, 2003.

Abel, Félix-Marie. *Les livres des Maccabées*. Paris: Librairie Lecoffre, 1949.

———. "Topographie des campagnes machabéennes." *RB* 34 (1925): 206–22.

Ackroyd, Peter R. *I and II Chronicles, Ezra, Nehemiah*. London: SCM, 1973.

———. "Criteria for the Maccabean Dating of Old Testament Literature." *VT* 3 (1953): 113–32.

———. *Exile and Restoration: A Study of Hebrew Thought of the Sixth Century BC*. London: SCM, 1968.

Aharoni, Yohanan. "Beth Haccherem." Pages 171–85 in *Archaeology and Old Testament Study*. Edited by Winston D. Thomas. Oxford: Clarendon, 1967.

———. *The Land of the Bible: A Historical Geography*. Philadelphia: Westminster Press, 1979.

Aharoni, Yohanan, and Michael Avi-Yonah. *The Macmillan Bible Atlas*. New York: Macmillian, 1993.

Ahituv, Shmuel. *Echoes from the Past*. Jerusalem: Carta, 2008.

Albertz, Rainer. *A History of Israelite Religion in the Old Testament*. Louisville: Westminster, 1994.

———. *Israel in Exile: The History and Literature of the Sixth Century B.C.E.* SBLStBL 3. Atlanta: Society of Biblical Literature, 2003.

Albright, William F. "Additional Note." *BASOR* 62 (1936): 25–26.

———. "Excavations at Jerusalem." *JQR* 21 (1930): 163–68.

———. "New Identifications of Ancient Towns." *BASOR* 9 (1923): 5–10.

Alt, Albrecht. "Das Taltor von Jerusalem." *PJ* 24 (1928): 74–98.

———. "Festungen und Levitenorte im Lande Juda." Pages 306–15 in *Kleine Schriften zur Geschichte des Volkes Israel*. Vol. 2. Munich: Beck, 1953.

———. "Judas Gaue unter Josia." *PJ* 21 (1925): 100–117.

———. *Kleine Schriften zur Geschichte des Volkes Israel*. Vol. 2. Munich: Beck, 1953.

———. "Zur Geschichte der Grenze zwischen Judäa und Samaria." *PJ* 31 (1953): 94–111.

Amiran, Ruth, and Avraham Eitan. "Excavations in the Courtyard of the Citadel, Jerusalem, 1968–1969 (Preliminary Report)." *IEJ* 20 (1970): 9–17.

Arbel, Yoav. "Lod." *ESI* 116 (2004): 40*.

Ariel, Donald T., Hannah Hirschfeld, and Neta Savir. "Area D1: Stratigraphic Report." Pages 33–72 in *Extramural Areas*. Vol. 5 of *Excavations at the City of David*. Edited by Donald T. Ariel. Qedem 40. Jerusalem: The Institute of Archaeology, The Hebrew University of Jerusalem, 2000.

Ariel, Donald T., and Yair Shoham. "Locally Stamped Handles and Associated Body Fragments of the Persian and Hellenistic Periods." Pages 137–71 in *Inscriptions*. Vol. 6 of *Excavations at the City of David 1978–1985*. Edited by Donald T. Ariel. Qedem 41. Jerusalem: The Institute of Archaeology, The Hebrew University of Jerusalem, 2000.

Avi-Yonah, Michael. "The Hasmonean Revolt and Judah Maccabee's War against the Syrians." Pages 147–82 in *The Hellenistic Age*. Vol. 6 of *The World History of the Jewish People*. Edited by Abraham Schalit. New Brunswick: Rutgers University, 1972.

———. *The Holy Land from the Persian to the Arab Conquests (536 B.C. to A.D. 640): A Historical Geography*. Grand Rapids: Baker, 1977.

———. "The Walls of Nehemiah: A Minimalist View." *IEJ* 4 (1954): 239–48.

Avigad, Nahman. *Discovering Jerusalem*. Nashville: Nelson, 1983.

———. "Jerusalem: The Second Temple Period." *NEAEHL* 2 (1993): 717–25.

Bar-Kochva, Bezalel. *Judas Maccabeus: The Jewish Struggle against the Seleucids*. Cambridge: Cambridge University Press, 1989.

Barkay, Gabriel, and Yitzhak Zweig. "The Temple Mount Debris Sifting Project: Preliminary Report" [Hebrew]. *NSJ* 11 (2006): 213–37.

Barrera, Julio T. "118.4Qchr." Pages 295–97 in *Qumran Cave 4.XI: Psalms to Chronicles*. Edited by Eugene Ulrich. DJD 16. Oxford: Clarendon, 2000.

Barstad, Hans M. "After the 'Myth of the Empty Land': Major Challenges in the Study of Neo-Babylonian Judah." Pages 3–20 in *Judah and the Judeans in the Neo-Babylonian Period*. Edited by Oded Lipschits and Joseph Blenkinsopp. Winona Lake, IN: Eisenbrauns, 2003.

———. *The Myth of the Empty Land: A Study in the History and Archaeology of Judah during the "Exilic" Period*. Oslo: Scandinavian University Press, 1996.

Beit-Arieh, Itzhaq. *Horvat 'Uza and Horvat Radum: Two Fortresses in the Biblical Negev*. MSIA 25. Tel Aviv: Tel Aviv University Institute of Archaeology, 2007.

Bellia, Giuseppe. "An Historico-Anthropological Reading of the Work of Ben Sira." Pages 49–78 in *The Wisdom of Ben Sira: Studies on Tradition, Redaction, and Theology*. Edited by Angelo Passaro and Giuseppe Bellia. DCLS 1. Berlin: de Gruyter, 2008.

Ben-Ami, Doron, and Yana Tchekhanovets. "The Seleucid Fortification System in the Givati Parking Lot, City of David" [Hebrew]. *New Studies in the Archaeology of Jerusalem and Its Region* 9 (2015): 313–22.

Ben Zvi, Ehud. "The Chronicler as a Historian: Building Texts." Pages 132–49 in *The Chronicler as Historian*. Edited by M. Patrick Graham, Kenneth G. Hoglund, and Steven L. McKenzie. JSNTSup 238. Sheffield: Sheffield Academic Press, 1997.

———. *History, Literature and Theology in the Book of Chronicles*. London: Equinox, 2006.

———. "A House of Treasures: The Account of Amaziah in 2 Chronicles 25; Observations and Implications." *SJOT* 22 (2008): 63–85.

———. "The List of the Levitical Cities." *JSOT* 54 (1992): 77–106.

———. "Observations on Josiah's Account in Chronicles and Implications for Reconstructing the Worldview of the Chronicler." Pages 89–106 in *Essays on Ancient Israel in Its Near Eastern Context: A Tribute to Nadav Na'aman*. Edited by Yairah Amit, Ehud Ben Zvi, Israel Finkelstein, and Oded Lipschits. Winona Lake, IN: Eisenbrauns, 2006.

Bergman, Avraham, and William F. Albright. "Soundings at the Supposed Site of Old Testament Anathoth." *BASOR* 62 (1936): 22–26.

Bergren, Theodore A. "Ezra and Nehemiah Square off in the Apocrypha and Pseudepigrapha." Pages 340–65 in *Biblical Figures Outside the Bible*. Edited by Michael E. Stone and Theodore A. Bergren. Harrisburg: Trinity Press International, 1998.

———. "Nehemiah in 2 Maccabees 1:10–2:18." *JSJ* 28 (1997): 249–70.

Berlin, Andrea. "The Pottery of Strata 8–7 (The Hellenistic Period)." Pages 5–30 in *Area E: The Finds*. Vol. 7B of *Excavations at the City of David 1978–1985 Directed by Yigal Shiloh*. By Alon De Groot and Hannah Bernick-Greenberg. Qedem 54. Jerusalem: The Institute of Archaeology, The Hebrew University of Jerusalem, 2012.

Beyer, Gustav. "Beiträge zur Territorialgeschichte von Südwestpalästina im Altertum: Festungssystem Rehabeams." *ZDPV* 54 (1931): 113–70.

Bianchi, Francesco, and Gabriele Rossoni. "L'armée d'Ozias (2 Ch 26, 11–15) entre fiction et réalité: Une esquisse philologique et historique." *Transeu* 13 (1997): 21–37.

Biran, Avraham. "On the Identification of Anathoth" [Hebrew]. *ErIsr* 18 (1985): 209–14.

Blair, Edward P. "Soundings at 'Anata (Roman Anathoth)." *BASOR* 62 (1936): 18–21.

Blenkinsopp, Joseph. *Ezra/Nehemiah: A Commentary*. Philadelphia: Westminster, 1988.

———. *Judaism: The First Phase; The Place of Ezra and Nehemiah in the Origins of Judaism*. Grand Rapids: Eerdmans, 2009.

Bliss, Frederick Jones, and Stewart R. A. Macalister. *Excavations in Palestine during the Years 1898–1900*. London: Palestine Exploration Fund, 1902.

Boda, Mark J. "Gazing through the Cloud of Incense: Davidic Dynasty and Temple Community in the Chronicler's Perspective." Pages 215–45 in *Chronicling the Chronicler: The Book of Chronicles and Early Second Temple Historiography*. Edited by Paul S. Evans and Tyler F. Williams. Winona Lake, IN: Eisenbrauns, 2013.

Böhler, Dieter. *Die heilige Stadt in Esdras α und Esra-Nehemia: Zwei Konzeptionen der Wiederherstellung Israels*. OBO 158. Fribourg: Universitätsverlag, 1997.

Boussett, Wilhelm. *Die Religion des Judentums im späthellenistischen Zeitalter*. HNT 21. Tübingen: Mohr, 1926.

Brand, Etty. "el-Haditha" [Hebrew]. *ESI* 19 (1997): 44*–46*.

———. *Salvage Excavation on the Margin of Tel Hadid, Preliminary Report*. [Hebrew]. Tel Aviv: Tel Aviv University Institute of Archaeology, 1998.

Braun, Roddy L. "1 Chronicles 1–9 and the Reconstruction of the History of Israel." Pages 92–105 in *The Chronicler as Historian*. Edited by M. Patrick Graham, Kenneth G. Hoglund, and Steven L. McKenzie. JSNTSup 238. Sheffield: Sheffield Academic Press, 1997.

———. "A Reconsideration of the Chronicler's Attitude toward the North." *JBL* 96 (1977): 59–62.
Brooke, George J. "The Books of Chronicles and the Scrolls from Qumran." Pages 35–48 in *Reflection and Refraction: Studies in Biblical Historiography in Honour of A. Graeme Auld*. Edited by Robert Rezetko, Timothy H. Lim, and W. Brian Aucker. VTSup 113. Leiden: Brill, 2007.
Broshi, Magen. "Excavations on Mount Zion, 1971–1972 (Preliminary Report)." *IEJ* 26 (1976): 81–88.
———. "Judeideh, Tell." *NEAEHL* 3 (1993): 837–38.
Broshi, Magen, and Israel Finkelstein. "The Population of Palestine in Iron Age II." *BASOR* 287 (1992): 47–60.
Broshi, Magen, and Shimon Gibson. "Excavations along the Western and Southern Walls of the Old City of Jerusalem." Pages 147–55 in *Ancient Jerusalem Revealed*. Edited by Hillel Geva. Jerusalem: Israel Exploration Society, 1994.
Bunimovitz, Shlomo, and Zvi Lederman. "The Archaeology of Border Communities: Renewed Excavations at Tel Beth-Shemesh, Part 1: The Iron Age." *NEA* 72 (2009): 114–42.
Cahill, Jane M., and David Tarler. "Excavations Directed by Yigal Shiloh at the City of David, 1978–1985." Pages 31–45 in *Ancient Jerusalem Revealed*. Edited by Hillel Geva. Jerusalem: Israel Exploration Society, 1994.
Callaway, Joseph A., and Murray B. Nicol. "A Sounding at Khirbet Hayian." *BASOR* 183 (1966): 12–19.
Campbell, Edward F. "Shechem, Tell Balatah." *NEAEHL* 4 (1993): 1345–54.
Car, David M. *The Formation of the Hebrew Bible: A New Reconstruction*. Oxford: Oxford Univerisy Press, 2011.
Carter, Charles E. *The Emergence of Yehud in the Persian Period: A Social and Demographic Study*. JSOTSup 294. Sheffield: Sheffield Academic Press, 1999.
Chen, Doron, Shlomo Margalit, and Bagil Pixner. "Mount Zion: Discovery of Iron Age Fortifications below the Gate of the Essens." Pages 76–81 in *Ancient Jerusalem Revealed*. Edited by Hillel Geva. Jerusalem: Israel Exploration Society, 1994.
Clancy, Frank. "Eupolemus the Chronographer and 141 B.C.E." *SJOT* 23 (1984): 274–81.
Clines, David J. *Ezra, Nehemiah, Esther*. Grand Rapids: Eerdmans, 1984.
Corley, Jeremy. "Searching for Structure and Redaction in Ben Sira: An Investigation of Beginnings and Endings." Pages 21–47 in *The Wisdom*

*of Ben Sira: Studies on Tradition, Redaction, and Theology*. Edited by Angelo Passaro and Giuseppe Bellia. DCLS 1. Berlin: de Gruyter, 2008.

Cotton, Hannah, and Michael Wörrle. "Seleukos IV to Heliodoros, A New Dossier of Royal Correspondence from Israel." *ZPE* 159 (2007): 191–205.

Crawford, Sidnie W. *Rewriting Scripture in Second Temple Times*. Grand Rapids: Eerdmans, 2008.

Cross, Frank M. "Aspects of Samaritan and Jewish History in Late Persian and Hellenistic Times." *HTR* 59 (1966): 201–11.

———. "The Discovery of the Samaria Papyri." *BA* 26 (1963): 110–21.

———. "A Reconstruction of the Judean Restoration." *JBL* 94 (1975): 4–18.

Crowfoot, John W., and Gerald M. Fitzgerald. *Excavations in the Tyropoeon Valley, Jerusalem 1927*. Palestine Exploration Fund Annual 5. London: Palestine Exploration Fund, 1929.

Dagan, Yehuda. "Khirbet Qeiyafa in the Judean Shephelah: Some Considerations." *TA* 36 (2009): 96–81.

———. "Results of the Survey: Settlement Patterns in the Lachish Region." Pages 2674–92 in *The Renewed Archaeological Excavations at Lachish (1973–1994)*. By David Ussishkin. Vol. 5. MSIA 22. Tel Aviv: Tel Aviv University Institute of Archaeology, 2004.

———. *The Shephelah during the Period of the Monarchy in Light of Archaeological Excavations and Surveys* [Hebrew]. MA thesis. Tel Aviv: Tel Aviv University, 1992.

———. "Tel Azekah: A New Look at the Site and Its 'Judean' Fortress." Pages 71–86 in *The Fire Signals of Lachish: Studies in the Archaeology and History of Israel in the Late Bronze Age, Iron Age and Persian Period in Honor of David Ussishkin*. Edited by Israel Finkelstein and Nadav Na'aman. Winona Lake, IN: Eisenbrauns, 2009.

Davies, Philip. *In Search of Ancient Israel*. Sheffield: JSOT Press, 1992.

Deboys, David G. "History and Theology in the Chronicler's Portrayal of Abijah." *Bib* 71 (1990): 48–62.

Demsky, Aaron. "Pelekh in Nehemiah 3." *IEJ* 33 (1983): 242–44.

Dever, William G. "Gezer." *NEAEHL* 2 (1993): 496–506.

Dinur, Uri. "Hizma." *ESI* 5 (1986): 53.

Dinur, Uri, and Nurit Feig. "Eastern Part of the Map of Jerusalem." [Hebrew] Page 339–427 in *Archaeological Survey of the Hill Country of Benjamin*. Edited by Israel Finkelstein and Yitzhak Magen. Jerusalem: Israel Antiquities Authority, 1993.

Dumbrell, William J. "The Tell El-Maskhuta Bowls and the 'Kingdom' of Qedar in the Persian Period." *BASOR* 203 (1971): 33–44.

Dušek, Jan. "Archaeology and Texts in the Persian Period: Focus on Sanballat." Pages 117–32 in *Congress Volume Helsinki 2010*. Edited by Martti Nissinen. Leiden: Brill, 2012.

Dvira (Zweig), Ittzhak, Gal Zigdon, and Lara Shilov. "Secondary Refuse Aggregates from the First and Second Temple Periods on the Eastern Slope of the Temple Mount" [Hebrew]. *NSJ* 17 (2011): 63–106.

Edelman, Diana. *The Origins of the 'Second' Temple: Persian Imperial Policy and the Rebuilding of Jerusalem*. London: Equinox, 2005.

———. "Seeing Double: Tobiah the Ammonite as an Encrypted Character." *RB* 113 (2006): 570–84.

Eisenberg, Emanuel, and David Ben-Shlomo. *The Tel Hevron 2014 Excavations: Final Report*. Ariel University Institute of Archaeology Monograph Series 1. Ariel: Ariel University Press, 2017.

Eisenberg, Emanuel, and Alla Nagorski. "Tel Hevron (er-Rumeidi)." *Hadashot Arkheologiyot/ESI* 114 (2002): 91–92.

Elliger, Karl. "Studien aus dem Deutschen Evang. Institut für Altertumswissenschaft des Heiligen Landes. 44. Die Heimat des Propheten Micha." *ZDPV* 57 (1934): 81–152.

Ephal, Israel. *The Ancient Arabs: Nomads on the Borders of the Fertile Crescent Ninth–Fifth Centuries B.C.* Jerusalem: Magnes, 1982.

Eshel, Hanan. "Jerusalem under Persian Rule: The City's Layout and the Historical Background." Page 327–44 in *The History of Jerusalem: The Biblical Period* [Hebrew]. Edited by Shmuel Ahituv and Amihai Mazar. Jerusalem: Yad Ben-Zvi, 2000.

———. "The Late Iron Age Cemetery of Gibeon." *IEJ* 37 (1987): 1–17.

Eskenazi, Tamara C. "Tobiah." *ABD* 6:584–85.

Faigenbaum-Golovin, Shira, Arie Shaus, Barak Sober, David Levin, Nadav Na'aman, Benjamin Sass, Eli Turkel, Eli Piasetzky, and Israel Finkelstein. "Algorithmic Handwriting Analysis of Judahite Military Correspondence Sheds Light on Composition of Biblical Texts." *Proceedings of the National Academy of Sciences* 113 (2016): 4664–69.

Fantalkin, Alexander, and Israel Finkelstein. "The Date of Abandonment and Territorial Affiliation of Khirbet Qeiyafa: An Update." *TA* 44 (2017): 53–60.

———. "The Sheshonq I Campaign and the Eighth Century B.C.E. Earthquake—More on the Archaeology and History of the South in the Iron I–IIA." *TA* 33 (2006): 18–42.

Fantalkin, Alexander, and Oren Tal. "The Persian and Hellenistic Pottery of Level I." Pages 2174–94 in *The Renewed Archaeological Excavations at Lachish (1973–1994)*. By David Ussishkin. MSIA 22. Tel Aviv: Tel Aviv University Institute of Archaeology, 2004.

Farès-Drappeau, Saba. *Dédan et Liḥyān: Histoire des Arabes aux confins des pouvoirs perse et hellénistique (IVe–IIe s. avant l'ère chrétienne)*. TMO 42. Lyon: Maison de l'Orient, 2005.

Feldstein, Amir. "Lod, Neve Yaraq (B)." *ESI* 19 (1997): 50*.

Feldstein, Amir, Giora Kidron, Nizan Hanin, Yair Kamaisky, and David Eitam. "Southern Part of the Maps of Ramallah and el-Bireh and Northern Part of the Map of 'Ein Kerem" [Hebrew]. Pages 133–264 in *Archaeological Survey of the Hill Country of Benjamin*. Edited by Israel Finkelstein and Yitzhak Magen. Jerusalem: Israel Antiquities Authority, 1993.

Finkelstein, Israel. "Archaeology and the List of Returnees in the Books of Ezra and Nehemiah." *PEQ* 140 (2008): 7–15.

———. "Archaeology as High Court in Ancient Israelite History: A Reply to Nadav Na'aman." *JHS* 10 (2010): art. 19.

———. "Ethno-historical Background: Land Use and Demography in Recent Generations." Pages 121–24 in *Highlands of Many Cultures: The Southern Samaria Survey*. Edited by Israel Finkelstein, Zvi Lederman, and Shlomo Bunimovitz. MSIA 14. Tel Aviv: Tel Aviv University Institute of Archaeology, 1997.

———. "The Expansion of Judah in II Chronicles: Territorial Legitimation for the Hasmoneans?" *ZAW* 127 (2015): 669–95.

———. "A Few Notes on Demographic Data from Recent Generations and Ethno-archaeology." *PEQ* 122 (1990): 47–52.

———. "The Historical Reality behind the Genealogical Lists in 1 Chronicles." *JBL* 131 (2012): 65–83.

———. "Jerusalem in the Persian (and Early Hellenistic) Period and the Wall of Nehemiah." *JSOT* 32 (2008): 501–20.

———. "Major Saviors, Minor Judges: The Historical Background of the Northern Accounts in the Book of Judges." *JSOT* 41 (2017): 431–49.

———. "Methods of the Field Survey and Data Recording." Pages 11–24 in *Highlands of Many Cultures, the Southern Samaria Survey*. Edited by Israel Finkelstein, Zvi Lederman, and Shlomo Bunimovitz. MSIA 14. Tel Aviv: Tel Aviv University Institute of Archaeology, 1997.

———. "Nehemiah's Adversaries: A Hasmonaean Reality." *Transeu* 47 (2015): 47–55.

———. "Penelope's Shroud Unraveled: Iron II Date of Gezer's Outer Wall Established." *TA* 21 (1994): 276–82.

———. "Persian Period Jerusalem and Yehud: A Rejoinder." *JHS* 9 (2009): art. 24.

———. "Rehoboam's Fortresses Cities (II Chr 11, 5–12): A Hasmonean Reality." *ZAW* 123 (2011): 92–107.

———. "The Rise of Jerusalem and Judah: The Missing Link." *Levant* 33 (2001): 105–15.

———. "Tell el-Ful Revisited: The Assyrian and Hellenistic Periods (With a New Identification)." *PEQ* 143 (2011): 106–18.

———. "The Territorial Extent and Demography of Yehud/Judea in the Persian and Early Hellenistic Periods." *RB* 117 (2010): 39–54.

Finkelstein, Israel, and Alexander Fantalkin. "Khirbet Qeiyafa: An Unsensational Archaeological and Historical Interpretation." *TA* 39 (2012): 38–63.

Finkelstein, Israel, Ze'ev Herzog, Lily Singer-Avitz, and David Ussishkin. "Has King David's Palace Been Found in Jerusalem?" *TA* 34 (2007): 142–64.

Finkelstein, Israel, Ido Koch, and Oded Lipschits. "The Mound on the Mount: A Solution to the 'Problem with Jerusalem'?" *JHS* 11 (2011): art. 12.

Finkelstein, Israel, Zvi Lederman, and Shlomo Bunimovitz, eds. *Highlands of Many Cultures: The Southern Samaria Survey*. MSIA 14. Tel Aviv: Tel Aviv University Institute of Archaeology, 1997.

Finkelstein, Israel, and Yitzhak Magen, eds. *Archaeological Survey of the Hill Country of Benjamin*. Jerusalem: Israel Antiquities Authority, 1993.

Finkelstein, Israel, and Nadav Na'aman. "The Judahite Shephelah in the Late Eighth and Early Seventh Centuries B.C.E." *TA* 31 (2004): 60–79.

———. "Shechem of the Amarna Period and the Rise of the Northern Kingdom of Israel." *IEJ* 55 (2005): 172–93.

Finkelstein, Israel, and Eli Piasetzky. "The Iron I/IIA Transition in the Levant: A New Perspective." *Radiocarbon* 52 (2010): 1667–80.

———. "Radiocarbon-Dated Destruction Layers: A Skeleton for Iron Age Chronology in the Levant." *OJA* 28 (2009): 255–74.

———. "Radiocarbon Dating Khirbet Qeiyafa and the Iron I–IIA Phases in the Shephelah: Methodological Comments and a Bayesian Model." *Radiocarbon* 57 (2015): 891–907.

———. "Radiocarbon Dating the Iron Age in the Levant: A Bayesian Model for Six Ceramic Phases and Six Transitions." *Antiquity* 84 (2010): 374–85.

Finkelstein, Israel, Thomas Römer, Christoph Nicolle, Zachary C. Dunseth, Assaf Kleiman, Juliette Mas and Noami Porat. "Excavations at Kiriath-Jearim Near Jerusalem, 2017: Preliminary Report." *Semitica* 60 (2018): 31–83.

Finkelstein, Israel, and Benjamin Sass. "The West Semitic Alphabetic Inscriptions, Late Bronze II to Iron IIA: Archeological Context, Distribution and Chronology." *HeBAI* 2 (2013): 149–220.

Finkelstein, Israel, and Lily Singer-Avitz. "Reevaluating Bethel." *ZDPV* 125 (2009): 33–48.

Fischer, Moshe, Israel Roll, and Oren Tal. "Persian and Hellenistic Remains at Tel Yaoz." *TA* 35 (2008): 123–63.

Fritz, Volkmar. "The 'List of Rehoboam's Fortresses' in 2 Chr 11:5–12—A Document from the Time of Josiah." *ErIsr* 15 (1981): 46*–53*.

Funk, Robert W. "Beth-Zur." *NEAEHL* 1 (1993): 259–61.

———. "The History of Beth-Zur with Reference to Its Defenses." Pages 4–17 in *The 1957 Excavation at Beth-Zur*. By Orvid R. Sellers, Robert W. Funk, John L. McKenzie, Paul Lapp, and Nancy Lapp. AASOR 38. Cambridge: American School of Oriental Research, 1968.

Galil, Gershon. "Pirathon, Parathon and Timnatha." *ZDPV* 109 (1993): 49–53.

Galling, Kurt. *Die Bücher der Chronik, Esra, Nehemia*. ATD 12. Göttingen: Vandenhoeck & Ruprecht, 1954.

———. "The 'Gōlā-List' according to Ezra 2 // Nehemiah 7." *JBL* 70 (1951): 149–58.

Garfinkel, Yosef. "2 Chr 11:5–10 Fortified Cities List and the Lmlk Stamps—Reply to Nadav Na'aman." *BASOR* 271 (1988): 69–73.

Garfinkel, Yosef, and Saar Ganor. *Excavation Report 2007–2008*. Vol. 1 of *Khirbet Qeiyafa*. Jerusalem: Israel Exploration Society, 2009.

Garfinkel, Yosef, Katharina Streit, Saar Ganor, and Paula J. Reimer. "King David's City at Khirbet Qeiyafa: Results of the Second Radiocarbon Dating Project." *Radiocarbon* 57 (2015): 881–90.

Gera, Dov. *Judaea and Mediterranean Politics 219 to 161 B.C.E.* Brill's Series in Jewish Studies 8. Leiden: Brill, 1998.

Geva, Hillel. "Excavations at the Citadel of Jerusalem, 1976–1980." Pages 156–67 in *Ancient Jerusalem Revealed*. Edited by Hillel Geva. Jerusalem: Israel Exploration Society, 1994.

———. "Excavations in the Citadel of Jerusalem, 1979–1980: Preliminary Report." *IEJ* 33 (1983): 55–71.

———. "The 'First Wall' of Jerusalem during the Second Temple Period— An Architectural-Chronological Note" [Hebrew]. *ErIsr* 18 (1985): 21–39.

———. "General Introduction to the Excavations in the Jewish Quarter." Pages 1–31 in *Jewish Quarter Excavations in the Old City of Jerusalem*. Vol. 1. Edited by Hillel Geva. Jerusalem: Israel Exploration Society, 2000.

———. "Jerusalem's Population in Antiquity: A Minimalist View." *TA* 41 (2014): 131–60.

———. "Summary and Discussion of Findings from Areas A, W and X-2." Pages 505–18 in *Jewish Quarter Excavations in the Old City of Jerusalem*. Edited by Hillel Geva. Vol. 2. Jerusalem: Israel Exploration Society, 2003.

———. "The Western Boundary of Jerusalem at the End of the Monarchy." *IEJ* 29 (1979): 84–91.

———. "Western Jerusalem at the End of the First Temple Period in Light of the Excavations in the Jewish Quarter." Pages 183–208 in *Jerusalem in the Bible and Archaeology: The First Temple Period*. Edited by Andrew G. Vaughn and Ann E. Killebrew. SymS 18. Atlanta: Society of Biblical Literature, 2003.

Gibson, Shimon. "The 1961–67 Excavations in the Armenian Garden, Jerusalem." *PEQ* 119 (1987): 81–96.

———. "The Tell ej-Judeideh (Tel Goded) Excavation: A Re-appraisel Based on Archival Rechords in the Palestine Exploration Fund." *TA* 21 (1994): 194–234.

Gichon, Mordechai. "The System of Fortifications in the Kingdom of Judah" [Hebrew]. Pages 410–25 in *The Military History of the Land of Israel in Biblical Times*. Edited by Jacob Liver. Tel Aviv: Maarachot, 1964.

Goldstein, Jonathan A. *1 Maccabees: A New Translation with Introduction and Commentary*. AB 41. Garden City: Doubleday, 1976.

———. "The Tales of the Tobiads." Pages 85–123 in *Christianity, Judaism and Other Greco-Roman Cults: Studies for Morton Smith at 60*. Edited by Jacob Neusner. SJLA 12. Leiden: Brill, 1975.

Gophna, Ram, and Itzhak Beit-Arieh. *Archaeological Survey of Israel: Map of Lod (80)*. Jerusalem: Israel Antiquities Authority, 1997.

Gophna, Ram, and Yosef Porat. "The Land of Ephraim and Manasseh" [Hebrew]. Page 196–241 in *Judaea, Samaria and the Golan, Archaeological Survey 1967–1968*. Edited by Mosheh Kochavi. Jerusalem: Carta, 1972.

Gophna, Ram, Itamar Taxel, and Amir Feldstein. "A New Identification of Ancient Ono." *BAIAS* 23 (2005): 167–76.

Goren, Yuval. "Scientific Examination of a Seleucid Limestone Stele." *ZPE* 159 (2007): 206–16.

Grabbe, Lester L. *Ezra-Nehemiah*. London: Routledge, 1998.

———. "Josephus and the Reconstruction of the Judean Restoration." *JBL* 106 (1987): 231–46.

———, ed. *Leading Captivity Captive: "The Exile" as History and Ideology*. JSOTSup 278. Sheffield: Sheffield Academic Press, 1998.

Graham, Patrick M. *The Utilization of 1 and 2 Chronicles in the Reconstruction of Israelite History in the Nineteenth Century*. SBLDS 116. Atlanta: Scholars Press, 1990.

Grätz, Sebastian. "The Adversaries in Ezra/Nehemiah—Fictitious or Real?" *Between Cooperation and Hostility: Multiple Identities in Ancient Judaism and the Interaction with Foreign Powers*. Edited by Rainer Albertz and Jakob Wöhrle. JAJSup 11. Göttingen: Vandenhoeck & Ruprecht, 2013.

Greenhut, Zvi, and Alon De Groot. *Salvage Excavations at Tel Moza: The Bronze and Iron Age Settlements and Later Occupations*. IAA Reports 39. Jerusalem: Israel Antiquities Authority, 2009.

De Groot, Alon. "Discussion and Conclusions." Pages 173–79 in *Area E: Stratigraphy and Architecture Text*. Vol. 7A of *Excavations at the City of David 1978–1985 Directed by Yigal Shiloh*. By Alon De Groot and Hannah Bernick-Greenberg. Qedem 53. Jerusalem: The Institute of Archaeology, The Hebrew University of Jerusalem, 2012.

———. "Jerusalem during the Persian Period" [Hebrew]. *NSJ* 7 (2001): 77–82.

———. "Jerusalem in the Early Hellenistic Period" [Hebrew]. *NSJ* 10 (2004): 67–70.

De Groot, Alon, David Cohen, and Arza Caspi. "Area A1." Pages 1–29 in *Stratigraphic, Environmental, and Other Reports*. Vol. 3 of *Excavations at the City of David 1978–1985*. Edited by Alan De Groot and Donald T. Ariel. Qedem 33. Jerusalem: The Institute of Archaeology, The Hebrew University of Jerusalem, 1992.

Halpern, Baruch. "Sacred History and Ideology: Chronicles' Thematic Structure—Identification of an Earlier Source." Pages 35–54 in *The Creation of Sacred Literature: Composition and Redaction of the Biblical Text*. Edited by Richard E. Friedman. Near Eastern Studies 22. Berkeley: University of California, 1981.

Hermann, Siegfried. "The So-Called 'Fortress System of Rehoboam', 2 Chron. 11:5–12: Theoretical Considerations." *ErIsr* 20 (1989): 72*–78*.

Herzog, Ze'ev, and Lily Singer-Avitz. "Redefining the Centre: The Emergence of State in Judah." *TA* 31 (2004): 209–44.

Hobbs, T. R. "The 'Fortresses of Rehoboam': Another Look." Pages 41–64 in *Uncovering Ancient Stones: Essays in Memory of H. Neil Richardson*. Edited by Lewis M. Hopfe. Winona Lake, IN: Eisenbrauns, 1994.

Hoglund, Kenneth G. *Achaemenid Imperial Administration in Syria-Palestine and the Missions of Ezra and Nehemiah*. SBLDS 125. Atlanta: Scholars Press, 1992.

Horsley, Richard A. "The Expansion of Hasmonean Rule in Idumea and Galilee: Toward a Historical Sociology." Pages 134–65 in *Second Temple Studies III: Studies in Politics, Class and Material Culture*. Edited by Philip R. Davies and John M. Halligan. JSOTSup 340. Sheffield: Sheffield Academic Press, 2002.

Japhet, Sara. *I and II Chronicles: A Commentary*. London: SCM, 1993.

———. "The Historical Reliability of Chronicles: The History of the Problem and Its Place in Biblical Research." *JSOT* 33 (1985): 83–107.

———. *The Ideology of the Book of Chronicles and Its Place in Biblical Thought*. BEATAJ 9. Frankfurt am Main: Lang, 1997.

———. "The Supposed Common Authorship of Chronicles and Ezra-Nehemiah Investigated Anew." *VT* 18 (1968): 330–71.

Johnson, Marshall D. *The Purpose of the Biblical Genealogies*. SNTSMS 8. Cambridge: Cambridge University Press, 1969.

Jones, Gwilym H. "From Abijam to Abijah." *ZAW* 106 (1994): 420–34.

Junge, Ehrhard. *Der Wiederaufbau des Heerwesens des Reiches Juda unter Josia*. BWANT 23. Stuttgart: Kohlhammer, 1937.

Kahana, Avraham. *Hasfarim Hahitzoniim II* [Hebrew]. Tel Aviv: Massada, 1960.

Kalimi, Isaac. *An Ancient Israelite Historian: Studies in the Chronicler, His Time, Place and Writing*. SSN 46. Assen: Van Gorcum, 2005.

———. "History of Interpretation the Book of Chronicles in Jewish Tradition from Daniel to Spinoza." *RB* 105 (1998): 5–41.

Kallai, Zechariah. "The Kingdom of Rehoboam" [Hebrew]. *ErIsr* 10 (1971): 245–54.

———. "The Land of Benjamin and Mt. Ephraim" [Hebrew]. Page 153–92 in *Judaea, Samaria and the Golan: Archaeological Survey 1967–1968*. Edited by Mosheh Kochavi. Jerusalem: Carta, 1972.

———. *The Northern Boundaries of Judah* [Hebrew]. Jerusalem: Magnes, 1960.

Kasher, Aryeh. "The Hasmonean Kingdom" [Hebrew]. Page 243–79 in *The Hasmonean State: The History of the Hasmoneans during the Hellenistic Period*. Edited by Uriel Rappaport and Israel Ronen. Jerusalem: Yad Ben-Zvi, 1993.

———. "Some Suggestions and Comments Concerning Alexander Macedon's Campaign in Palestine" [Hebrew]. *Beit Miqra* 20 (1975): 187–208.

Katz, Haya. "A Note on the Date of the 'Great Wall' of Tell en-Nasbeh." *TA* 25 (1998): 131–33.

Kegler, Jürgen. "Prophetengestalten im Deuteronomistischen Geschichtswerk und in den Chronikbüchern: Ein Beitrag zur Kompositions- und Redaktionsgeschichte der Chronikbücher." *ZAW* 105 (1993): 481–97.

Kellermann, Ulrich. "Anmerkungen zum Verständnis der Tora in den chronistischen Schriften." *BN* 42 (1988): 49–92.

———. *Nehemia: Quellen Überlieferung und Geschichte*. BZAW 102. Berlin: Töpelmann, 1967.

Kelly, Brian E. "Manasseh in the Books of Kings and Chronicles (2 Kings 21:1–18; 2 Chron 33:1–20)." Pages 131–46 in *Windows into Old Testament History: Evidence, Argument, and the Crisis of "Biblical Israel."* Edited by V. Philips Long, David W. Baker, and Gordan J. Wenham. Grand Rapids: Eerdmans, 2002.

Kelso, James L. *The Excavation of Bethel (1934–1960)*. AASOR 39. Cambridge: American Schools of Oriental Research, 1968.

Kennett, Robert H. *Old Testament Essays*. Cambridge: Cambridge University Press, 1928.

Kenyon, Kathleen M. *Digging Up Jerusalem*. London: Ernest Benn, 1974.

———. "Excavations in Jerusalem, 1963." *PEQ* 96 (1964): 7–18.

———. "Excavations in Jerusalem, 1964." *PEQ* 97 (1965): 9–20.

———. "Excavations in Jerusalem, 1965." *PEQ* 98 (1966): 73-88.

———. *Jerusalem: Excavating Three Thousand Years of History*. London: Thames & Hudson, 1967.

Khalaily, Hamoudi, and Avi Gopher. "Lod." *ESI* 19 (1997): 51*.

King, Philip J., and Lawrence E. Stager. *Life in Biblical Israel*. Louisville: Westminster, 2001.
Klausner, Joseph. "John Hyrcanus I." Pages 211–21 in *The Hellenistic Age*. Vol. 6 of *The World History of the Jewish People*. Edited by Abraham Schalit. New Brunswick: Rutgers University, 1972.
Klein, Ralph W. *1 Chronicles: A Commentary*. Minneapolis: Fortress, 2006.
———. *2 Chronicles: A Commentary*. Minneapolis: Fortress, 2012.
———. "Abijah's Campaign against the North (II Chr 13)—What Were the Chronicler's Sources?" *ZAW* 95 (1983): 210–17.
———. "Reflections on Historiography in the Account of Jehoshaphat." Pages 643–58 in *Pomegranates and Golden Bells: Studies in Biblical, Jewish, and Near Eastern Ritual, Law, and Literature in Honor of Jacob Milgrom*. Edited by David P. Wright, David Noel Freedman and Avi Hurvitz. Winona Lake, IN: Eisenbrauns, 1995.
Kletter, Raz. "Pots and Polities: Material Remains of Late Iron Age Judah in Relation to Its Political Borders." *BASOR* 314 (1999): 19–54.
Kloner, Amos. *Archaeological Survey of Israel, Survey of Jerusalem: The Northwestern Sector, Introduction and Indices*. Jerusalem: Israel Antiquities Authority, 2003.
———. "Jerusalem's Environs in the Persian Period" [Hebrew]. *NSJ* 7 (2001): 91–96.
———. *Maresha Excavations Final Report I: Subterranean Complexes 21, 44, 70*. IAA Reports 17. Jerusalem: Israel Antiquities Authority, 2003.
Knauf, Axel E. *Ismael: Untersuchungen zur Geschichte Palastinas und nordarabiens im 1. Jahrtausend v. Chr*. Wiesbaden: Harrassowitz Verlage, 1989.
———. "Jerusalem in the Late Bronze and Early Iron Ages: A Proposal." *TA* 27 (2000): 75–90.
———. "Pireathon–Ferata." *BN* 51 (1990): 19–24.
Knoppers, Gary N. *I Chronicles 1–9: A New Translation with Introduction and Commentary*. AB 12. New York: Doubleday, 2004.
———. "Intermarriage, Social Complexity, and Ethnic Diversity in the Genealogy of Judah." *JBL* 120 (2001): 15–30.
———. "Israel or Judah? The Shifting Body Politic and Collective Identity in Chronicles." Pages 173–88 in *Rethinking Israel: Studies in the History and Archaeology of Ancient Israel in Honor of Israel Finkelstein*. Edited by Oded Lipschits, Yuval Gadot, and Matthew J. Adams. Winona Lake, IN: Eisenbrauns, 2017.

———. "Reform and Regression: The Chronicler's Presentation of Jehoshaphat." *Bib* 72 (1991): 500–24.

———. "Rehoboam in Chronicles: Villain or Victim?" *JBL* 109 (1990): 423–40.

Koch, Ido. "The Geopolitical Organization of the Judean Shephelah during the Iron Age I–IIA (1150–800 B.C.E.)" [Hebrew]. *Cathedra* 143 (2012): 45–64.

Kochavi, Moshe. "The Land of Judah" [Hebrew]. Page 19–89 in *Judea, Samaria and the Golan, Archaeological Survey 1967–1968*. Edited by Moshe Kochavi. Jerusalem: Carta, 1972.

Kofoed, Jens B. *Text and History: Historiography and the Study of the Biblical Text*. Winona Lake, IN: Eisenbrauns, 2005.

Kohut, Alexander. *Aruch Completum*. Vienna: Hebräischer Verlag Menorah, 1926.

Konkel, August H. *Hezekiah in Biblical Tradition*. Ann Arbor: University Microfilms International, 1989.

Kratz, Reinhard G. *The Composition of the Narrative Books of the Old Testament*. London: T&T Clark, 2005.

———. "Rewriting Torah in the Hebrew Bible and the Dead Sea Scrolls." Pages 273–92 in *Wisdom and Torah: The Reception of "Torah" in the Wisdom Literature of the Second Temple Period*. Edited by Bernd Ulrich Schipper and D. Andrew Teeter. JSJSup 163. Leiden: Brill, 2013.

Lapp, Paul W. "Bethel Pottery of the Late Hellenistic and Early Roman Periods." Pages 77–80 in *The Excavation of Bethel (1934–1960)*. By James Leon Kelso. AASOR 39. Cambridge: American Schools of Oriental Research, 1968.

———. "The Excavation of Field II." Pages 26–34 in *The 1957 Excavation at Beth-Zur*. By Orvid R. Sellers, Robert W. Funk, John L. McKenzie, Paul W. Lapp, and Nancy Lapp. AASOR 38. Cambridge: American Schools of Oriental Research, 1968.

Lapp, Paul W., and Nancy Lapp. "Iron II—Hellenistic Pottery Groups." Pages 54–79 in *The 1957 Excavation at Beth-Zur*. By Orvid R. Sellers, Robert W. Funk, John L. McKenzie, Paul W. Lapp, and Nancy Lapp. AASOR 38. Cambridge: American Schools of Oriental Research, 1968.

Lee-Sak, Itzhak. "The Lists of Levitical Cities (Joshua 21, 1 Chronicles 6) and the Propagandistic Map for the Hasmonean Territorial Expansion." *JBL* 136 (2017): 783–800.

Lehmann, Gunnar, Michael H. Niemann, and Wolfgang Zwickel. "Zora und Eschtaol." *UF* 28 (1996): 343–442.

Lemaire, André. *Les ostraca hébreux de l'époque royale israélite.* PhD thesis. Paris: Université de Paris, 1973.
Levin, Yigal. "Who Was the Chronicler's Audience? A Hint from His Genealogies." *JBL* 122 (2003): 229–45.
Lipschits, Oded. "Achaemenid Imperial Policy, Settlement Processes in Palestine, and the Status of Jerusalem in the Middle of the Fifth Century B.C.E." Pages 19–52 in *Judah and the Judeans in the Persian Period.* Edited by Oded Lipschits and Manfred Oeming. Winona Lake, IN: Eisenbrauns, 2006.
———. "Bethel Revisited." Pages 233–46 in *Rethinking Israel: Studies in the History and Archaeology of Ancient Israel in Honor of Israel Finkelstein.* Edited by Oded Lipschits, Yuval Gadot, and Matthew J. Adams. Winona Lake, IN: Eisenbrauns, 2017.
———. "Demographic Changes in Judah between the Seventh and the Fifth Centuries B.C.E." Pages 323–76 in Pages 3–20 in *Judah and the Judeans in the Neo-Babylonian Period.* Edited by Oded Lipschits and Joseph Blenkinsopp. Winona Lake, IN: Eisenbrauns, 2003.
———. *The Fall and Rise of Jerusalem: Judah under Babylonian Rule.* Winona Lake, IN: Eisenbrauns, 2005.
———. "The History of the Benjaminite Region under Babylonian Rule" [Hebrew]. *Zion* 64 (1999): 2878–291.
———. "Nehemiah 3: Sources, Composition and Purpose." Pages 73–100 in *New Perspectives on Ezra-Nehemiah: History and Historiography, Text, Literature, and Interpretation.* Edited by Isaac Kalimi. Winona Lake, IN: Eisenbrauns, 2012.
———. "Persian Period Finds from Jerusalem: Facts and Interpretations." *JHS* 9 (2009): art. 20.
———. *The 'Yehud' Province under Babylonian Rule (586–539 B.C.E.): Historic Reality and Historiographic Conceptions* [Hebrew]. PhD thesis. Tel Aviv: Tel Aviv University, 1997.
Lipschits, Oded, Yuval Gadot, and Manfred Oeming. "Tel Azekah 113 Years After: Preliminary Evaluation of the Renewed Excavations at the Site." *NEA* 75 (2012): 196–206.
Lipschits, Oded, and David S. Vanderhooft. *The Yehud Stamp Impressions: A Corpus of Inscribed Impressions from the Persian and Hellenistic Periods in Judah.* Winona Lake, IN: Eisenbrauns, 2011.
———. "Yehud Stamp Impressions: History of Discovery and Newly-Published Impressions." *TA* 34 (2007): 3–11.

Lods, Adolphe. *Israel: From Its Beginning to the Middle of the Eight Century.* New York: Knopf, 1932.

Macalister, Robert A. S., and John G. Duncan. *Excavation on the Hill of Ophel, Jerusalem, 1923-1925.* Palestine Exploration Fund Annual 4. London: Palestine Exploration Fund, 1926.

Maeir, Aren M. "The Historical Background and Dating of Amos VI 2: An Archaeological Perspective from Tell Es-Safi/Gath." *VT* 54 (2004): 319-34.

Magen, Yitzhak. *A Temple City.* Vol. 2 of *Mount Gerizim Excavations.* Jerusalem: Israel Antiquities Authority, 2008.

Magen, Yitzhak, Haggai Misgav, and Levana Tsfania. *The Aramaic, Hebrew and Samaritan Inscriptions.* Vol. 1 of *Mount Gerizim Excavations.* Jerusalem: Israel Antiquities Authority, 2004.

Marböck, Johannes. "Structure and Redaction History in the Book of Ben Sira Review and Proposals." Pages 61-79 in *The Book of Ben Sira in Modern Research.* Edited by Pancratius Cornelis Beentjes. BZAW 255. Berlin: de Gruyter, 1997.

Mazar, Amihai. "The Excavations of Khirbet Abu et-Twein and the System of Iron Age Fortresses in Judah" [Hebrew]. *ErIsr* 15 (1981): 229-49.

Mazar, Amihai, and Christopher Bronk Ramsey. "$^{14}$C Dates and the Iron Age Chronology of Israel: A Response." *Radiocarbon* 50 (2008): 159-80.

Mazar, Benjamin. "The Excavations in the Old City of Jerusalem near the Temple Mount—Second Preliminary Report, 1969-1970 Seasons" [Hebrew]. *ErIsr* 10 (1971): 1-34.

———. "The Tobiads." *IEJ* 7 (1957): 137-45.

Mazar, Benjamin, and Hanan Eshel. "Who Built the First Wall of Jerusalem?" *IEJ* 48 (1998): 265-68.

Mazar, Eilat. *The Excavations in the City of David, 2005* [Hebrew]. Jerusalem: Shoham, 2007.

———. *Preliminary Report on The City of David Excavations 2005 at the Visitors Center Area* [Hebrew]. Jerusalem: Shoham Academic Research and Publication, 2007.

———. *The Summit of the City of David: Excavations 2005-2008.* Jerusalem: Shoham Academic Research and Publication, 2015.

Mazar, Eilat, and Benjamin Mazar. *Excavations in the South of the Temple Mount: The Ophel of Biblical Jerusalem.* Qedem 29. Jerusalem: The Institute of Archaeology, The Hebrew University of Jerusalem, 1989.

McKenzie, Steven L. *1-2 Chronicles.* Nashville: Abingdon, 2004.

———. "The Chronicler as Redactor." Pages 70–90 in *The Chronicler as Author*. Edited by M. Patrick Graham and Steven L. McKenzie. JSOTSup 263. Sheffield: Sheffield Academic Press, 1999.

———. *The Chronicler's Use of the Deuteronomistic History*. HSM 33. Atlanta: Scholars Press, 1984.

———. "The Trouble with King Jehoshaphat." Pages 299–314 in *Reflection and Refraction: Studies in Biblical Historiography in Honour of A. Graeme Auld*. Edited by Robert Rezetko, Timothy H. Lim, and W. Brian Aucker. VTSup 113. Leiden: Brill, 2007.

Mendels, Doron. *The Land of Israel as a Political Concept in Hasmonean Literature: Recourse to History in Second Century B.C. Claims to the Holy Land*. TSAJ 15. Tübingen: Mohr, 1987.

———. *The Rise and Fall of Jewish Nationalism*. New York: Doubleday, 1992.

Meyers, Carol L., and Eric M. Meyers. *Haggai, Zechariah 1–8*. AB 25B. Garden City: Doubleday, 1987.

Michaeli, Frank. *Les Livres des Chroniques, d'Esdras et de Néhémie*. Commentaire de l'Ancien Testament 16. Paris: Delachaux, 1967.

Miller, Maxwell J. "Rehoboam's Cities of Defense and the Levitical City List." Pages 273–86 in *Archaeology and Biblical Interpretation: Essays in Memory of D. Glenn Rose*. Edited by Leo G. Perdue, Lawrence E. Toombs, and Gary Lance Johnson. Atlanta: John Knox, 1987.

Mittman, Siegried. "Hiskia und die Philister." *JNSL* 16 (1990): 91–106.

———. "Tobia, Sanballat und die persische Provinz Juda." *JNSL* 26.2 (2000): 1–49.

Möller, Christa, and Gotz Schmitt. *Siedlungen Palästinas nach Flavius Josephus*. Wiesbaden: Reichert, 1976.

Mowinckel, Sigmund. *Studien zu dem Buche Ezra-Nehemia*. Oslo: Universitetsforlaget, 1964.

Myers, Jacob M. *Ezra Nehemiah*. AB 14. Garden City: Doubleday, 1965.

Na'aman, Nadav. *Borders and Districts in Biblical Historiography*. Jerusalem: Simor, 1986.

———. "Does Archaeology Really Deserve the Status of a 'High Court' in Biblical Historical Research?" Pages 165–84 in *Between Evidence and Ideology: Essays on the History of Ancient Israel Read at the Joint Meeting of the Society for Old Testament Study and the Oud Testamentisch Werkgezelschap, Lincoln, July 2009*. Edited by Bob Becking and Lester L. Grabbe. OtSt 59. Leiden: Brill, 2010.

———. "Hezekiah and the Kings of Assyria." *TA* 21 (1994): 235–54.

———. "Hezekiah's Fortified Cities and the *LMLK* Stamps." *BASOR* 261 (1986): 5–21.
———. "The Inheritance of the Sons of Simeon." *ZDPV* 96 (1980): 136–52.
———. "The Jacob Story and the Formation of Biblical Israel." *TA* 41 (2014): 95–125.
———. "Khirbet Qeiyafa in Context." *UF* 42 (2010): 497–526.
———. "The Kingdom of Judah under Josiah." *TA* 18 (1991): 3–71.
———. "Pirathon and Ophrah." *BN* 50 (1989): 11–16.
———. "Sources and Redaction in the Chronicler's Genealogies of Asher and Ephraim." *JSOT* 49 (1991): 99–111.
———. "Text and Archaeology in a Period of Great Decline: The Contribution of the Amarna Letters to the Debate on the Historicity of Nehemiah's Wall." Pages 20–30 in *The Historian and the Bible: Essays in Honour of Lester L. Grabbe*. Edited by Philip R. Davies and Diana Vikander Edelman. New York: T&T Clark, 2010.
———. "Was Khirbet Qeiyafa a Judahite City? The Case Against It." *JHS* 17 (2017): art. 7.
Na'aman, Nadav, and Ran Zadok. "Assyrian Deportations to the Province of Samaria in the Light of the Two Cuneiform Tablets from Tel Hadid." *TA* 27 (2000): 159–88.
Nagorsky, A. "Tel Hadid." *ESI* 117 (2005). http://www.hadashot-esi.org.il/report_detail_eng.aspx?id=173&mag_id=110.
Nashef, Khaled. "Khirbet Birzeit 1996, 1998–1999: Preliminary Report." *Journal of Palestinian Archaeology* 1 (2000): 25–27.
Netzer, Ehud. *Hasmonean and Herodian Palaces at Jericho I*. Jerusalem: Israel Exploration Society, 2001.
North, Robert S. "Does Archaeology Prove Chronicle's Sources?" Pages 375–401 in *A Light unto My Path: Studies in Honor of J. M. Meyers*. Edited by Howard N. Bream, Ralph Daniel Heim, and Carey A. Moore. Gettysburg Theological Studies 4. Philadelphia: Temple University Press, 1974.
Noth, Martin. "Eine palästinische Lokalüberlieferung in 2 Chr. 20." *ZDPV* 67 (1945): 45–71.
———. *The Chronicler's History*. JSOTSup 50. Sheffield: Sheffield Academic Press, 1987.
Oeming, Manfred. *Das wahre Israel: Die "genealogische Vorhalle" 1 Chronik 1–9*. BWANT 8. Stuttgart: Kohlhammer, 1990.
———. "Rethinking the Origins of Israel: 1 Chronicles 1–9 in the Light of Archaeology." Pages 303–18 in *Rethinking Israel: Studies in the History*

*and Archaeology of Ancient Israel in Honor of Israel Finkelstein.* Edited by Oded Lipschits, Yuval Gadot, and Matthew J. Adams. Winona Lake, IN: Eisenbrauns, 2017.

Ofer, Avi. "Hebron." *NEAEHL* 2 (1993): 606–9.

———. *The Highland of Judah during the Biblical Period* [Hebrew]. PhD thesis, Tel Aviv: Tel Aviv University, 1993.

Olavarri, Emilio. "Aroer (in Moab)." *NEAEHL* 1 (1993): 92–93.

Onn, Alexander, and Yehuda Rapuano. "Jerusalem, Khirbet El-Burj." *ESI* 14 (1994): 88–90.

Passaro, Angelo, and Giuseppe Bellia. "Sirach, or Metamorphosis of the Sage." Pages 355–73 in *The Wisdom of Ben Sira: Studies on Tradition, Redaction, and Theology.* Edited by Angelo Passaro and Giuseppe Bellia. DCLS 1. Berlin: de Gruyter, 2008.

Peltonen, Kay. "A Jigsaw Without a Model? The Date of Chronicles." Pages 225–73 in *Did Moses Speak Attic? Jewish Historiography and Scripture in the Hellenistic Period.* Edited by Lester L. Grabbe. JSOTSup 317. Sheffield: Sheffield Academic Press, 2001.

Peterson, John L. *A Topographical Surface Survey of the Levitical 'Cities' of Joshua 21 and 1 Chronicles 6: Studies on the Levites in Israelite Life and Religion.* Chicago: Institute of Advanced Theological Studies; Evanston: Western Theological Seminary, 1977.

Porten, Bezalel. *The Elephantine Papyri in English: Three Millennia of Cross-Cultural Continuity and Change.* DMOA 22. Leiden: Brill, 1996.

Prag, Kay. "Bethlehem, A Site Assessment." *PEQ* 132 (2000): 169–81.

Pritchard, James B. "Gibeon." *NEAEHL* 2 (1993): 511–14.

———. *Gibeon, Where the Sun Stood Still: The Discovery of the Biblical City.* Princeton: Princeton University Press, 1962.

———. *Winery, Defenses and Soundings at Gibeon.* Philadelphia: University Museum, University of Pennsylvania, 1964.

Rabinowitz, Isaac. "Aramaic Inscriptions of the Fifth Century B.C.E. from a North-Arab Shrine in Egypt." *JNES* 15 (1956): 1–9.

Rainey, Anson F. "The Chronicles of the Kings of Judah: A Source Used by the Chronicler." Pages 30–72 in *The Chronicler as Historian.* Edited by M. Patrick Graham, Kenneth G. Hoglund, and Steven L. McKenzie. JSNTSup 238. Sheffield: Sheffield Academic Press, 1997.

———. "The Identification of Philistine Gath: A Problem in Source Analysis for Historical Geography." *ErIsr* 12 (1975): 63*–76*.

Rajak, Tessa. "The Jews under Hasmonean Rule." *CAH* 9 (1999): 274–309.

Rappaport, Uriel. *The First Book of Maccabees: Introduction, Hebrew Translation, and Commentary* [Hebrew]. Jerusalem: Yad Ben-Zvi, 2004.

———. "The Hasmonean State (160–37 B.C.E.)." [Hebrew] Page 193–273 in vol. 3 of *The History of Eretz Israel: The Hellenistic Period and the Hasmonean State (332–37 B.C.E.)*. Edited by Menahem Stern. Jerusalem: Yad Ben-Zvi, 1981.

Reich, Ronny. "The Beth-Zur Citadel II—A Persian Residency?" *TA* 19 (1992): 113–23.

———. "Local Seal Impressions of the Hellenistic Period." Pages 256–62 in vol. 2 of *Jewish Quarter Excavations in the Old City of Jerusalem*. Edited by Hillel Geva. Jerusalem: Israel Exploration Society, 2003.

Reich, Ronny, and Eli Shukron. "The History of the Gihon Spring in Jerusalem." *Levant* 36 (2004): 211–23.

———. "The Urban Development of Jerusalem in the Late Eight Century B.C.E." Pages 209–18 in *Jerusalem in the Bible and Archaeology: The First Temple Period*. Edited by Andrew G. Vaughn and Ann E. Killebrew. SymS 18. Atlanta: Society of Biblical Literature, 2003.

———. "The Yehud Seal Impressions from the 1995–2005 City of David Excavations." *TA* 34 (2007): 59–65.

Roll, Israel. "Bacchides' Fortifications and the Arteries of Traffic to Jerusalem in the Hellenistic Period" [Hebrew]. *ErIsr* 25 (1996): 509–14.

Römer, Thomas. *The So-Called Deuteronomistic History*. London: T&T Clark, 2005.

Ronen, Yigal. "Some Observations on the Coinage of Yehud." *Israel Numismatic Journal* 15 (2003–2006): 29–30.

Rosenberg, Aryeh, and Alon Shavit. "Lod, Newe Yaraq." *ESI* 13 (1993): 54*–56*.

Rudolph, Wilhelm. *Chronikbücher*. HAT 1. Tübingen: Mohr Siebeck, 1955.

Safrai, Zeev. *Borders and Government in the Land of Israel in the Period of the Mishna and the Talmud* [Hebrew]. Tel Aviv: Hakibbutz Hameuchad, 1980.

Saller, Sylvester J., and Bellarmino Bagatti. *The Town of Nebo (Khirbet El-Mekhayyat), with a Brief Survey of Other Ancient Christian Monuments in Transjordan*. Publications of the Studium Bibilicum Franciscanum 7. Jerusalem: Franciscan Press, 1949.

Schniedewind, William M. *How the Bible Became a Book: The Textualization of Ancient Israel*. Cambridge: Cambridge University Press, 2004.

———. "Jerusalem, the Late Judaean Monarchy and the Composition of the Biblical Texts." Pages 375–93 in *Jerusalem in the Bible and Archae-*

*ology: The First Temple Period*. Edited by Andrew G. Vaughn and Ann E. Killebrew. SymS 18. Atlanta: Society of Biblical Literature, 2003.

Schorch, Stefan. "The Construction of Samaritan Identity from the Inside and from the Outside." Pages 135–49 in *Between Cooperation and Hostility: Multiple Identities in Ancient Judaism and the Interaction with Foreign Powers*. Edited by Rainer Albertz and Jakob Wöhrle. JAJSup 11. Göttingen: Vandenhoeck & Ruprecht, 2013.

Schwartz, Daniel R. *The Second Book of Maccabees: Introduction, Hebrew Translation, and Commentary* [Hebrew]. Jerusalem: Yad Ben-Zvi, 2004.

Schwartz, Joshua J. *Lod (Lydda), Israel: From Its Origins through the Byzantine Period, 5600 B.C.E.–640 C.E.* BARIS 571. Oxford: B.A.R, 1991.

Schwartz, Seth. "Israel and the Nations Roundabout: I Maccabees and the Hasmonean Expansion." *JJS* 42 (1991): 16–38.

Schweitzer, Steven J. *Reading Utopia in Chronicles*. LHBOTS 442. New York: T&T Clark, 2007.

Segal, Michael. *The Book of Jubilees: Rewritten Bible, Redaction, Ideology and Theology*. JSJSup 117. Leiden: Brill, 2007.

Sellers, Ovid R. *The Citadel of Beth-Zur*. Philadelphia: Westminster, 1933.

Sellers, Ovid R., Robert W. Funk, John L. McKenzie, Paul W. Lapp, and Nancy Lapp. *The 1957 Excavation at Beth-Zur*. AASOR 38. Cambridge: American Schools of Oriental Research, 1968.

Shalev, Yiftah. "The Early Persian Period Pottery." Pages 203–41 in *The Summit of the City of David: Excavations 2005–2008*. By Eilat Mazar. Jerusalem: Shoham Academic Research and Publication, 2015.

Sharon, Ilan, Ayelet Gilboa, Timothy A. J. Jull, and Elisabetta Boaretto. "Report on the First Stage of the Iron Age Dating Project in Israel: Supporting a Low Chronology." *Radiocarbon* 49 (2007): 1–46.

Shatzman, Israel. *The Armies of the Hasmonaeans and Herod from Hellenistic to Roman Frameworks*. Tübingen: Mohr, 1991.

———. "The Hasmonean Army" [Hebrew]. Page 21–44 in *The Hasmonean Period*. Edited by David Amit and Hanan Eshel. Jerusalem: Yad Ben-Zvi, 1995.

Shavit, Alon. *The Ayalon Valley and Its Vicinity during the Bronze and Iron Ages* [Hebrew]. MA thesis. Tel Aviv: Tel Aviv University, 1996.

Shiloh, Yigal. *Excavations at the City of David*. Vol. 1. Qedem 19. Jerusalem: The Institute of Archaeology, The Hebrew University of Jerusalem, 1984.

Sivan, Renee, and Giora Solar. "Excavations in the Jerusalem Citadel, 1980-1988." Pages 168-76 in *Ancient Jerusalem Revealed*. Edited by Hillel Geva. Jerusalem: Israel Exploration Society, 1994.

Sparks, James T. *The Chronicler's Genealogies: Towards an Understanding of 1 Chronicles 1-9*. AcBib 28. Atlanta: Society of Biblical Literature, 2008.

Spinoza, Baruch de. *Theological-Political Treaties*. Cambridge: Cambridge University Press, 2007.

Steiner, Richard C. "The Aramaic Text in Demotic Script: The Liturgy of a New Year's Festival Imported from Bethel to Syene by Exiles from Rash." *JAOS* 111 (1991): 362-63.

Steins, Georg. *Die Chronik als kanonisches Abschlussphänomen: Studien zur Entstehung und Theologie von 1/2 Chronik*. BBB 93 Weinheim: Beltz Athenaum, 1995.

———. "Zur Datierung der Chronik: Ein neuer methodischer Ansatz." *ZAW* 109 (1997): 84-92.

Stern, Ephraim. *The Assyrian, Babylonian, and Persian Periods (732-332 B.C.E.)*. Vol. 2 of *Archaeology of the Land of the Bible*. New York: Doubleday, 2001.

———. *Material Culture of the Land of the Bible in the Persian Period, 538-332 B.C.* Warminster: Aris & Phillips, 1982.

Stern, Menahem. *The Documents on the History of the Hasmonaean Revolt*. [Hebrew]. Tel Aviv: Hakibbutz Hameuchad, 1965.

Strübind, Kim. *Tradition als Interpretation in der Chronik: König Josaphat als Paradigma chronistischer Hermeneutik und Theologie*. BZAW 201. Berlin: de Gruyter, 1991.

Tal, Oren. *The Archaeology of Hellenistic Palestine: Between Tradition and Renewal*. [Hebrew]. Jerusalem: Bialik Institute, 2006.

———. "Coin Denominations and Weight Standards in Fourth Century B.C.E. Palestine." *Israel Numismatic Research* 2 (2007): 17-28.

Tammuz, Oded. "Will the Real Sanballat Please Stand Up?" Pages 51-58 in *Samaritans: Past and Present, Current Studies*. Edited by Menahem Mor and Friedrich V. Reiterer. SJ 53. Berlin: de Gruyter, 2010.

Tavger, Aharon. "E.P. 914 East of Beitin and the Location of the Ancient Cult Site of Bethel" [Hebrew]. *In the Highland's Depth* 5 (2015): 49-69.

Throntveit, Mark A. *Ezra-Nehemiah*. Louisville: John Knox, 1992.

———. "The Relationship of Hezekiah to David and Solomon in the Books of Chronicles." Pages 105-21 in *The Chronicler as Theologian: Essays in Honor of Ralph W. Klein*. Edited by M. Patrick Graham, Steven L.

McKenzie, and Gary N. Knoppers. JSOTSup 271. London: T&T Clark, 2003.
Torrey, Charles C. "The Chronicler as Editor and as Independent Narrator." *AJSL* 25 (1908): 157–73.
———. *The Composition and Historical Value of Ezra-Nehemiah*. Giessen: Ricker, 1896.
———. *Ezra Studies*. Chicago: University of Chicago Press, 1910.
Tufnell, Olga. *Lachish III: The Iron Age*. The Wellcome Archaeological Research Expedition to the Near East Publications 1. London: Oxford Univerisy Press, 1953.
Tzafrir, Yoram. "The Walls of Jerusalem in the Period of Nehemiah" [Hebrew]. *Cathedra* 4 (1977): 31–42.
Tzafrir, Yoram, Leah Di Segni, and Judith Green. *Tabula Imperii Romani Judaea Palaestina, Maps and Gazetteer*. Jerusalem: Israel Academy of Sciences and Humanities, 1994.
Tzur, Yoav. *The History of the Settlement at Tel Socho in Light of Archaeological Survey* [Hebrew]. MA thesis. Tel Aviv: Tel Aviv University, 2015.
Ulrich, Eugene, ed. *The Biblical Qumran Scrolls: Transcriptions and Textual Variants*. VTSup 134. Leiden: Brill, 2010.
Ussishkin, David. "The Borders and *De Facto* Size of Jerusalem in the Persian Period." Pages 147–66 in *Judah and the Judeans in the Persian Period*. Edited by Oded Lipschits and Manfred Oeming. Winona Lake, IN: Eisenbrauns, 2006.
———. "A Synopsis of the Stratigraphical, Chronological and Historical Issues." Pages 50–122 in *The Renewed Archaeological Excavations at Lachish (1973–1994)*. By David Ussishkin. Monograph Series of the Institute of Archaeology Tel Aviv University 22. Tel Aviv: Tel Aviv University Institute of Archaeology, 2004.
Vanderhooft, David, and Oded Lipschits. "A New Typology of the Yehud Stamp Impressions." *TA* 34 (2007): 12–37.
VanderKam, James C. *The Book of Jubilees*. Sheffield: Sheffield Academic Press, 2001.
Vaughn, Andrew G. *Theology, History, and Archaeology in the Chronicler's Account of Hezekiah*. ABS 4. Atlanta: Scholars Press, 1999.
Vriezen, Karel J. H. "Hirbet Kefire—Eine Oberflächenuntersuchung." *ZDPV* 91 (1975): 135–58.
Wacholder, Ben Zion. *Eupolemus: A Study of Judaeo-Greek Literature*. Monographs of the Hebrew Union College 3. Cincinnati: Hebrew Union College, 1974.

Weinberg, Joel P. *The Citizen-Temple Community*. JSOTSup 151. Sheffield: Academic Press, 1992.

———. "Jerusalem in the Persian Period." Page 307–26 in *The History of Jerusalem: The Biblical Period* [Hebrew]. Edited by Shmuel Ahituv and Amihai Mazar. Jerusalem: Yad Ben-Zvi, 2000.

Weinfeld, Moshe. "Pelekh in Nehemiah 3." Pages 249–50 in *Studies in Historical Geography and Biblical Historiography*. Edited by Gershon Galil and Moshe Weinfeld. VTSup 81. Leiden: Brill, 2000.

Weissenberg, Hanne von. "'Canon' and Identity at Qumran: An Overview and Challenges for Future Research." Pages 635–46 in *Scripture in Transition: Essays on Septuagint, Hebrew Bible, and Dead Sea Scrolls in Honour of Raija Sollamo*. Edited by Anssi Voitila and Jutta Jokiranta. JSJSup 126. Leiden: Brill, 2008.

Welch, Adam C. *The Work of the Chronicler: Its Purpose and Date*. London: Milford, 1939.

Welten, Peter. *Die Königs-Stempel: Ein Beitrag zur Militarpolitik Judas unter Hiskia und Josia*. Abhandlungen des Deutschen Palästina-Vereins. Wiesbaden: Harrassowitz, 1969.

———. *Geschichte und Geschichtsdarstellung in den Chronikbüchern*. WMANT 42. Neukirchen-Vluyn: Neukirchener Verlag, 1973.

Wightman, Gregory J. *The Walls of Jerusalem: From the Canaanites to the Mamluks*. Sydney: Meditarch, 1993.

Willi, Thomas. *Chronik*. Göttingen: Vandenhoeck & Ruprecht, 1972.

Williamson, Hugh G. M. *1 and 2 Chronicles*. Grand Rapids: Eerdmans, 1982.

———. *Ezra, Nehemiah*. WBC 16. Waco, TX: Word Books, 1985.

———. "The Historical Value of Josephus' Jewish Antiquities XI." *JTS* 28 (1977): 49–66.

———. *Israel in the Books of Chronicles*. Cambridge: Cambridge University Press, 1977.

———. "Nehemiah's Walls Revisited." *PEQ* 116 (1984): 81–88.

———. "Sources and Redaction in the Chronicler's Genealogy of Judah." *JBL* 98 (1979): 351–59.

Wright, Jacob L. "A New Model for the Composition of Ezra-Nehemiah." Pages 333–48 in *Judah and the Judeans in the Fourth Century B.C.E.* Edited by Oded Lipschits, Gary N. Knoppers, and Rainer Albertz. Winona Lake, IN: Eisenbrauns, 2007.

———. "David, King of Judah (Not Israel)." The Bible and Interpretation, 2014. https://tinyurl.com/SBL2637a.

———. *Rebuilding Identity: The Nehemiah Memoir and Its Earliest Readers.* BZAW 348. Berlin: de Gruyter, 2004.
Wright, John W. "Remapping Yehud: The Borders of Yehud and the Genealogies of Chronicles." Pages 67–89 in *Judah and the Judeans in the Persian Period.* Edited by Oded Lipschits and Manfred Oeming. Winona Lake, IN: Eisenbrauns, 2006.
Yeivin, Shemuel. "The Benjaminite Settlement in the Western Part of Their Territory." *IEJ* 21 (1971): 141–54.
Young, Robb A. *Hezekiah in History and Tradition.* VTSup 155. Leiden: Brill, 2012.
Zadok, Ran. "On the Reliability of the Genealogical and Prosopographical Lists of the Israelites in the Old Testament." *TA* 25 (1998): 228–54.
Zertal, Adam. "The Pahwah of Samaria (Northern Israel) during the Persian Period: Types of Settlement, Economy, History and New Discoveries." *Transeu* 2 (1989): 9–30.
Zevit, Ziony. "Is There an Archaeological Case for Phantom Settlements in the Persian Period?" *PEQ* 141 (2009): 124–37.
Zorn, Jeffrey R. "Estimating the Population Size of Ancient Settlements: Methods, Problems, Solutions, and a Case Study." *BASOR* 295 (1994): 31–48.
Zsengellér, József., ed. *Rewritten Bible after Fifty Years: Texts, Terms, or Techniques? A Last Dialogue with Geza Vermes.* JSJSup 166. Leiden: Brill, 2014.
Zuckerman, Sharon. "The Pottery of Stratum 9 (the Persian Period)." Pages 31–50 in *Area E: The Finds.* Vol. 7B of *Excavations at the City of David 1978–1985 Directed by Yigal Shiloh.* By Alon De Groot and Hannah Bernick-Greenberg. Qedem 54. Jerusalem: The Institute of Archaeology, The Hebrew University of Jerusalem, 2012.
Zukerman, Alexander, and Itzhak Shai. "The Royal City of the Philistines in the 'Azekah Inscription' and the History of Gath in the Eighth Century B.C.E." *UF* 38 (2006): 1–50.

# Biblical References Index

| Genesis | |
|---|---|
| 12:8 | 48 |
| 13:3 | 48 |

| Judges | |
|---|---|
| 1:27 | 92, 151 |

| Joshua | |
|---|---|
| 15 | 113, 116, 118 |
| 15:59a | 38 |
| 15:60 | 39 |
| 17 | 92, 151 |
| 18:14 | 39 |
| 18:21 | 36 |
| 18:22 | 35, 142 |
| 18:23 | 143 |
| 18:24 | 42 |
| 18:25 | 34, 41 |
| 18:26 | 40 |
| 19 | 92, 94, 104 n. 108 |
| 19:1–7 | 92, 151 |
| 21 | 85 |

| 2 Samuel | |
|---|---|
| 10 | 139 n. 50 |

| 1 Kings | |
|---|---|
| 15 | 141 |
| 15:22 | 117 |
| 22:49 | 145 |

| 2 Kings | |
|---|---|
| 12:3 | 149 |
| 12:21–24 | 125 n. 92 |
| 18:8 | 146 |
| 18:9–10 | 146 |
| 18:16 | 146 |
| 19:8 | 117 n. 40 |
| 23 | 35 |
| 23:19 | 150 |

| Jeremiah | |
|---|---|
| 26:18 | 113 |
| 26:20 | 39 |
| 28:1 | 34 |
| 31:15 | 41 |
| 31:38 | 19 n. 96 |
| 31:40 | 19 n. 96 |
| 40:1 | 41 |
| 41:16 | 34 |
| 41:17 | 38 |

| Micah | |
|---|---|
| 1:1 | 113 |
| 1:10 | 111 |

| Zechariah | |
|---|---|
| 7:2 | 35 |

| Daniel | |
|---|---|
| 1:2 | 133, 135 |
| 3:27 | 19 n. 99 |

| Ezra | |
|---|---|
| 2:1–67 | 1, 29, 68, 71, 98 n. 80, 159 |
| 3:10 | 135 |

| Nehemiah | |
|---|---|
| 1:3 | 18 |
| 2:4 | 18 |

*Nehemiah (cont.)*

| | | | |
|---|---|---|---|
| 2:8 | 18 | 2:42 | 85 |
| 2:10 | 72 | 2:43 | 86 |
| 2:13 | 18 | 2:45 | 86 |
| 2:19 | 72–73 | 2:46 | 88 |
| 3 | 1, 5–6, 14–16, 16 n. 84, 17–19, 19 n. 97, 20, 22, 25, 25 n. 124, 29, 34, 46, 52–56, 68, 69 n. 85, 70–71, 72 n. 7, 81, 94–95, 97, 159 | 2:53 | 86 |
| | | 2:54 | 86, 88 |
| | | 4:3 | 86 |
| | | 4:4 | 87 |
| | | 4:5 | 85 |
| 3:1–32 | 71 | 4:14 | 87 |
| 3:7 | 19, 21, 54, 96 | 4:16 | 85 |
| 3:11 | 19 | 4:17 | 87 |
| 3:13 | 14 | 4:18 | 87 |
| 3:16 | 20, 53, 96 | 4:19 | 87 |
| 3:33 | 18 | 4:21 | 85 |
| 3:33–35 | 73 | 5:8 | 89, 104 |
| 3:33–36 | 72 | 6 | 85 n. 10 |
| 3:38 | 18 | 7:8 | 87 |
| 4:1 | 73 | 7:21 | 103 n. 106, 151 n. 78 |
| 4:1–3 | 72–73 | 7:24 | 89 |
| 4:5 | 18, 72 | 7:28 | 89 |
| 4:9 | 18, 72 | 7:29 | 92, 151 |
| 5:16 | 18 | 7:31 | 89 |
| 6:1 | 18 | 8:6 | 88 |
| 6:1–14 | 72 | 8:12 | 88 |
| 6:2 | 79 n. 41 | 8:13 | 88, 103 n. 106, 151 n. 78 |
| 6:6 | 18 | 8:29 | 88 |
| 6:15 | 18 | 8:36 | 87–88 |
| 6:16 | 72 | 9:2–34 | 93, 144, 151 |
| 6:17–19 | 72 | 9:3 | 93, 151 |
| 7 | 34 | 9:35 | 88 |
| 7:1 | 18 | 9:42 | 87–88 |
| 7:4 | 5 | 10–9 | 156, 163 |
| 7:6–68 | 1, 29, 68, 71, 98 n. 80, 159 | 15:16–21 | 133 |
| 11:1 | 5 | 16:4–42 | 133 |
| 12:24 | 135 | 19:7 | 139 n. 50 |
| 12:27 | 18 | 22:8 | 133 |
| 13:4–14 | 5 | 24:7 | 138 |
| 13:7 | 74 | 25:1–31 | 133 |
| 13:28 | 74 | | |

*2 Chronicles*

| | | | |
|---|---|---|---|
| | | 10–36 | 156–157 |
| 1 Chronicles | | 11 | 117–120 |
| 2–9 | 1, 83, 85, 90–91, 98, 105, 125, 150, 160 | 11:1–4 | 125 n. 92 |
| 2:24 | 85 | 11:5–11 | 125 |

## Biblical References Index

| | | | |
|---|---|---|---|
| 11:5–12 | 1, 109, 113, 117–18, 120, 124–25, 160 | 1 Maccabees | |
| | | 1:11 | 79 |
| 11:8 | 111, 113 | 3:10 | 79 |
| 11:10 | 118 | 3:17–22 | 153 |
| 11:12 | 140 | 3:24 | 79 |
| 11:23 | 140 | 3:25 | 145 |
| 12:1 | 140 | 3:41 | |
| 12:12 | 140 | 4:6 | 65 |
| 13 | 137, 141 | 4:10–11 | 154 |
| 13:15–18 | 142 | 4:15 | 79, 146 |
| 13:19 | 106, 142 | 4:22 | 79 |
| 13:22 | 142 n. 54 | 4:29 | 65, 79 |
| 14:6 | 143 | 4:30–33 | 154 |
| 14:9–13 | 144 | 4:61 | 60 n. 51, 99 n. 86, 119 n. 49, 141 n. 53 |
| 14:19 | 143 | | |
| 15:9–10 | 143 | 5:1 | 145 |
| 16:6 | 115 | 5:3 | 79 |
| 16:7–12 | 143 | 5:6 | 79 |
| 17:2 | 144–45 | 5:8 | 145 |
| 17:10 | 145 | 5:9 | 79 |
| 17:12 | 145 n. 61 | 5:13 | 74 |
| 19:2–3 | 144 | 5:20 | 65 |
| 19:4 | 145 | 5:58 | 146 |
| 20 | 145 | 5:65 | 79, 121 |
| 21:16–17 | 149 | 5:66 | 145 |
| 24:2 | 149 | 5:66–68 | 79 |
| 24:17–22 | 149 | 5:68 | 145 |
| 25:13 | 149 | 6 | 150 n. 70 |
| 25:14–16 | 149 | 6:7 | 60 n. 51, 99 n. 86, 119 n. 49, 141 n. 53 |
| 26:6–7 | 146 | | |
| 26:9 | 19 n. 96 | 6:31 | 79 |
| 26:9–10 | 146 | 7:8 | 19 n. 99 |
| 26:15 | 138 n. 46 | 7:40 | 65 |
| 26:16 | 149 | 7:41 | 147, 154 |
| 27:5 | 149 | 8:17 | 134 |
| 28:17–19 | 149 | 9 | 112, 150 n. 70 |
| 29:1–3 | 138 | 9:4 | 41 |
| 30 | 137 | 9:5–6 | 65 |
| 30:1 | 146 | 9:33 | 120, 145 |
| 30:5 | 146 | 9:35–42 | 139 n. 50 |
| 33:14 | 19 n. 96 | 9:36 | 145 |
| 34:6 | 150 | 9:50 | 35 |
| 36:7 | 133, 135 | 9:50–52 | 2, 61, 77 n. 32, 100, 119 |
| | | 9:52 | 61 n. 51, 100 n. 86, 119 n. 49, 141 n. 53 |

*1 Maccabees* (*cont.*)

| | |
|---|---|
| 9:73 | 42 |
| 10:69 | 146 |
| 10:76–84 | 146 |
| 10:77–86 | 144 |
| 10:78–84 | 79 |
| 10:89 | 65, 78, 102 |
| 11:4 | 79, 146 |
| 11:34 | 37, 46, 65, 78, 102, 143 |
| 11:65 | 61 n. 51, 100 n. 86, 119 n. 49, 141 n. 53 |
| 12:38 | 36, 79 n. 41 |
| 12:53 | 145 |
| 13:13 | 36, 79 n. 41 |
| 13:20 | 79 |
| 13:43 | 65, 78, 103 |
| 13:48 | 65, 78, 103 |
| 14:5 | 65, 78, 103, 153 |
| 14:7 | 141 n. 53, 153 |
| 14:10 | 145 n. 61 |
| 14:33 | 61 n. 51, 99 n. 86, 119 n. 49, 141 n. 53 |
| 14:34 | 79 |
| 15:28–31 | 153 |
| 15:33 | 103 |
| 15:33–34 | 153 |
| 15:35 | 153 |
| 15:40 | 146 |
| 15:40–41 | 144 |
| 16:1–10 | 144 |
| 16:10 | 79, 146 |

2 Maccabees

| | |
|---|---|
| 3:11 | 74 |
| 4:11 | 134 |
| 8:1 | 65 |
| 8:19 | 146 |
| 9 | 150 n. 70 |
| 12:38 | 62, 101, 121 |
| 13:25 | 144 |

Ben Sira

| | |
|---|---|
| 47:8–10 | 133, 135 |
| 49:13 | 20 n. 100 |

# Modern Authors Index

Abadie, Philippe 149 n. 70
Abel, Félix-Marie 61, 61 nn. 52 and 55, 62 n. 61, 100, 100 nn. 87–88, 101 n. 94
Ackroyd, Peter R. 35 n. 40, 131 n. 11, 132 n. 17, 138 n. 44
Aharoni, Yohanan 45 n. 90, 68 n. 83, 98 n. 82, 109 n. 3, 111 n. 8, 113, 113 n. 16, 115, 115 n. 24, 147 n. 67
Ahituv, Shmuel 3 n. 2, 74 n. 19
Albertz, Rainer 19 n. 97, 59 n. 44, 136 n. 32, 137 n. 36, 155 n. 91, 162 n. 3
Albright, William F. 14 n. 72, 38 nn. 55–56, 48, 49, 143 n. 57
Alt, Albrecht 14, 14 n. 73, 34 n. 28, 35 n. 37, 36 n. 47, 38 n. 54, 39 n. 66, 40 n. 69, 41 nn. 75 and 78, 42 n. 81, 60 n. 50, 92 n. 54, 99 n. 85, 110 n. 5, 115 n. 30, 116 n. 32, 119 n. 48, 151 n. 77
Amiran, Ruth 7 n. 26
Arbel, Yoav 37 n. 50
Ariel, Donald T. 9 nn. 31 and 34, 10 n. 40, 11, 11 nn. 49–50, 31, 31 nn. 7 and 11–12, 67 n. 80, 78 n. 35
Avigad, Nahman 7 nn. 23–24, 12 n. 53, 13 n. 57, 14 n. 68, 16 n. 86, 32 n. 17, 84 n. 6
Avi-Yonah, Michael 61, 61 n. 55, 62, 62 n. 60, 64, 64 n. 68, 65, 65 nn. 72 and 74–76, 77 n. 33, 78 nn. 36–38, 100, 100 nn. 88–89 and 92, 101 n. 97, 102 nn. 102–3, 103 n. 104, 119 n. 52, 121 n. 62, 146 n. 62, 147 n. 67
Bagatti, Bellarmino 98 n. 47
Barkay, Gabriel 11 nn. 47 and 51, 24 n. 123, 71 n. 5, 162 n. 4

Bar-Kochva, Bezalel 64, 64 nn. 68–69, 65, 65 nn. 71 and 73, 77 n. 33
Barrera, Julio T. 138 n. 45
Barstad, Hans M. 60 n. 44
Beit-Arieh, Itzhaq 37 nn. 48–49, 116 n. 35
Bellia, Giuseppe 135 nn. 29 and 31
Ben Zvi, Ehud 111 n. 7, 117 n. 31, 131 n. 3, 133 n. 20, 135 n. 28, 138 n. 46, 149 n. 69, 150 n. 71
Ben-Ami, Doron 26 n. 129
Ben-Shlomo, David 106 n. 115, 127 n. 99
Bergman, Avraham 39 n. 56
Bergren, Theodore A. 19, 20 n. 100
Berlin, Andrea 26 n. 127
Beyer, Gustav 109 nn. 2–3, 110 n. 6
Bianchi, Francesco 138 n. 46
Biran, Avraham 38, 38 nn. 57 and 59
Blair, Edward P. 38 n. 55
Blenkinsopp, Joseph 17 n. 92, 18 n. 93, 45 n. 94, 53 n. 10, 71 n. 2, 72 nn. 6 and 8, 73 n. 10, 74 n. 17, 75 nn. 20 and 23–24, 79 n. 40, 95 n. 67
Bliss, Frederick Jones 122 nn. 74–75, 123, 124 nn. 87–88
Boaretto, Elisabetta 114 n. 18
Boda, Mark J. 130 n. 7
Böhler, Dieter 19, 19 n. 98, 22 n. 116, 53 n. 12, 81 n. 47, 96 n. 69
Brand, Etty 36 n. 41, 36 n. 43
Braun, Roddy L. 93 n. 57, 137 n. 37
Bronk Ramsey, Christopher 114 n. 18
Brooke, George J. 137 n. 34, 138 n. 56
Broshi, Magen 7 n. 23, 8 n. 27, 13 n. 62, 59 n. 42, 121 n. 59

Bunimovitz, Shlomo    86 n. 19, 90 nn. 39–40 and 45, 117 n. 39, 121 n. 66, 142 n. 56, 143 n. 57
Cahill, Jane M.    15 n. 78
Callaway, Joseph A.    43 n. 84
Campbell, Edward F.    89 n. 43
Car, David M.    81 n. 47
Carter, Charles E.    3 n. 2, 4, 4 nn. 3–7, 12 n. 53, 13, 13 nn. 57, 60 and 62, 20, 20 n. 103, 22 n. 115, 30 nn. 2–3, 32 n. 17, 45 n. 92, 51 n. 1, 52 nn. 5–6, 53, 53 n. 13, 55 n. 28, 57, 57 nn. 31 and 35, 58, 58 n. 37, 59, 59 n. 41, 76 nn. 26 and 29, 94 n. 63, 95 n. 64, 96, 96 n. 72, 98, 98 n. 81, 122 n. 72
Caspi, Arza    10 n. 40
Chen, Doron    7 n. 23
Clancy, Frank    135 n. 22
Clines, David J.    74 n. 10
Cohen, David    10 n. 40
Corley, Jeremy    135, 135 n. 30
Cotton, Hannah    118 n. 47
Crawford, Sidnie W.    136 n. 34
Cross, Frank M.    73 n. 13, 74 nn. 16–17, 83 n. 3, 151 n. 74
Crowfoot, John W.    10, 11 n. 44, 14, 14 n. 71, 15, 26
Dagan, Yehuda    21 n. 115, 64, 64 n. 67, 66, 66 n. 77, 86 nn. 19–20, 87 nn. 27–28, 92, 92 n. 51, 114 n. 19, 121 n. 57, 122 n. 65, 124, 124 n. 89
Davies, Philip    59 n. 47
De Groot, Alon 8, 8 nn. 33 and 35, 10 nn. 38 and 40, 12 n. 52, 14 n. 68, 15, 15 n. 76, 26 nn. 127–28, 32 n. 15, 85 n. 8, 88 n. 38
Deboys, David G.    142 n. 54
Demsky, Aaron    19 n. 99
Dever, William G.    89 n. 42
Di Segni, Leah    37 n. 47
Dinur, Uri    38 n. 58 and 60–61, 39, 39 nn. 62 and 64–65, 87 nn. 29–30
Dumbrell, William J.    73 n. 11, 75 n. 21
Duncan, John G.    11, 11 n. 45, 14, 14 n. 65, 15, 15 n. 79 and 81

Dušek, Jan    74 n. 16
Dvira (Zweig), Ittzhak    24 n. 123, 71 n. 5, 162 n. 4
Edelman, Diana    3 nn. 1–2, 5, 5 nn. 13–15, 17 n. 89, 19 n. 99, 30 n. 2, 72 n. 8, 73 n. 12, 74 n. 18, 81 n. 46
Eisenberg, Emanuel    86 n. 14, 106 n. 115, 122 n. 68, 126 n. 99
Eitan, Avraham    7 n. 26
Elliger, Karl    115 n. 28
Ephal, Israel    75 n. 23
Eshel, Hanan    3 n. 2, 4–5, 5 n. 8, 15 n. 74, 16 n. 87, 32 n. 20
Eskenazi, Tamara C.    74 n. 18
Faigenbaum-Golovin, Shira    161 n. 2
Fantalkin, Alexander    114 n. 19, 116 n. 34, 123, 123 n. 85, 126 nn. 94 and 97
Farès-Drappeau, Saba    75 n. 22
Feig, Nurit    38 nn. 58 and 60–61, 39, 39 n. 62 and 64, 87 nn. 29–30
Feldstein, Amir    37 n. 50, 40, 40 nn. 68 and 73, 41, 41 n. 77, 42, 42 n. 80 and 82–83, 43, 43 nn. 86–88, 88 nn. 31 and 33
Finkelstein, Israel    12 nn. 54–55, 13 n. 62, 15 nn. 77 and 81, 23 n. 118, 24 n. 120, 25 n. 124, 29 n. 1, 31 n. 13, 46 n. 100, 47 nn. 101–3, 49 nn. 107 and 109, 51 n. 4, 52 n. 8, 53 n. 12, 55 n. 30, 57 nn. 32 and 36, 58 nn. 38 and 40, 59 nn. 42–43, 63 n. 66, 64 n. 70, 68 n. 81, 70, 71 nn. 1 and 4–5, 72 n. 8, 76 n. 25, 77 n. 32, 84 n. 5, 85 n. 7, 86 nn. 17–18, 87 n. 28, 88 nn. 34 and 36–37, 89 nn. 39–41 and 44–45, 94 n. 60, 95 n. 66, 96 n. 69, 98 n. 80, 101 n. 93, 106 nn. 116 and 118–19, 114 nn. 18–19 and 22, 116 n. 34, 117 n. 39, 120 n. 56, 122 n. 72, 125 n. 90, 126 nn. 94 and 97, 127 n. 102, 130 n. 4, 131 nn. 9–10, 138 nn. 42–43, 140 n. 52, 142 nn. 56–57, 150 n. 72
Fischer, Moshe    100 n. 88, 119 n. 51
Fitzgerald, Gerald M.    11 n. 44, 14 n. 71
Fritz, Volkmar    108 nn. 1–2, 110 n. 5, 111, 111 n. 9

# Modern Authors Index

Funk, Robert W.   20, 20 nn. 101 and 104, 53, 53 nn. 13–14, 85 n. 9, 96, 96 nn. 72–73, 122 n. 70
Gadot, Yuval   126 n. 98
Galil, Gershon   61 n. 57, 62, 62 nn. 59 and 63, 101 n. 96
Galling, Kurt   45 n. 93, 131 n. 11, 137 n. 36
Ganor, Saar   114 n. 19
Garfinkel, Yosef   114 n. 19, 118 n. 44, 126 n. 93
Gera, Dov   75 n. 20
Geva, Hillel   7 nn. 23–25, 8 n. 28, 15 n. 78, 16 nn. 86–87, 30 n. 4, 32 n. 18, 84 n. 6, 138 n. 43
Gibson, Shimon   7 nn. 23 and 25, 122 nn. 75–77
Gichon, Mordechai   109 nn. 2–3, 110 n. 6
Gilboa, Ayelet   114 n. 18
Goldstein, Jonathan A.   61 n. 55, 75 n. 20, 100 n. 88, 132 n. 13
Gopher, Avi   37 n. 50
Gophna, Ram   37 nn. 48–49, 43, 43 nn. 87–88, 88 nn. 33 and 35, 121 n. 67
Goren, Yuval   118 n. 47
Grabbe, Lester L.   17 n. 92, 59 n. 44, 72 n. 6, 74 n. 17
Graham, Patrick M.   111 n. 7
Grätz, Sebastian   72 n. 8, 73 n. 12, 81 n. 45
Green, Judith   36 n. 47
Greenhut, Zvi   85 n. 8, 88 n. 38
Halpern, Baruch   110 n. 7, 129 n. 2
Hermann, Siegfried   110 n. 5, 111 nn. 8 and 10
Herzog, Ze'ev   15 n. 81, 116 n. 34
Hirschfeld, Hannah   8 nn. 31 and 34, 31 n. 7
Hobbs, T. R.   109 n. 3, 110 n. 6
Hoglund, Kenneth G.   18 n. 89
Japhet, Sara   83 n. 2, 105 n. 114, 109 n. 3, 110 n. 7, 115 n. 26, 129 n. 1, 130, 130 n. 6, 133 nn. 17 and 21, 137 nn. 37 and 41, 138, 139 nn. 47–48, 140 n. 51, 143 n. 58, 146 n. 63, 156 n. 98

Johnson, Marshall D.   83 nn. 1–2, 150 n. 73
Jones, Gwilym H.   142 n. 54
Jull, Timothy A. J.   114 n. 18
Junge, Ehrhard   110 n. 5, 115 n. 29
Kahana, Avraham   62 n. 62, 101 n. 95
Kalimi, Isaac   132 n. 16, 133 nn. 19–20, 138 n. 45
Kallai, Zechariah   39, 39 n. 63, 40, 40 n. 72, 41, 41 n. 79, 43, 43 n. 85, 61 n. 53, 88 n. 31, 89 n. 45, 102 n. 102, 109 nn. 2–3, 113 n. 16, 115 n. 28, 142 n. 55
Kasher, Aryeh   60 n. 50, 99 n. 85, 103 n. 105
Katz, Haya   117 n. 37
Kegler, Jürgen   155, 155 n. 92
Kellermann, Ulrich   74 nn. 14 and 17, 75 nn. 20 and 23, 133, 133 n. 18, 155, 155 n. 90
Kelly, Brian E.   149 n. 70
Kelso, James L.   34 nn. 29–31, 35, 35 nn. 32–36, 48 n. 105
Kennett, Robert   130, 131 nn. 8 and 12, 132 n. 15
Kenyon, Kathleen   5, 5 n. 12, 10, 10 n. 41, 14, 14 nn. 64 and 67, 15, 15 nn. 75 and 83, 25
Khalaily, Hamoudi   38 n. 50
King, Philip J.   12 n. 56, 59 n. 47, 149 n. 70
Klausner, Joseph   79 n. 39, 103 n. 105
Kleiman, Assaf   2
Klein, Ralph W.   133 n. 19, 136 n. 34, 138 n. 46, 142 n. 54, 145 n. 59, 147 n. 64
Kletter, Raz   113 n. 15, 116 n. 33
Kloner, Amos   13 n. 59, 85 n. 13, 104 n. 107, 114 n. 23, 118 n. 46, 121 n. 60, 123, 123 nn. 78–80 and 82
Knauf, Axel E.   24 n. 120, 61 n. 54, 75 n. 23
Knoppers, Gary N.   83 n. 1, 84 n. 4, 92 n. 53, 93 nn. 55 and 58, 94 n. 62, 104 nn. 112–13, 132 n. 16, 133 nn. 19 and 21, 136 n. 33, 138 n. 44, 140 n. 51,

*Knoppers, Gary N. (cont.)* 144 n. 59, 149 n. 70, 151 nn. 75–76, 153 nn. 81–82, 157, 157 n. 99, 158 n. 100

Koch, Ido 2, 24, 24 n. 120, 25 n. 124, 47, 47 n. 101, 71 n. 5, 126 n. 96

Kochavi, Moshe 21 n. 115, 85 nn. 11–12, 86 nn. 15–16 and 22, 87 n. 23–24, 26 and 28, 120 n. 54, 121 nn. 61 and 63

Kofoed, Jens B. 138 n. 46

Kohut, Alexander 19 n. 99

Konkel, August H. 146 n. 63

Kratz, Reinhard 71 n. 2, 73 n. 9, 131 n. 11, 132 n. 14, 133, 133 n. 17, 136 n. 34

Lapp, Nancy 20, 20 n. 102, 53, 53 n. 13

Lapp, Paul W. 20, 20 n. 102, 35 n. 36, 53, 53 n. 13

Lederman, Zvi 64 n. 70, 86 n. 19, 89 nn. 39–40 and 45, 117 n. 38, 121 n. 66, 142 n. 56, 143 n. 57

Lee-Sak, Itzhak 127, 127 n. 101

Lehmann, Gunnar 86 nn. 19–20, 90 n. 49, 92 n. 50

Lemaire, Andre 116 n. 35

Levin, Yigal 84 n. 4, 93 nn. 58 and 62

Lipschits, Oded 3 n. 2, 4 n. 5, 5–6, 6 nn. 18–22, 12 n. 53, 13, 13 nn. 57 and 61, 17 nn. 89–90, 21 nn. 109, 112 and 115, 23, 23 n. 117, 24, 24 nn. 119–20, 25 n. 124, 30 nn. 2–3, 32 n. 17, 34 nn. 21, 23 and 26, 36 n. 44, 44 n. 89, 45, 45 nn. 91–92 and 95–97, 46 n. 99, 47, 47 nn. 101 and 103, 48, 48 n. 104, 51 n. 3, 52 nn. 5–7, 54 nn. 19, 21 and 24–25, 55, 55 nn. 26 and 29, 57, 57 n. 35, 58, 58 nn. 37 and 39, 59, 59 nn. 41 and 44–45, 60 n. 49, 67 nn. 78 and 80, 69, 69 n. 84, 70, 71 n. 5, 73 nn. 6–7, 76, 76 nn. 26–27 and 29, 77 nn. 31 and 34, 78 n. 35, 90 n. 48, 94 n. 63, 95, 95 nn. 74–75 and 77–78, 98 nn. 79 and 83, 99 n. 84, 101 n. 99, 114 n. 23, 127 n. 98

Lods, Adolphe 131 n. 11, 132 n. 14

Macalister, Robert A. S. 11, 11 n. 45, 14, 14 n. 65, 15, 15 nn. 79 and 81, 122 nn. 74–75, 123, 124 nn. 87–88

Maeir, Aren M. 111 n. 13, 123 n. 77

Magen, Yitzhak 7 n. 23, 8 n. 27, 13 n. 62, 59 n. 42, 63 n. 66, 121 n. 59, 137 n. 39

Malkin, Irad 18 n. 95

Marböck, Johannes 135 n. 31

Margalit, Shlomo 7 n. 23

Mazar, Amihai 61 n. 57, 100 n. 90, 114 n. 18

Mazar, Benjamin 10, 10 nn. 42–43, 16 n. 87, 74 n. 18, 75 n. 20

Mazar, Eilat 10, 10 n. 42, 15, 15 n. 80, 24 n. 123, 25, 25 nn. 125–26, 72 n. 5, 162 n. 4

McKenzie, Steven L. 130 n. 3, 132 n. 16, 145 n. 59, 156 n. 98,

Mendels, Doron 104 nn. 109–11, 134 n. 25, 136 nn. 26, 32 and 35, 137 n. 40, 147 n. 68, 150 n. 70, 152 nn. 79–80, 154, 154 nn. 83–89

Meyers, Carol L. 35 n. 39

Meyers, Eric M. 35 n. 39

Michaeli, Frank 17 nn. 92–93

Miller, Maxwell J. 109 n. 3, 111 n. 8, 113 n. 16

Misgav, Haggai 137 n. 39

Mittman, Siegried 74 n. 15, 111 n. 14

Möller, Christa 62 n. 63, 101 n. 96

Mowinckel, Sigmund 18 n. 94, 53 n. 11, 72 n. 6, 96 n. 68

Myers, Jacob M. 45 n. 93

Na'aman, Nadav 23 n. 118, 24 n. 121, 34 n. 28, 35 n. 37, 36 nn. 42 and 46, 38 n. 54, 39 n. 66, 40 n. 69, 41 nn. 75 and 78, 42 n. 81, 47, 47 n. 103, 62, 62 n. 58, 92 n. 54, 93 n. 57, 94 nn. 60–61, 100, 100 n. 91, 109 n. 2, 110 n. 4, 111 nn. 8 and 11, 113 nn. 14 and 17, 114 n. 20, 115 nn. 25 and 30, 116, 116 n. 32, 117, 117 nn. 36 and 39–41, 118 n. 44, 119 n. 48, 126 n. 96

Nagorsky, Alla 36 n. 43

Nashef, Khaled 89 n. 45

Netzer, Ehud 19 n. 115, 36 n. 45

Nicol, Murray B. 43 n. 84

Niemann, Michael H.   86 nn. 19-20, 90, 90 n. 49, 92 n. 50
North, Robert S.   110 n. 7
Noth, Martin   83 n. 3, 110 n. 7, 125 n. 91, 131 n. 11, 132 nn. 14 and 17, 133, 135 n. 28, 145 n. 60, 150 n. 74, 155
Oeming, Manfred   83 nn. 1-2, 106-8, 106 n. 120, 107 nn. 121-22, 127 n. 98, 133 n. 17, 150 n. 73
Ofer, Avi   13 n. 26, 21 n. 115, 37, 37 n. 53, 63 n. 66, 85 nn. 11-12 and 14, 86 nn. 15-16 and 21-22, 87 nn. 23-26, 120 nn. 53-55, 61 and 68
Olavarri, Emilio   89 n. 46
Onn, Alexander   41 n. 74
Passaro, Angelo   135 n. 31
Peltonen, Kay   136 n. 32, 137 n. 37
Peterson, John L. A   87 n. 25
Piasetzky, Eli   114 nn. 18-19 and 22, 116 n. 34, 126 n. 94, 127 n. 102, 161
Pixner, Bagil   7 n. 23
Porat, Yosef   88 n. 35, 121 n. 67
Porten, Bezalel   24 n. 122
Prag, Kay   37 nn. 50 and 52
Pritchard, James B.   21, 21 nn. 111 and 113-14, 34, 34 nn. 22, 24-25 and 27, 54, 54 nn. 20 and 22-23, 85 n. 7, 97, 97 nn. 75-76
Rabinowitz, Isaac   73 n. 11, 75 n. 21
Rainey, Anson F   110 n. 7, 111 n. 12
Rajak, Tessa   80 n. 39, 103 n. 105
Rappaport, Uriel   19 n. 99, 41 n. 76, 79 nn. 39 and 41, 103 n. 105, 132 n. 12, 147 n. 66
Rapuano, Yehuda   41 n. 74
Reich, Ronny   7 n. 23, 8, 8 n. 36, 11, 11 nn. 46 and 48, 20, 20 n. 106, 30 n. 4, 31, 31 nn. 9-10, 53, 53 n. 16, 66 nn. 79-80, 78 n. 35, 96, 96 n. 71, 101 n. 100, 102 n. 101, 122, 122 n. 71
Roll, Israel   61, 61 nn. 55-56, 62 n. 65, 77 n. 32, 100, 100 nn. 88-89, 101 n. 98, 119 n. 51
Römer, Thomas   59 n. 44, 59 n. 46, 156 n. 97

Ronen, Yigal   57 n. 33
Rosenberg, Aryeh   37 n. 50
Rossoni, Gabriele   138 n. 46
Rudolph, Wilhelm   83 n. 3, 93 n. 54, 109 n. 3, 125 n. 91, 137 n. 36, 151 n. 77
Safrai, Zeev   62, 62 n. 58, 100, 100 n. 91
Saller, Sylvester J.   89 n. 47
Sass, Benjamin   106 n. 117, 130 n. 4
Savir, Neta   8 nn. 31 and 34, 31 n. 7
Schmitt, Gotz   62 n. 63, 101 n. 96
Schniedewind, William M.   3 n. 1, 4 n. 6, 51 n. 2, 59 n. 48
Schorch, Stefan   137 n. 38
Schwartz, Daniel R.   79 n. 43
Schwartz, Joshua J.   65 n. 74, 102 n. 102
Schwartz, Seth   78 n. 36, 79 n. 42, 104 n. 113, 152 n. 82
Schweitzer, Steven J.   83 n. 2, 93 n. 56, 130 n. 7
Segal, Michael   136 n. 34
Sellers, Ovid R.   20 n. 107, 54 n. 17
Shai, Itzhak   113 n. 14, 113 n. 15
Shalev, Yiah   25 n. 125
Sharon, Ilan   114 n. 18
Shatzman, Israel   61 n. 53, 65, 65 nn. 71 and 73
Shavit, Alon   37 n. 50, 88 n. 35
Shiloh, Yigal 8, 8 nn. 29-30, 32 and 37, 9 nn. 39 and 41, 11-12, 14-15, 14 n. 68, 15 n. 78, 23, 26, 31, 31 nn. 5-6 and 8, 32 nn. 14 and 16
Shilov, Lara   24 n. 123, 72 n. 5, 162 n. 4
Shoham, Yair   11, 11 nn. 49-50, 31, 31 nn. 11-12, 66 n. 80, 78 n. 35
Shukron, Eli   7 n. 23, 8, 8 n. 36, 11, 11 nn. 46 and 48, 30 n. 4, 31, 31 nn. 9-10, 53, 53 n. 16, 66 nn. 79-80, 78 n. 35, 96, 96 n. 71, 101 n. 100, 102 n. 101, 122, 122 n. 71
Singer-Avitz, Lily   15 n. 81, 47, 47 n. 102, 84 n. 5, 89 n. 41, 116 n. 34
Sivan, Renee   7 n. 23
Solar, Giora   7 n. 23
Sparks, James T.   83 nn. 1-2, 84 n. 4
Spinoza, Baruch de.   132 n. 15, 133, 133 n. 20

Stager, Lawrence E.   12 n. 56
Steiner, Richard C.   36 n. 38
Steins, Georg 131 n. 11, 134 n. 24, 135 n. 27, 136 nn. 32 and 44, 155, 155 nn. 93 and 95
Stern, Ephraim 3 n. 2, 5, 5 nn. 10–11, 14, 14 n. 69, 17 n. 91, 20, 20 nn. 105 and 108, 21, 21 nn. 110 and 115, 33 n. 21, 34, 34 nn. 21, 26 and 31, 36 n. 44, 50 n. 114, 52 n. 6, 53, 53 n. 14, 54, 54 nn. 18–19 and 24, 76 n. 26, 95 n. 64, 96, 96 nn. 70 and 74, 97 n. 75
Stern, Menahem   60 n. 50, 99 n. 85
Tal, Oren   57 n. 33, 100 n. 88, 119 n. 51, 120 n. 73, 123, 123 nn. 81, 83 and 85
Tammuz, Oded   74 nn. 15 and 17
Tarler, David   15 n. 78
Tavger, Aharon   48 n. 106
Taxel, Itamar   43, 43 nn. 87–88, 89 n. 33
Tchekhanovets, Yana   26 n. 129
Torrey, Charles C.   17 n. 92, 18 n. 94, 53 nn. 10–11, 72 n. 6, 95 nn. 67–68, 96 n. 68, 129 n. 3, 137 n. 36
Tsfania, Levana   137 n. 39
Tufnell, Olga   123 n. 86
Tzafrir, Yoram   14 n. 74, 36 n. 47
Tzur, Yoa   126 n. 100
Ulrich, Eugene   138 n. 45
Ussishkin, David   4 n. 2, 6, 6 nn. 16–17, 13 n. 63, 14, 14 n. 70, 15, 15 nn. 81–83, 16, 16 n. 85, 17 n. 88, 26, 52 n. 9, 114 nn. 20–21, 121 n. 64, 123, 123 n. 84
Vanderhooft, David   21 n. 109, 36 n. 44, 43 n. 89, 46 n. 99, 51 n. 3, 52 n. 5, 54 n. 25, 55, 55 nn. 26 and 29, 60 n. 49, 66 nn. 78 and 80, 69, 69 n. 84, 70, 76, 76 n. 27, 77 nn. 31 and 34, 78 n. 35, 94 n. 63, 97 n. 78, 98 nn. 79 and 83, 99 n. 84, 101 n. 99, 102 n. 101
VanderKam, James C.   104 nn. 109–10, 154 n. 87
Vaughn, Andrew G.   110 n. 7, 117 n. 38
Vriezen, Karel J. H.   40, 40 n. 67

Wacholder, Ben   134 n. 23
Weinberg, Joel P.   5 n. 9, 13 n. 58, 19 n. 97, 57 n. 34
Weinfeld, Moshe   19 n. 99
Weissenberg, Hanne von   138 n. 46
Welch, Adam C.   83 n. 3, 125 n. 91
Welten, Peter   109 n. 3, 110 n. 7, 129 n. 3, 132 n. 17, 138 n. 46, 155 n. 94
Wightman, Gregory J.   7 n. 23, 32 n. 18
Willi, Thomas   132 n. 17, 137 n. 37
Williamson, Hugh G. M.   15 n. 74, 17 n. 92, 18 n. 93, 19 n. 97, 53 n. 10, 71 n. 3, 72 nn. 6 and 10, 74 nn. 10 and 17, 75 nn. 20 and 23, 81 n. 47, 83 n. 2, 84 n. 4, 93 n. 57, 95 n. 67, 104 n. 113, 115 n. 27, 129 nn. 1–2, 130, 130 n. 5, 132 n. 17, 133 n. 19, 137 n. 37, 140 n. 51, 143 n. 58, 146 n. 63, 147 n. 64, 151 n. 71, 152 n. 82, 156 n. 98
Wörrle, Michael   118 n. 47
Wright, Jacob L.   19 n. 97, 46 n. 98, 68 n. 82, 72 n. 6, 73 n. 9, 81 n. 44, 81 n. 47
Wright, John W.   55 n. 27, 84 n. 4, 93 n. 58, 94 n. 62, 139 nn. 48–49
Yeivin, Shemuel.   40 nn. 70–71, 117 n. 42
Young, Robb A.   129 n. 2, 146 n. 63, 148 n. 65
Zadok, Ran   36 n. 42, 92 n. 52, 94 n. 59, 103 n. 107, 106 n. 117
Zertal, Adam   77 n. 30
Zevit, Ziony 49–50, 49 nn. 108 and 110, 50 nn. 111–13
Zigdon, Gal   25 n. 123, 72 n. 5, 162 n. 4
Zorn, Jeffrey R.   12 n. 54
Zsengellér, Józse   136 n. 34
Zuckerman, Sharon   26 n. 127
Zukerman, Alexander   113 nn. 14–15
Zweig, Yitzhak   11 nn. 47 and 51, 24 n. 123, 71 n. 5, 162 n. 4
Zwickel, Wolfgang   86 nn. 19–20, 90 n. 49, 93 n. 50

# Place Names Index

Abu-Ghosh  39
Adasa  60, 65, 67, 99
Adoraim  57, 60, 67, 77–78, 98–99, 103, 112, 118–21, 124, 140, 157
Adulam  62, 101, 111–12, 113, 121
Ai  33, 42–44
Aijalon  88, 91, 112, 118, 121
Akra  26, 51, 100–101, 119
al-Aqsa Mosque  24, 162 n. 4
Alemeth  87, 91
Ammon  74–75, 79, 81, 139 n. 50, 145, 157, 161
Ammonitis  74, 78
'Anata  38, 39 n. 62, 50, 87
Anathoth  33, 38–39, 44, 87, 91
Apheraema  67, 102
Arad  116, 116 n. 35, 117
Aram  148
'Ara'ir  89
Armenian Garden  7
Armenian Quarter  26, 77
Aroer  89, 91, 104, 107
Ashdod  62, 75, 79, 101, 111, 144–46, 157, 160–61
Asher  89, 92, 151
Ayyah  89–91, 107
Azekah  68, 102, 111–12, 113 n. 14, 114 n. 23, 121, 124, 127, 140
Azmaveth  33, 39, 44, 88, 91
Baal-meon  89, 91, 104
Babylon  55 n. 27, 133, 162
Beeroth  33, 40–41, 44, 46, 117 n. 42
Beer-sheba  116, 116 n. 35, 117, 139, 145–47, 150

Beer-sheba Valley  92, 94, 104 n. 108, 114, 116, 117
Beit 'Ur el-Fauqa  89
Beit 'Ur et-Tahta  89
Beit Lahm  86
Beit Nattif  62, 101
Beitin  34–35, 89
Benjamin  30, 34–36, 39–42, 87–88, 93–94, 125, 140–41, 143, 147, 151
Bethel  33–35, 44, 47–48, 61–62, 67–68, 78, 84, 89–91, 93–94, 98, 100, 101–2, 108, 91, 112, 116, 119–20, 142–43, 151
Beth-haccherem  45, 52, 56, 68, 95, 98
Beth-horon  60–62, 67, 73, 89–101, 112, 120
Bethlehem  30, 33, 37–38, 43, 86, 91, 112, 120
Beth-shean  92
Beth-shemesh  117
Beth-zacharia  60, 67, 99
Beth-zur  2, 20–21, 52–53, 55–56, 58, 60–62, 60 n. 51, 65, 68–69, 69 n. 85, 76–78, 84, 86, 91, 95–97, 99–103, 107, 111, 112, 118–20, 119 n. 49, 122, 140–41, 141 n. 53
Birzaith  89, 91, 93, 98, 103, 151
Burj el-Lisaneh  143
Chephirah  33, 40, 44
Christian Quarter  26
Church of Nativity  37
City of David  4, 5, 8, 10–14, 16, 24–26, 30–32, 47, 53, 55, 66, 72, 78, 95, 97, 101
Coastal Plain  17, 81, 131, 144

| | |
|---|---|
| Dan | 139, 146–47, 150 |
| Dead Sea | 58, 92 |
| Dedan | 75 |
| Deir Dibwan | 42–44 |
| Deir el-'Azar | 39, 50, 86 |
| Dor | 92 |
| Dothaim | 105 |
| edh-Dhahiriya | 111 |
| Egypt | 17 |
| Ein Duk | 89 |
| Ekron | 57, 62, 65, 67, 78, 81, 98, 101–3, 113 n. 14 |
| Elah Valley | 61–62, 100–101, 111, 114 n. 19 |
| Elasa | 65, 154 |
| Elephantine | 57, 73 |
| el-Bireh | 142 |
| el-Haditheh | 36 |
| el-Jib | 88 |
| el-Ludd | 88 |
| el-Malhah | 88 |
| el-Ula | 75 |
| Emmaus | 61–62, 65, 100–101, 112, 120 |
| En Gedi | 45, 55, 60, 69, 76–77, 97–99 |
| Ephraim (Apheraema) | 65, 78, 89, 93, 94, 102, 137, 142, 143 |
| Ephron | 106, 142–45, 147–51 |
| er-Ram | 39 n. 62, 41, 50 |
| Eshtaol | 86, 90–91 |
| Eshtemoa | 87, 91, 93, 119, 151 |
| es-Samuʿ | 87, 111 |
| Etam | 86, 91, 112, 119–20 |
| et-Taiyibeh | 106, 143 |
| et-Tell | 42 |
| Ezion-geber | 145 |
| Farkha | 62, 100 |
| Galilee | 65, 147–48 |
| Gath | 111–13, 120–22, 145 |
| Gazara | 61, 61 n. 55, 100, 100 n. 88, 119–20, 153 |
| Geba | 33, 41–42, 44, 88, 91, 115 |
| Gedor | 87, 91 |
| Gerar | 144 |
| Gezer | 15 n. 77, 52, 55, 57, 61 n. 55, 62, 65, 67–69, 78, 81, 89–91, 94–95, |
| *Gezer (cont.)* | 97–98, 101–4, 107, 117 n. 42, 112, 119, 148, 151, 153 |
| Gibeon | 2, 20–21, 32–34, 43, 54, 60, 84, 88, 91, 96–97, 99, 107, 117 n. 42, 126 |
| Gihon Spring | 8, 11, 16, 31, 71 |
| Gilead | 65, 79 |
| Givati Parking Lot | 26 |
| Hadid | 33, 36, 44, 46, 68 |
| Hebron | 60, 62, 77, 78, 85, 91, 98–99, 101–4, 106–7, 111–12, 121, 122 n. 69, 127, 141 |
| Hizma | 39, 39 n. 62, 88 |
| Horonaim | 74 |
| Idumea | 57, 60, 77–79, 81, 98–99, 103–4, 118–19, 123–24, 131, 140–41, 144, 151, 157, 161 |
| Ishwaʿ | 86, 90 |
| Issachar | 105, 151 |
| Israel | 1, 49, 101, 105, 113, 115, 116, 129, 130, 139–40, 142–43, 145–49, 151–53, 155, 158 |
| Jaba | 39 n. 62, 41, 50, 88 |
| Jaffa | 148, 153 |
| Jamnia (Jabneh) | 144–46 |
| Jattir | 119 |
| Jazer | 145 |
| Jericho | 21 n. 115, 30, 33, 36, 44, 52, 55, 60–62, 67, 69, 76–77, 92, 95, 97–101, 112, 119–20 |
| Jerusalem | 3–7, 9–10, 13 n. 58, 16–17, 19, 22–24, 25 n. 124, 27, 29–30, 32–33, 39–43, 45, 47, 52–53, 55–63, 66–73, 75–77, 80–81, 84, 93, 95, 97, 99–101, 112, 115, 117, 119–20, 122, 124, 126, 137–38, 140–41, 146–49, 152, 155 |
| Jeshanah | 142 |
| Jewish Quarter | 7 |
| Jezreel Valley | 79, 103, 105, 152 |
| Joppa | 65–68, 78, 102–3, 152–53 |
| Jordan Valley | 58, 146 |
| Judah | 1–2, 38–39, 59, 66, 70, 85–87, 92–94, 105–6, 109–11, 113–16, 118, 124–27, 129–32, 134, 139–55, 157–58, 160–62 |

## Place Names Index

Judea  1, 51, 57, 60–62, 61 n. 55, 64–66, 68–69, 75–79, 80–82, 93, 98–105, 100 n. 88, 103 n. 106, 111, 118–19, 125, 131, 131 n. 9, 133, 135, 138, 141, 143, 145–46, 148, 151, 151 n. 78, 152, 155, 157, 160–62
Juttah  119
Kadesh-barnea  55 n. 26, 161
Kafar Salama  60, 67, 99
Kafr Ana  43
Kafr Juna  43, 88
Keilah  19 n. 21, 52, 56, 68, 87, 91, 93, 95
Khirbet ʿAbbad  111, 121 n. 57, 127
Khirbet ʿAlmit  87
Khirbet Bad-Faluh  62, 101
Khirbet Bir Zeit  89
Khirbet Deir es-Sidd  38
Khirbet el-Burj  39 n. 62, 40, 117 n. 42
Khirbet el-Fire  62
Khirbet el-Haiyan  42–44, 89
Khirbet el-Hara el-Fauqa  42
Khirbet el-Kafira  39 n. 62, 40, 50
Khirbet el-Khawkh  86
Khirbet el-Mukhayyat  89
Khirbet esh-Sheikh Madkur  121 n. 57
Khirbet et-Tawil  61 n. 57
Khirbet et-Tayyibe  87
Khirbet et-Tubeiqeh  86
Khirbet et-Tuqu  85
Khirbet Judur  87
Khirbet Main  89
Khirbet Maʿin  86
Khirbet Qeiyafa  126
Khirbet Qila  87
Khirbet Shuweike  87, 111
Khirbet Tibna  61, 100
Khirbet Zanuʿ  87
Kidron Valley  8, 31
Kirjath-jearim  33, 39, 44, 49, 86, 106–7
Lachish  74 n. 19, 92, 92 n. 52, 94, 111–12, 114, 121, 123, 140, 144, 161
Lod  30, 33, 36–37, 44, 46, 57, 62, 64 n. 70, 65, 67–69, 78, 88, 91, 94, 98, 101–4, 143, 151

Madaba  78, 93, 103–4, 139 n. 50, 145, 148, 151, 157
Manahath  88, 91
Manasseh  85 n. 10, 92–93, 115–16, 137, 143, 147, 149–51, 149 n. 70
Maon  86, 91, 93, 119, 151
Mareshah  57, 60, 67, 77–78, 85, 91, 93, 98–99, 103, 107, 112–13, 114 n. 23, 118, 121, 123–24, 140–41, 144–45, 151
Marisa  104, 118
Megiddo  92, 147, 150
Michmash  33, 42, 44, 46
Mishor  93
Mizpah  5, 45, 52, 55–56, 58, 60, 62, 68–69, 76–77, 95, 97–99, 102–3, 115, 117
Moab  145
Moresheth-gath  113
Mount Gerizim  78, 103, 137, 147
Mount Zemaraim  142
Moza  84, 88, 91, 107
Mt. Zion  8
Mukhmas  39 n. 62, 42, 50
Naaran  89, 91
Nahal Shiloh  62, 65, 100, 103
Naphtali  105, 146, 150–51
Nebi Samuel  45, 55–56, 60, 77, 98–99, 115 n. 27
Nebo  30, 89, 91, 104, 107
Negev  79
Netophah  30
Neve Yarak  37
Ono  33, 43–44, 46, 68, 79 n. 41, 88, 91, 94, 98, 102–4
Ophel  23–24
Ophrah  87, 91, 106, 143
Peraea  65–67, 78–79, 102–3
Pharathon  61–62, 70, 100, 106, 112, 119–20
Philistia  79, 146, 157, 161
Pirathon (Farʾata)  61, 100
Qalunyah  88
Qedar  73
Qumran  133, 138
Ramah  33, 41, 44

Ramallah 143
Ramat Rahel 45, 45 n. 90, 55–56, 58, 60, 68–69, 76–77, 97–99, 117 n. 42
Ramathaim 65, 67, 78, 102, 143
Ramat-negeb 116 n. 35
Ramot 40
Rantis 143
Ras el-Kharubeh 38
Ras et-Tahune 142
Reuben 89, 93, 151
Samaria 46, 61, 73–75, 77, 79, 81, 87 n. 28, 100, 103, 105, 116, 124, 131, 137, 143, 147, 149–51, 157–58, 161
Scythopolis 105
Sar'ah 86
Senaah 30
Shechem 61–62, 78, 89, 91, 93, 100–101, 103–14, 107, 137, 147, 149, 151
Shephelah 52, 55, 57–60, 62–64, 66, 68–69, 77, 92–95, 97–99, 102, 111, 114, 117, 126–27, 140–41, 144
Siloan Pool 10
Simeon 85 n. 10, 104 n. 108, 143, 150
Soco 87, 111–12, 120–21, 121 n. 57, 127
Taanach 92
Tafuh 86
Tapuah 62, 86, 91, 101
Tekoa 21 n. 115, 62, 85, 91, 101, 112, 120, 140, 145
Tel Harasim 55, 97
Tel Ira 116 n. 35
Tell Balata 89
Tell el-Ful 101
Tell el-Maskhuta 73, 75 n. 21
Tell el-Rumeideh 85, 106, 122 n. 69, 127
Tell es-Safi 111
Tell es-Sultan 36
Tell Judeideh 113, 122
Tell Nasbeh 12 n. 54
Tell Sandahannah 85
Tell Zif 85
Temple Mount 9–11, 12 n. 53, 23–24, 25 n. 124, 27, 32 n. 17, 47, 71, 159, 162
Tephon 61–62, 67, 100–101, 112, 121

Thamnatha 61, 61 n. 57, 100, 112
Timna 61, 100–101
Timnath-heres (Khirbet Tibne) 61, 100
Transjordan 65, 78, 102–3, 105, 126, 131, 151
Tulul Abu el-Alayiq 36
Valley of Zephathah 144
Wadi ed-Daliyeh 73
Wadi Fara 62, 100
Yalu 88
Yehud 1, 3–6, 13, 16, 21–22, 29–31, 34, 36, 44–46, 51–52, 55, 57, 59, 62–64, 69, 74–79, 84, 93–95, 97–98, 105, 131, 137, 159–62
Zanoah 87, 91
Ziph 85, 91, 112, 119, 121, 140
Zorah 86, 91, 93, 111–12, 121

# Ancient Figures Index

Abd govenor of Dedan 75
Abijah/Abijam 137, 139, 141, 142, 142 n. 54, 143, 144, 148
Abraham 48
Adonijah 133
Ahab 144
Ahaz 149
Ahaziah 148
Alexander Jannaeus 123, 124, 146, 148
Alexander Polyhistor 134
Alexander the Great 99 n. 85
Amaziah 148, 149, 149 n. 69
Amon 149
Antiochus III 17 n. 87, 34
Antiochus IV 155
Antiochus VII/Sidetes 124, 126, 141, 147, 152, 153
Aristobolus 148
Artaxerxes I 5
Asa 115, 117, 139, 143, 143 n. 58, 144, 145, 148
Asher 92, 151
Athaliah 148
Baasha of Israel 143
Bacchides 2, 35, 60, 61, 61 n. 51, 67, 77, 77 n. 32, 99, 100, 100 n. 86, 112, 119, 119 n. 49, 120, 124, 141 n. 53, 145
Ben-hadad of Damascus 143
Clement of Alexandria 134
Dan 92 n. 53, 105, 151
Darius III 73
David 129, 133, 135, 136, 139, 139 n. 50, 140, 146, 147, 148, 154, 156
Demetrius 143
Eliashib 74

Eupolemus 133–35
Eusebius 134
Gashmu king of Qedar 73
Geshem the Arab 72, 75, 79 n. 41, 81
Hezekiah 110–11, 116–17, 117 n. 40, 118, 126, 130, 132, 137, 139–40, 146, 146 n. 63, 147, 147 n. 64, 148–51, 157
Issachar 92, 105, 151
Jacob 105
Jasm son of Sahr 75
Jehoash 148–49
Jehoiada 149
Jehoiakim 133
Jehoram 148–49
Jehoshaphat 139, 144–45, 144 n. 59, 148
Jeroboam 48, 125, 142–43, 148
John Hyrcanus 34, 78–79, 103, 103 n. 105, 104, 105, 119, 124–25, 131–32, 140–41, 144, 146–48, 151–52, 154, 157, 160–61
John Hyrcanus I 105, 118, 123–24, 132
Jonathan the Hasmonean 42, 55, 57, 62, 65, 78–79, 97–98, 101–3, 120, 143–44, 151
Josiah 35, 94, 110, 115–16, 118, 140, 147–48, 150
Jotham 148–49
Judah Aristobulus 105
Judas Maccabeus 19, 60, 60 n. 51, 64–65, 67, 69, 99, 99 n. 86, 119 n. 49, 132 n. 15, 134, 141 n. 53, 143, 153
Lysias 60 n. 51, 99 n. 86, 119 n. 49, 141 n. 53
Manasseh 92, 115–16, 149, 151

Mattathias the Hasmonean 138
Naphtali 92, 151
Nehemiah 1, 3–6, 12 n. 56, 13, 13 n. 58, 14–20, 22, 29, 45, 72, 79, 79 n. 41, 158, 160
Rehoboam 1–2, 106, 109, 111–13, 115–16, 118, 124–27, 132, 139–41, 148, 160
Sanballat the Horonite 72–74, 74 n. 17, 79 n. 41, 81
Sargon II 111
Sennacherib 113, 113 n. 14, 115, 117 n. 40, 126, 147, 154
Seron 153
Shishak 110 n. 3, 126, 140
Simeon the Hasmonean 36, 55, 57, 61 n. 51, 62, 65, 66, 68, 78–79, 85 n. 10, 92, 97–98, 99 n. 86, 101–3, 104 n. 108, 119 n. 49, 141 n. 53, 143–44, 150–53
Solomon 125, 129, 136, 139–140, 146–47, 147 n. 64, 148, 154, 156
Tiglath-pileser III 149
Tobiah the Ammonite 72, 74, 75 n. 20, 81 n. 46
Uzziah 139, 145–47, 149
Zebulun 92, 105, 151
Zerah the Cushite 143–44

www.ingramcontent.com/pod-product-compliance
Lightning Source LLC
Chambersburg PA
CBHW030622230426
43661CB00053B/2109